Department of Economic and Social Affairs
Division for Public Administration and Development
Management

Building Trust
Through Civic Engagement

Publication based on the 7th Global Forum workshop on
Building Trust Through Civic Engagement
26 to 29 June 2007
Vienna, Austria

United Nations
New York, 2008

DESA

The Department of Economic and Social Affairs of the United Nations Secretariat is a vital interface between global policies in the economic, social and environmental spheres and national action. The Department works in three main interlinked areas: (i) it compiles, generates and analyses a wide range of economic, social and environmental data and information on which Member States of the United Nations draw to review common problems and to take stock of policy options; (ii) it facilitates the negotiations of Member States in many intergovernmental bodies on joint courses of action to address ongoing or emerging global challenges; and (iii) it advises interested Governments on the ways and means of translating policy frameworks developed in United Nations conferences and summits into programmes at the country level and, through technical assistance, helps build national capacities.

Note

The designations employed and the presentation of the material in this publication do not imply the expression of any opinion whatsoever on the part of the Secretariat of the United Nations concerning the legal status of any country, territory, city or area, or of its authorities, or concerning the delimitation of its frontiers or boundaries.

The views expressed are those of the individual authors and do not imply any expression of opinion on the part of the United Nations.

Enquiries concerning this publication may be directed to:
Ms. Haiyan Qian
Acting Director, Division for Public Administration and
Development Management, Department of Economic and Social Affairs
United Nations, New York, NY 10017, USA
Fax: (212)963-9681 Email:qianh@un.org

ST/ESA/PAD/SER.E/120
United Nations publication

No loan

UN2

ST/ESA/PAD/SER.E/120

Foreword

Trust is at the nexus of the compact between governments and their citizens. Public trust emanates from a socially-centered government that is responsive and capable of articulating public needs through pro-poor policies and delivering necessary services in a transparent and accountable way. This synergy acts as both a precondition and a result of good governance. However, falling levels of trust in government have become an increasingly significant issue of global scale, affecting governments in both developing and developed regions. Survey after survey in recent times have demonstrated a growing lack of public trust by citizens and significant gaps between expectations held by citizens on the responsibilities of their governments and actual governmental actions.

This publication is the result of the Workshop on Building Trust through Civic Engagement, held as part of the 7th Global Forum on Reinventing Government: Building Trust in Government, which took place at the United Nations Headquarters in Vienna from 26 to 29 June 2007. The Workshop was organized by the United Nations Department of Economic and Social Affairs (UNDESA), with the support of partner institutions including the Eastern Regional Organization for Public Administration (EROPA), Kyung Hee University (Republic of Korea), the International Budget Project of Washington, D.C., Queensland (Australia) Community Engagement Alliance, and the New York University Wagner Graduate School of Public Service

UNDESA and its partners chose the topic of Building Trust through Civic Engagement in recognition of the need to explore the options and means to articulate and advocate the role that citizen engagement in public policy, services delivery and public accountability can have in bringing citizens closer to the government and government closer to the citizens. It is envisioned that addressing the issues of building trust through civic engagement will greatly help in instilling in public governance a sense of shared vision in development, help to produce a mutually re-enforcing mechanism of transparency and accountability, and aid in delivering services that meet priorities set by citizen themselves. The Workshop provided a space to explore the role of civic engagement in building trust in government, highlight best practices and lessons learned from previous experiences in civic participation, and address the institutional forms and capacity building issues related to forging ongoing partnerships to foster civic engagement in government processes.

This resulting publication, *Building Trust through Civic Engagement*, addresses these issues with the goal of advancing the understanding of successful civic participation in public governance. Part One of the publication introduces the concepts and issues regarding civic engagement in government, including the role of public participation in empowerment and capacity building, the formalization of civic engagement using NGOs and the concepts of trust, structure and order in the public policy process, and the relationship between governments and citizens in the context of representative democratic structures. Part Two of the publication highlights best practices and lessons learned from previous examples of civic engagement in the governmental process, including case studies from Austria, Philippines, Rwanda, India, and Australia.

While civic engagement is not an alternative to representative government, the cases highlighted herein provide a roadmap toward utilizing public participation to aid government leadership in becoming more effective and accountable, increasing genuine communication, and ultimately, building trust and creating an enabling environment for all involved stakeholders. This publication is an important addition to the ongoing research done by UNDESA to facilitate technical cooperation support for capacity building for governments and to provide a deeper understanding of how civic participation can improve governance, service delivery, accountability and trust in all levels of government.

Guido Bertucci
Director, Division for Public Administration
and Development Management
Department of Economic and Social Affairs

Acknowledgments

The Workshop on Building Trust through Civic Engagement and the resulting publication on Civic Engagement for Building Trust in Government were undertaken as part of the United Nations Programme on Public Administration managed by Mr. Guido Bertucci, Director, Division for Public Administration and Development (DPADM) of DESA.

DPADM/DESA would like to thank and acknowledge the work of the contributing authors of the publication, namely Mr. Adil Khan, Mr. Siddiqur Osmani, Mr. Herrington Bryce, Mr. Patrick Bishop, Mr. Andreas Henkel, Mayor Jesse Robredo, Minister Protais Musoni, Mr. Warren Krafchik, Mr. Vivek Ramkumar, Mr. Amitabh Mukhopadhyay, Mr. Neil Doyle, Mr. Peter Oliver, Mr. Greg Hoffman, Mr. Alan Morton and Ms. Desley Renton, as well as the other panelists who participated in the Workshop and contributed valuable insight and expertise.

DESA wishes to acknowledge Mr. Adil Khan, Chief, Socio-Economic Governance and Management Branch (SGMB) of DPADM, who provided the over-all framework of this project, as well as Mr. Jacinto de Vera, Chief, Policy Analysis and Coordination Unit (PACU) of SGMB, who acted as Workshop Coordinator. For the resulting publication, DESA wishes to acknowledge the project team led by Mr. De Vera, who acted as primary editor and supervised the production of this project, and was assisted in the compilation, finalization and proofreading of the publication by Ms. Mary Christine Ong-Reyes, Research Assistant and Ms. Lilian Haney, Intern. The contributions of all other concerned SGMB staff members during the publication process are also duly acknowledged.

Contents

Abbreviations and Acronyms

ABS	- Australian Bureau of Statistics
ACIJ	- La Asociación Civil por la Igualdad y la Justicia (Argentina)
ALGA	- Australian Local Government Association
ARC	- Australian Research Council
AUD	- Australian Dollar
BAC	- Bids and Awards Committee (Philippines)
BAI	- Board of Audit and Inspection (South Korea)
BAK	- Federal Chamber of Labor (Austria)
BNDES	- Brazil's National Economic and Social Development Bank
CAG	- Comptroller and Auditor General (India)
CCAGG	- Concerned Citizens of Abra for Good Government
CCEJ	- Concerned Citizens for Economic Justice (South Korea)
CEO	- Chief Executive Officer
CMEF	- Collaboration Monitoring and Evaluation Framework
COA	- Commission on Audit (Philippines)
COAG	- Council of Australian Governments
COPE	- Community Organizers of the Philippines Enterprises (Philippines)
CQRMCN	- Central Queensland Regional Managers' Coordination Network
CSO	- Civil society organization
CSRS	- Community Service and Research Center (Australia)
DLGPS	- Department of Local Government Planning and Sport (Australia)
DISHA	- Development Initiatives for Social and Human Action
EDP	- Electronic Data Processing
EMEF	- Collaboration, Monitoring and Evaluation Framework (Australia)
EU	- European Union
FUNDAR	- Centro de Análisis e Investigación
HIV/AIDS	- Human Immuniency Virus/Acquired Immune Deficiency Syndrome
IAP2	- The International Association for Public Participation
IBASE	- Instituto Brasileiro de Análises Sociais e Econômicas
IBP	- International Budget Project (United States)
ICASA	- Issue, Context and Stakeholder System (Australia)
ICC	- International Criminal Court

ICM	- Ideal Collaboration Model
IDASA	- Institute for Democracy in South Africa
IDS	- Institute for Development Studies
ILO	- International Labour Organization
INTOSAI	- International Organization of Supreme Audit Institutions
IPF	- Institute for Public Finance
IRTPs	- Integrated Regional Transport Plans (Australia)
JADF	- Joint Action Development Forum (Rwanda)
LAMP	- Local Area Multicultural Partnership (Australia)
LG	- Local Government
LGA	- Local Government Area (Australia)
LGAQ	- Local Government Association of Queensland Inc. (Australia)
LRRS	- Local Roads of Regional Significance (Australia)
MDGs	- Millennium Development Goals
MKSS	- Mazdoor Kisan Shakti Sangathan (India)
MR	- Main Roads (Australia)
MRCF	- Ministerial Regional Community Forum (Australia)
NCPC	- Naga City People's Council (Philippines)
NGM	- Naga Governance Model (Philippines)
NGO	- Non-governmental Organization
NHS	-National Health Service
NPM	- New Public Management
NREGA	- National Rural Employment Guarantee Act
NRM	- Natural Resource Management
OECD	- Organisation for Economic Cooperation and Development
OESR	- Office of Economic and Statistical Research
ÖGB	- Trade Union Federation (Austria)
PDR	- Process Documentation and Reporting
PGS	- Public Governance Scorecard (Philippines)
PO	- Poverty Observatory
PPAs	- Projects and Activities
PSAM	- Public Service Accountability Monitor (South Africa)
PWI	- Procurement Watch, Inc (Philippines)
RCQ	- Roads Connecting Queenslanders (Australia)
RMCN	- Regional Managers' Coordination Networks (Australia)
RRGs	- Regional Road Groups (Australia)
RSM	- Road System Manager Framework (Australia)
RTI	- Right to Information Act
SAI	- Supreme Audit Institution
SCARP	- Social Capital Action Research Project (Australia)

SEQIPP	- South East Queensland Infrastructure Plan and Program (Australia)
SOG	- International Political Science Association
SSS	- Size, Shape, and Sustainability Program (Australia)
TCP	- Transport Coordination Plan (Australia)
UBC SCARP	- British Columbia School of Community and Regional Planning (Canada)
UDN	- Uganda Debt Network
UK	- United Kingdom
UN	- United Nations
UNESCAP	- The United Nations Economic and Social Commission for Asia and the Pacific
UNESCO	- United Nations Educational, Scientific and Cultural Organization
UNDP	- United Nations Development Programme
UNSW	- University of New South Wales (Australia)
UQ	- University of Queensland (Australia)
US	- United States of America
VFM	- Value for Money
WEF	- World Economic Forum
WKÖ	- Federal Economic Chamber (Austria)

Part One

Building Trust in Government: Concepts and Issues

M. Adil Khan

Public trust in institutions, especially in government is key to achieving the triangle of freedom - stability, peace and development- in each and every nation. Trust enhances confidence in institutions and consequently, attracts cooperation of citizens to the agreed policies and programmes of the governments.

The trend

In recent times, however, trust in institutions, especially in governments seems to be experiencing a downward trend. The recent World Economic Forum Trust Survey 2006 as well similar surveys that concern the current state of public governance reveal the following trends (World Economic Forum, 2006):

(i) trust in governments, international organizations and global companies are at its lowest;

(ii) trust in governments worsened since 2004;

(iii) though United Nations enjoy considerably higher level of trust than other institutions, it also experienced setbacks in recent years (most likely due to Iraq situation);

(iv) trust in companies eroded in last two years and currently, at its lowest;

(v) 75% of the world population detect inconsistencies between public policies and public expectations; and finally

(vi) non-government organizations are leaders in trust, but they too have suffered setbacks in recent years.

Factors and concerns

A variety of reasons have been forwarded for this falling trend. However, at the global level the following factors seem to contribute most to this falling trend (WEF, 2006):

(i) Peace and safety: 29%

(ii) Poverty: 13%

(iii) Human rights abuses: 13%

(iv) Inequality: 11%

(v) Environment: 10%

(vi) Drugs and crime: 6%

(vii) HIV/AIDS: 3%

Though these factors are inextricably linked to one another, a broad categorization of these into 'development' and 'governance' related issues highlight that 65% of the factors that contribute to falling trust are 'development' related (poverty: 13%; inequality: 11%; environment: 10%; social/gender: 5% and HIV/AIDS: 3%) and of the rest, 35% are 'governance' related (peace and security: 29%; drugs and crime: 6%).

'Development' related factors of falling trust reveal the following general concerns:
(i)   almost one billion people continue to remain poor;
(ii)   5% of the world's rich earns 114 times more than the 5% of the world's poor;
(iii) of the world's 854 million illiterate, 544 million are women;
(iv)   every day more than 30,000 children die of preventable diseases, worldwide;
(v)   by 2002, 22 million died of HIV/HIDS and currently, about 40 million are living with HIV/AIDS;
(vi)   global warming has increased the spectre of natural disasters and significantly altered the world ecology and economy; and
(vii) Internet use remains low in developing countries; OECD countries, which represent only 14% of the world population, account for 72% of internet users.

On the 'governance' side the key concerns are:
(i)   though there has been a surge in democratization of countries, of the 81 newly democratic countries, only 41 are fully democratic;
(ii)   61 countries still do not have free press;
(iii) 106 countries restrict important civil and political liberties;
(iv)   the "war on terror" and the resulting curbing of civil liberties is regressing progress towards democracy and aggravating mistrust;
(v)   an increasing number of citizens fear for their safety;
(vi)   there is mistrust in how governments allocate and spend public resources and see corruption as a rising scourge – 90% of countries (surveyed) do not meet transparency and accountability criteria in budget preparation and more than third of these countries provide minimal or no budget information to their citizens (International Budget Project, 2006);
(vii) NGOs and civil society organizations are not included in many of the decision-making processes of the state.

In general, failure to achieve equitable development on the one hand, and the lack of success in guaranteeing full democratic rights to the citizens and absence of accountability and transparency in public governance on the other, continues to dent public faith in governments. Against this backdrop, the key questions that must be asked are the following: (i) what should be done to restore trust? and (ii) in addition to the governments, do the civil societies and other stakeholders have a role to play? Before these questions are answered, it may be useful to get a clear conception of the idea of trust and how this concept relates to public governance.

The concept of trust and civic engagement

Oxford Dictionary defines trust as a concept that has to do with:
  (i)   to have or place confidence in: *rely*
  (ii) to expect: *hope*
  (iii) to entrust: *custody*
  (iv) something given to one's care for the benefit of another: *charge/ authority*
  (v)   to account for entrusted power and authority: *accountability*

The significance of this comprehensive definition of *trust* is that there is more than one factor that contributes to building or denting trust and when this multi-dimensional concept of trust is linked to the concept of public governance, it becomes clear that the institutions, processes, rules, regulations, the aspect of relationships between the government and the citizens, information sharing etc., impact directly on trust. For example, whether a citizen shall *rely* on a particular government very much depends on the extent to which she or he sees how government systems, procedures, rules, regulations etc. address his or her needs. Similarly, a citizen's *hope* of a government doing something good for him or her will depend, among other things, on the latter's capacity to produce and deliver quality public goods.

So in all these, where does the issue of civic engagement fit in and how, if at all, shall civic engagement in public governance enhance citizen trust in government? The simple answer would be that as is the case in interpersonal relationships, trust becomes an achievable target when two concerned parties become open and engaging to each other. Trust becomes a problem when engagement becomes a casualty. Similarly, in public governance, citizens start to lose trust in government when they get the feeling that they have no clue what the latter is doing (even though it could be doing some good things) or have a perception that the government heeds more to the rich and the powerful and to their needs rather than those of the poor and the disadvantaged.

These days, there is also an overwhelming belief that due to changing patterns of relationships induced by globalization and liberalization, the emerging global power games caused by economic and security interests, and rising unequal power relationships at the country level, governments, especially the governments of the aid-dependent countries, are either becoming too powerless to respond to the needs of the less powerful or they are being hijacked by the forces of vested interest. In either case, governments are becoming increasingly alien and as a result, distancing themselves away from the ordinary citizens of their own countries.

To overcome these challenges, there is now an increasing demand for greater citizen/government synergy in public governance. The World Economic Forum Trust Survey 2006 also confirms this demand. When asked by the Survey how to recover trust in public institutions, it revealed the following consensus:

(i)   7% say, "reconnect with the stakeholders"
(ii)   8% say, "make the institutions more relevant"
(iii) 13% say "dialogue with the consumers (citizens"
(iv)   30% say "punishment of fraudulent behaviour"
(v)   32% say "greater transparency in governance"

When one leaves out the issue of "punishment of fraudulent behaviour" above, one could easily argue that nearly 68% of the citizens believe that engagement with public institutions is key to enhancing trust in government.

While democracy is important for creating opportunities for greater civic engagement, this is not sufficient. The emerging socio-economic dynamic and their related challenges indicate that there is a need to engage citizens beyond political systems, at different tiers of public governance more directly. In recognition of this governance need and ranging from policy development to community projects, many countries, both developed and developing, have now embarked on a variety of engagement initiatives with the expectations that engagements will make public governance more relevant and accountable and bolster citizen trust.

Engagement initiatives

Direct civic engagements in public governance are now taking place at different levels – at policy development through formation of multi-stakeholder national economic and social councils (NESCs); at sub-national level for improved and citizen-sensitive service delivery; in local government planning and development; and in budgeting and auditing (United Nations, 2007).

Through adoption of locally suited institutional frameworks, these initiatives co-opt the civil society organizations as partners of public decisions. Challenges remain, and these need to be overcome since initiatives of civic engagement demonstrate that multi-stakeholder participation in policy development, direct citizen or civil society participation in budgeting and auditing and mainstreaming of civil society participation in local government councils help in enhancing transparency and accountability in public policies, promote sustained economic growth, reduce corruption and improve service delivery. It is expected that these positive outcomes will gain the capacity to enhance trust as well.[1]

Table 1 presents the relationship between civic engagement initiatives, impacts and also the challenges.

Table 1: Civic Engagement Initiatives, Impacts and Challenges

CG Initiatives	Impact on trust	Impact on accountability	Challenges
NESC (in properly operated countries: Ireland, Mauritius, South Korea etc.)	Sustained economic growth with better equity; low gini coeff.	Low Corruption Perception Index (CPI)	Tension with the parliamentary process; fear of elite capture; capacity
Participatory budgeting	Pro-poor allocations;	Low CPI; higher resource mobilization	Tension with the parliamentary process; fear of elite capture; capacity
Participatory sub	Improved social development performance; improved community endorsement	Low CPI; increased hits on government portals etc.	Conflict about CSO representativeness, capacity
Participatory audit	Greater programme delivery, corruption control	Low CPI	SAIs uncomfortable about CSO participation; capacity, enabling governance environment

However, civic engagements cannot happen in a vacuum. These initiatives have to be fully supported by a number of enabling factors such as democratization of societies, decentralization, rule of law, freedom of expression and capacity building (United Nations, 2007). Civic engagement initiatives also require adjustments to institutions, introduction of new rules and regulations, value change and most importantly, mentoring from within. Media also has a very important and responsible role to play, in both

---

[1] In recent times, available facts demonstrate that governments and leaders that promote participation also seem to win elections more frequently and revealingly, without the allegations of fraud.

highlighting genuine public issues, as well as connecting citizens to public institutions.

In summary, the rationale of civic engagement as an instrument of building trust in government stems from a number of values and these include: its intrinsic value in the sense that participation enhances ownership and thus contributes to strengthened mutual confidence; its instrumental value in that it produces relevant development outcomes and thus earns citizen appreciation; and finally, its constructive values (and in understanding the force and feasibility of claims, rights and duties) in the sense that it builds visions of shared goals and responsibilities .

These values are culture or situation neutral and are therefore, applicable to all situations- east, west, developed, developing countries. Considering its rising appeal, it would appear that the logic of civic engagement like the mission of democracy is gaining momentum and waiting to achieve the value of universality.

References

International Budget Project (2006). Open Budget Initiative 2006: More Public Information Needed to Hold Governments to Account. Washington, DC: International Budget Project. Available from *http://www.openbudgetindex. org/SummaryReport.pdf* (accessed 28 September 2007).

United Nations (2008). People Matter: Civic Engagement in Public Governance. World Public Sector Report. ST/ESA/PAD/SER.E/108. New York : United Nations.

World Economic Forum   (2006). Global Survey on Trust 2006. Toronto: GlobalScan International.

Participatory Governance: An Overview of Issues and Evidence

Siddiqur R. Osmani[2]

1. Introduction

The idea of participatory governance has gained enormous popularity in recent times, both in academic discourse and actual practice. Analysts have used theoretical constructs such as 'deliberative democracy' and 'empowered participatory governance' to scrutinise the scope and limitations of people's participation in the process of governance.[3] At the same time, some high-profile examples of successful participatory governance such as those of Porto Alegre in Brazil and the states of Kerala and West Bengal in India, and to a lesser extent South Africa, have aroused great expectations among activists and policymakers all over the world.

More generally, the recent emphasis on good governance as the foundation for sustained and equitable development has generated widespread interest in participation in the development circle, as effective participation by all stakeholders, especially at local levels of government, has come to be viewed as a necessary condition for promoting good governance.[4] In the developed world too, people's participation in social decision-making processes is increasingly being emphasized as a means of combating a range of social malaise, including the problems of social exclusion, political apathy and so on. Finally, in post-conflict, post-transition and other fragile societies, broad-based participation in public affairs is being promoted as a means of creating the social capital necessary for building a cohesive society (e.g. Brown 2006).

---

[2] Mr. Osmani was one of the panelists of the workshop on Building Trust through Civic Engagement. His paper is also featured at the United Nations publication on Participatory Governance and the Millennium Development Goals (2008). He is currently a Professor at the University of Ulster, UK, 2007.

[3] The idea of deliberative democracy has been explored extensively in a number of recent contributions, which include Bohman & Rehg (1997), Elster (1998), Freeman (2000) & Conover et al. (2002). For an authoritative account of the notion of Empowered Participatory Governance, see Fung & Wright (2003a).

[4] Mansuri & Rao (2004), Hickey & Mohan (2005) and Bardhan & Mookherjee (2006) contain detailed discussion of recent experience.

A huge burden of expectation is thus being placed on the slender shoulders of participation, which almost inevitably has begun to produce a backlash; so much so that some have even begun to speak of the 'tyranny' of participation (e.g., Cooke and Kothari, 2001). Yet the fact remains that for all the enthusiasm being shown in its support, examples of genuinely effective participation by all the relevant stakeholders, especially by the marginalised, socially excluded and disadvantaged groups, are still more of an exception than the rule.[5] Social action that is necessary to turn the idea of effective participation into reality is only beginning to emerge in most parts of the world. No less importantly, much of the analytical work that is necessary to guide that social action – in terms of clarifying the relevant conceptual issues and distilling the lessons of experience – also remains to be done, even though a good deal of work has already been done. The present chapter seeks to make a contribution towards this analytical task, by building on the work that has been done so far.[6]

The chapter proceeds by clarifying some conceptual issues related to the rationale of participation and varieties of its manifestation in Section 2. Section 3 discusses the evidence for the claimed benefits of electoral participation at national level, by drawing upon the burgeoning literature on democracy and development. Sections 4 and 5 examine the evidence on participation at local levels of government, focussing on the links between participation and decentralization. Section 4 is concerned with the efficiency effects of participatory decentralization, while Section 5 is concerned with the equity effects. Section 6 attempts to draw some lessons for effective participation based on the evidence discussed in the preceding sections. This discussion identifies three gaps – called the capacity gap, the incentive gap and the power gap – which must be bridged by appropriate social action and institution-building for effective participation to be possible. The chapter ends by offering some concluding observations in Section 7, drawing particular attention to the need for fostering synergies between the pre-conditions for effective participation and the practice of participation.

---

[5]   We define 'effective' participation as one in which all the relevant stakeholders take part in decision-making processes and are also able to influence the decisions in the sense that at the end of the decision-making process all parties feel that their views and interests have been given due consideration even if they are not always able to have their way.

[6]   In particular, the paper draws heavily upon a number of background papers written for the Division for Public Administration and Development Management (DPADM) of the United Nations Department of Economic and Social Affairs' (UNDESA) Expert Group Meeting on Engaged Governance: Citizen Participation in the Implementation of the Development Goals including the Millennium Development Goals November 1-2, 2006 and chapters in this volume – viz. Blair (2007), Commins (2006), Manor (2006), Platteau (2007) and Przeworski (2007).

2. The Rationale and Varieties of Participation: Some Conceptual Issues

Participation is valued for both intrinsic and instrumental reasons. The intrinsic value refers to the idea that the act of participation is valuable in itself, quite apart from any value it may have in helping to achieve other good things. Amartya Sen's forceful exposition of the idea of 'development as freedom' clearly recognises the intrinsic value of participation in the development process (Sen 1999). In this perspective, development consists of the expansion of a range of freedoms to do and to be the things that human beings have reasons to value, and the freedom to participate meaningfully in public affairs is seen as one of those valuable freedoms.

Sen (2002) makes a distinction between the opportunity aspect and the process aspect of freedom that is especially relevant in this context. The opportunity aspect refers to the freedom to achieve valuable outcomes - such as the ability to lead a life free from hunger, disease, illiteracy and so on, while the process aspect refers to the manner in which these outcomes are achieved - in particular, whether people have the freedom to influence the process that leads to the valuable outcomes. Development consists in the expansion of both these aspects of freedom because people attach value not just to the final outcomes but also to the process through which these outcomes are achieved.

The freedom to participate is related to the process aspect of freedom, and as such it is very much a constituent of development, not just a means of achieving it. As a constituent it may be valued just as much as the final outcomes. For instance, while people value freedom from hunger, they are not indifferent to the process through which this outcome is achieved. In particular, they have reason to value a process in which they have the freedom to participate actively in the choice of pathways leading to freedom from hunger as compared to a process in which this outcome is gifted to them by a benevolent dictator. This value of the freedom to participate in the process is distinct from and in addition to any value people may attach to the outcomes that may be achieved through participation. The intrinsic value of participation derives from the value people attach to this process aspect of freedom.

The argument that the freedom to participate in the development process is a valuable freedom in its own right has not remained confined to the philosopher's domain. The force of the argument has been recognised, for example, by the international human rights discourse, in which the right to participate is enshrined alongside rights to other civil-political and socio-economic freedoms. This recognition is quite explicit in the Declaration of the Right to Development adopted by the United Nations in 1986, which says: 'The right to development is an inalienable human right by virtue of which every human person and all peoples are *entitled to participate in*, contribute to and enjoy economic, social, cultural and political development, in which all human rights and fundamental freedoms can be fully realised.' (UN 1986, Paragraph 1 of Article 1; italics added) It is evident from this statement that the right to development is to be seen not simply as a right to 'enjoy' the fruits of development, but also as a right to participate in the process of realizing them.

The right to participate is not limited, however, to the context of development. It's a very general right that has a bearing on all spheres of public affairs, and as such it is equally applicable to developed as well as developing countries. This is evident from the following excerpt from Article 25 of the International Covenant on Civil and Political Rights: 'Every citizen shall have the right and the opportunity ... *To take part* in the conduct of public affairs, directly or through freely chosen representatives ...' (italics added). Thus the universality of the right to participate has been recognized beyond dispute, underlining the intrinsic value of participation in all spheres of public life.

It's a welcome bonus that in addition to being intrinsically valuable, participation can also be a powerful instrument for achieving a range of valuable outcomes. In particular, participation has the potential to achieve more efficient and equitable outcomes in many different contexts of decision-making, such as allocation of budgetary resources among alternative uses, management of common property resources, delivery of community services, and so on.

Both allocative and technical efficiency can be enhanced through participation. Crucial to the achievement of allocative efficiency is success in ensuring that resources are allocated in accordance with the preferences of the people concerned. But ascertaining what the preferences are is not a simple task. Markets have their own ways of eliciting information on preferences (even though it can sometimes go awry), but this can be a seriously tricky affair in non-market spheres such as bureaucratic decision-making processes, which may have no reliable mechanism for revealing the preferences of those likely to be affected by the decisions. Decisions based on wrong perceptions of what people actually want can result in wastage of scarce resources – that is, in the loss of allocative efficiency. This is one of the pitfalls of top-down bureaucratic decision-making. By contrast, participation by relevant stakeholders in the decision-making process may make it easier to achieve allocative efficiency by facilitating the process of preference revelation. When people are able to exercise their voice in the conduct of public affairs, they will have an opportunity to reveal their true preferences. Only participation can allow this exercise of voice.[7]

---

[7]   As we shall see in Section IV, participation does not guarantee that allocations will be made on the basis of true preferences; for various reasons, distortion of preferences can occur even in participatory processes. All that is being claimed here is that participation makes allocation based on true preferences more likely than would otherwise be the case.

Technical efficiency – which refers to the efficiency with which resources are used for a given end[8] – can also be improved through participation in a number of ways. One of them hinges on the notion of informational asymmetry and another on the idea of accountability. Informational asymmetry is a common problem in the typical top-down procedures of designing and implementing community-level projects, where those in charge of the projects may not possess some relevant information that local people may have. Two types of problems can follow from such asymmetric information – known as 'hidden information' and 'hidden action' problems respectively. Both of them are relevant in the present context.

The 'hidden information' problem arises because the bureaucrats and technocrats responsible for the projects do not often have access to the details of local-level information that may be necessary for proper design and implementation of projects. Local people may possess the necessary information, but if the project is to achieve efficient outcomes, this information needs to be harnessed and used in tandem with the technical knowledge possessed by others. Thus in principle the problem of hidden information can be solved by a co-operative decision-making framework that involves all those who possess relevant information. Participation of local people in the design and implementation of community-level projects is essential for this purpose.

Participation can also help deal with the 'hidden action' aspect of informational asymmetry that often stands in the way of the efficient execution of projects. In a top-down bureaucratic framework, implementation of local-level projects will typically involve local people working for remuneration. If these workers choose to be negligent in their duties, this will have an adverse effect on the outcome of the project, but the bureaucrats may find it hard to detect the offenders through the arm's length monitoring methods they typically employ. Nor is it always possible to detect negligence *ex post* by observing project outcomes, because even if the outcomes happen to be poor, the bureaucrats may not have the information necessary to decide whether it is the workers' negligence or some extraneous factors that are responsible for poor outcomes. This is a typical moral hazard problem – one that entails loss of efficiency through harmful hidden action. Participation of the local community in all stages of the project cycle can help circumvent this problem in at least two ways. First, the community may employ the method of 'peer monitoring' to prevent negligence, which has a greater likelihood of success than the arm's length method employed by the bureaucrats. Secondly, the sense of ownership that participation can bring may itself act as a deterrent – after all people don't normally cheat in the tasks they consider their own.

The other route through which participation can improve efficiency is by strengthening the institutions of accountability. Politicians and govern-

---

8   Strictly speaking, this definition is somewhat broader than what economists call technical efficiency as it also includes the related but distinct concept of X-efficiency.

ment officials who take decisions and implement them - supposedly for the benefit of the people - are often subject to pressures that might conflict with the goal of serving the public interest. However, the more accountable they are for their actions, the less likely they are to succumb to those pressures and the greater the likelihood of more efficient outcomes.

There are many different ways of ensuring accountability. Some of them are quite formal – for example, administrative and judicial procedures for scrutinising the performance of government officials and holding periodic elections for politicians. The latter is one of the channels through which people can participate in accountability procedures. If elected representatives do not perform to the satisfaction of the voters, the latter have the option of removing them from office in the next election. It is because of this accountability-enforcing property of elections that democracy is sometimes claimed to be more conducive to development than its alternatives such as autocracy. There are, however, arguments on the other side as well, and the relationship between development and the type of government remains a matter of lively debate.[9]

Election in any case is a rather blunt instrument for holding politicians accountable for specific actions. This is partly because of the long time lag between successive elections, and partly because of the fact that elected representatives are expected to perform many different tasks some of which they might do rather well while failing in others. Elections can, however, be supplemented by other participatory mechanisms with more direct and immediate impact on accountability – for example, by holding a village meeting in which the elected officials are required to explain to the public how they spent the money entrusted to them for the benefit of the villagers. As a supplement to the standard administrative procedures for ensuring accountability, these participatory mechanisms can help strengthen the overall institutional framework for holding the duty-bearers accountable for their actions, and thereby improve the likelihood of efficient outcomes.

In addition to encouraging more efficient use of resources, participation also has the potential of improving the likelihood of more equitable outcomes. Efficiency and equity are both qualities that are worth aspiring for, but unfortunately in most cases of public policy one has to face a trade-off between the two. For instance, while carrying out redistributive policies that transfer resources from the rich to the poor, some efficiency may have to be sacrificed for the sake of equity. In reality, there are not too many policy instruments that can improve efficiency and equity at the same time. Fortunately, participation is one of those rare instruments than can potentially do so.[10]

---

[9]   The evidence on the relationship between democracy and development is examined in section III.

[10]   Section 4 reviews the evidence on the efficiency effect of participation. The equity outcomes of participation are examined in section 5.

In fact, some of the pathways through which participation can lead to higher efficiency are also the ones that can lead to more equitable outcomes. For example, when people exercise their voice to reveal their preferences over alternative outcomes and policies to achieve them, it not only helps improve allocative efficiency but also creates an opportunity for the weaker and marginalised groups of the society to press for their interest in a way that is seldom possible in the standard practice of governance. The same principle applies to the pathways that allow participation to strengthen the institutions of accountability. While helping to achieve technical efficiency, participatory mechanisms of accountability also provide an opportunity to the weaker segments of the society to ensure that the duty-bearers cannot get away with policies and practices that are unjust and unfair towards them. As a result, when it comes to taking policy decisions with distributive consequences, such as how to use the resources at the disposal of the local government or how to choose beneficiaries of services to be delivered by the government, participatory mechanisms are likely to achieve more equitable outcomes compared to non-participatory ones.

The instrumental role of participation can be further clarified by examining its relationship with two other concepts - namely, empowerment and social capital. These two may be thought of as intermediate variables through which participation promotes efficiency and equity.

The causal link between participation and empowerment is quite straightforward. In normal processes of governance, in which decisions are taken by an elite coterie consisting of politicians, bureaucrats and technocrats, ordinary people are powerless to influence the decisions that may have far-reaching consequences for their lives and livelihoods. Even if those decisions happen to be favourable to them, the fact remains that they are at the mercy of a distant group of decision-makers over whom they have very little control. Participation can change all that. The very presence of ordinary people at the discussion table will give them some power to influence the decision-making processes and their outcomes – even if they are not always able to participate on equal terms with the elite decision-makers. One would thus expect participatory mechanisms to be more empowering than non-participatory ones, even though the degree of empowerment may well vary depending on circumstances.

Participation also has obvious implications for the formation of social capital, which consists of the networks of relationships between different individuals and groups operating outside the market sphere. Through the very act of bringing people together and allowing them to interact with each other in the course of decision-making activities outside the market, participatory governance gives people an opportunity to strengthen these networks and build new ones. The result is an expansion of social capital – both the 'bonding' type that ties people from similar social status and the 'bridging' type that allows people from different stations in life to get closer to each other.

These effects of participation - namely, empowerment and expansion of social capital - can in turn have salutary effects on the efficiency and equity of the outcomes that decision-making processes are meant to achieve. Both of them can enable people to express their preferences better and to make them count, thereby enhancing allocative efficiency; to improve the accountability of those who are responsible for implementing decisions, thereby improving technical efficiency; and to ensure that the interests of those suffering from marginalisation and social exclusion are not ignored or trampled over, thereby promoting the cause of equity.

Of course, it is not guaranteed that participation will always be able to achieve these desirable outcomes, and even when it does so the degree of success can vary widely. Much will depend on the extent to which participation can actually lead to greater empowerment and stronger social capital. However, that in turn will depend, among other things, on the initial levels of empowerment and social capital that different social groups bring to the process of participation. The higher the initial endowments of these two entities, the more potent will participation be to engender further empowerment and social capital, and thereby to achieve more efficient and equitable outcomes of decision-making processes. It is indeed arguable that participation can achieve very little in a situation where the endowment of empowerment and social capital is practically non-existent to begin with. One of the concerns of this paper will be to examine the strategies and actions that can be help enhance these initial endowments.

However, the point that needs to be emphasised at this stage is that there exists a synergistic relationship between participation on the one hand and empowerment and social capital on the other – they can mutually reinforce each other, thereby engendering a virtuous cycle.[11] An important implication of this point is that there is no need to wait for a very high level of empowerment and social capital to emerge before participatory governance can be allowed to proceed. All that may be necessary is to cross a critical minimum threshold of these two endowments beyond which the synergy mentioned above would be able to render participation a self-reinforcing process. This will of course have to be supplemented by an appropriate institutional framework for participation so that the self-reinforcing process can achieve its full potential.[12]

The actual practice of participatory governance varies enormously in its form and effectiveness, depending on the initial endowments and the quality of the institutions for participation. One way of making sense of this diversity is to compare the varieties of practice along two dimensions, namely the scope and the intensity of participation. In terms of scope, participation can

---

[11]   The issue of synergy is discussed more fully in section 7.

[12]   Some of the most important classes of actions that are needed to ensure success of participatory processes are examined in details in section 6.

in principle encompass four distinct types of activities, which together might be said to constitute the act of governance – namely (a) ascertaining people's preferences over alternative social outcomes and alternative processes of achieving those outcomes, (b) formulation of policies, rules and institutions based on those preferences, (c) implementation of the proposed policies, rules and institutions, and (d) monitoring, evaluation and ensuring accountability of policy formulation and implementation.[13] Participation can be said to be the most extensive in scope when it occurs in each of these phases. Such comprehensive participation is, however, rare in real life; most instances of participatory governance cover a subset of the four phases (Blair 2007).

The scope of participation is not of course an adequate measure of the effectiveness or quality of participation, as it also depends on the intensity of participation. In each of the four phases, the intensity of participation can vary from the superficial to the deeply engaged form of involvement by the relevant stakeholders. The degree of intensity is in turn a function of the institutional framework within which participation is embedded. The institutional framework embodies the rules of the game that determine, for example, who will be allowed to participate in decision-making process, how they will express their preferences, how the preferences of different stakeholders will be reconciled, and how they will be involved in the processes of implementation, monitoring, evaluation and accountability. It is the quality of these institutional processes that ultimately determines the quality of participation.

Thus although intuitively participation would appear to be a simple idea, its institutional manifestation can be quite complex. Its scope can vary widely depending on which of the four stages of policy cycle it happens to encompass, and its intensity can span a wide spectrum depending on the institutional framework that defines the rules of the game for participation in each phase. One consequence of this complexity is that participation cannot be seen as an 'all or nothing' affair – rather it is a matter of degree, reflecting variations in both scope and intensity. This also means that if the quality of participation in some specific instance falls short of whatever one thinks to be the 'ideal type', that is not necessarily a reason for despair. What matters is whether the existing form and structure of participation makes for a quality of participation that is good enough for the purpose at hand.[14] Once a minimum threshold of quality is ensured, the self-reinforcing property of participation discussed earlier can be expected to take over.

---

[13]   In the context of specific policies, these may be seen as four phases of the policy cycle. See Osmani (2002).

[14]   This is not an argument for being complacent with the status quo or against trying to improve things further, but a reason for not resigning oneself to nihilism at the first sight of imperfection – a point that resonates with Merilee Grindle's idea of 'good enough governance' (Grindle, 2004).

Yet another consequence of the complexity mentioned above is that the institutional details of participation cannot be expected to be identical everywhere, even if the immediate objective of participation is the same (for example, providing a particular type of service to a community, or deciding on the pattern of resource allocation at the level of local government). The same objective may call for different forms of participation in different contexts, and this is true in both positive and normative senses. The positive sense is that the institutional structure that is most likely to emerge to foster participation in a specific context would vary depending, among other things, on the 'initial conditions' – that is, the number and quality of the people involved, the balance of forces between different social groups, the overall socio-political environment, the level of economic development, and so on. The normative sense is that the structure of participation that may be deemed appropriate for a specific purpose may also vary depending on these initial conditions. The context-specificity of the structure of participation is, therefore, an inescapable fact of life. Any attempt to transfer lessons of successful participation from one context to another ought to be conscious of this fact.

3. Electoral Participation in National Governance: The Instrumental Value

Participation is expected to achieve many good things, but what is the evidence in this regard? One of the problems of assessing the evidence is that participation can occur in many different forms and in many different contexts, and its effect can also vary accordingly. Making sense of the evidence, after allowing for the contextual differences, is therefore not a simple task. Some of the most rigorous analysis of the evidence carried out so far relates to the effect of participation as embodied in the nature of political regimes that govern the nation states – a body of literature that has come to be known as the 'democracy and development' debate. The issue in question is whether democracy promotes development better than autocracy and the answer is sought by comparing the experience of countries with different political regimes.

The relevance of this debate in the present context is that democracy represents a basic form of participation by ordinary people in the act of governance, while autocracy represents its absence. Any evidence in favour of democracy can, therefore, be adduced as evidence in favour of participation. In most democracies, however, people participate only indirectly through elected representatives; as such, a democratic political regime governing at the national level can be said to embody participation only at a minimum level of intensity. Still it is interesting to know whether even this minimalist type of participation has any instrumental value in promoting development. If the answer is yes, that would provide at least a *prima facie* case for the view that more intense types of participation at national and local levels would promote development even better.

Development of course has many dimensions and it is conceivable that the effect of democracy might be different for different dimensions. The dimension that has been investigated most extensively is the rate of economic growth, and yet the evidence accumulated so far is by no means conclusive.[15] During the second half of the twentieth century, democracies as a group have enjoyed a slightly faster rate of growth of per capita income than autocracies as a group. But even this small difference disappears when one controls for the different initial conditions and extraneous influences under which different political regimes have operated. Thus on the average democracy does not seem to have any edge over autocracy in terms of economic growth.

However, this result does not necessarily imply that the nature of a political regime has no causal influence on economic growth. What is more likely is that democracy and autocracy have their respective strengths and weaknesses, with each having some positive and some negative effects on growth, and that on average the net effects do not differ very much. It may be true for example, that autocracies use the coercive state power more ruthlessly to depress consumption so as to extract more savings and thereby accumulate more capital than democracies can manage to do. On the other hand, it's possible that by being more accountable through periodic elections, democracies do better in curbing growth-retarding rent-seeking activities than autocracies do. On balance, these effects may cancel each other out.

The average picture also hides the fact that compared to democracies autocracies differ more widely amongst themselves in terms of growth performance. The best of the growth miracles (e.g., in East Asia) and the worst of the growth disasters (e.g., in sub-Saharan Africa) are both to be found almost exclusively in autocracies, while democracies are on the whole characterised by middling performances, with the result that on the average the two regimes do not seem to perform very differently.

Democracy and autocracy do not seem to differ much in terms of income distribution either – the income share of the bottom quintile is found to be similar in the two types of regimes, after controlling for per capita income and other contextual factors. Thus democracy does not seem to have an advantage over autocracy in terms of ensuring higher incomes for the poorest segment of the population. However this is the average picture, encompassing both rich and poor nations. Focussing only on the countries at low levels of income, one does find a significant difference – the poorest

---

[15]   Most of the findings reported in this section are drawn from the comprehensive review of the recent literature by Przeworski (2007). For further analysis of the links between democracy and development, see, among others, Sirowy & Inkeles (1990), Przeworski & Limongi (1993), Sen (1999), Przeworski *et al.* (2000), Tavares & Wacziarg (2001), Varshney (2002), Lee (2003), Keefer & Khemani (2005), Ross (2006), Persson & Tabellini (2006) and Sinmazdemir (2006).

quintile of the population enjoys a higher level of income in poor democracies as compared with poor autocracies. As the problem of absolute poverty is concentrated mostly in the poorest nations of the world, this finding suggests that democracy may have an advantage over autocracy in handling the problem of absolute poverty, so long as the countries remain poor. Since, as noted above, the two regimes do not differ much in terms of rates of growth, this advantage presumably derives from the greater propensity of democracies to adopt either redistributive policies in favour of the poor or more pro-poor growth policies, or a combination of the two.

The pro-poor edge of democracy is evident even more when one considers acute deprivation, for example as manifested in the occurrence of famines, and dimensions of poverty other than income. As Amartya Sen has famously observed, famines never occur in independent well-functioning democracies endowed with free media and a vibrant political climate that allows for public debate and political opposition.[16] As an imminent famine looms large, the media, civil society and political adversaries begin to demand immediate remedial action by the government, which in a democracy the rulers can ignore only at their peril in the next election. Two attributes of democracy are at work here – namely, the scope for open debate as an accountability-demanding mechanism and the presence of election as an accountability-enforcing mechanism. The possibilities of demanding accountability through a free media, and then enforcing it through election together ensure that democratic politicians cannot allow famine to reach a stage where it would cost a huge number of lives. In the absence of similar mechanisms for demanding and enforcing accountability, autocratic regimes can, by contrast, easily let a nascent famine get out of control.

This contrast is most strikingly evident in the comparative history of India and China in the second half of the twentieth century. Before gaining political independence from the British in 1947, India was repeatedly ravaged by famines, the latest being the Great Bengal famine of 1944 that cost two to three million lives. However, since independence, democratic India has not endured a single famine, although the threat of famine did emerge several times. On every occasion that such a threat appeared, the pressure created in the arena for public debate was strong enough to spur the government into immediate action to avert the famine. This is in sharp contrast to the behaviour of the communist rulers of China. They had used their autocratic power to great benefit of the poor Chinese by meeting their basic needs in normal times, and yet allowed a temporary food scarcity caused by the Great Leap Forward of 1958 to degenerate into the most devastating famine of the twentieth century. In the absence of the accountability mechanisms

---

[16]   One of his earliest analyses of the relationship between democracy and famine can be found in Sen (1983); the argument is elaborated and illustrated more fully in Dreze & Sen (1989, 1995).

afforded by democracy, they faced no compulsion to take remedial measures, and indeed were probably not even aware of the magnitude of the problem until it was too late. And once they did become aware, their instinctive reaction was to hide the tragedy from the rest of the world instead of pursuing all options to save lives, including seeking help from outside. The consequence was the tragic loss of close to thirty million lives! The absence of democratic accountability has seldom been so expensive in the history of mankind.

The spectacular success of democracy in averting famines is unfortunately not mirrored in the fight against chronic but relatively mild hunger, although as noted earlier the problem of absolute poverty is probably somewhat less severe in poor democracies as compared to poor autocracies. The superior, if unspectacular, performance of democracy in dealing with the problem of chronic deprivation in nutrition and healthcare is also reflected in the better survival chances of the people living in democracies. Cross-country evidence shows that democracies in general perform better than autocracies in reducing the infant mortality rate. This is especially true about the poorer countries of the world. For all income levels below $15,000 per capita, democracies have on the average lower infant mortality rates than autocracies. Democracy, evidently, can save lives not just in the face of short term crisis of famine-threats, but also in the long haul by lessening chronic deprivation in nutrition and healthcare. To put some numbers to the extent of this success, it has been estimated that after controlling for other factors that have a bearing on the survival chances of infants, democracy makes a difference of 4.6 fewer deaths per thousand as compared with autocracies (Navia & Zweifel, 2003).

One obvious problem with this kind of binary comparison between democracy and autocracy is that it ignores variations within each type of regime in the degree of participation and their consequences. Not all autocracies, for example, are characterised by complete absence of participation; some of them do allow periodic elections, even if they are usually non-competitive. On the other hand, democracies, which do allow competitive elections, differ amongst each other in terms of the proportion of the electorate who actually participate in voting. One of the most interesting findings of recent research is that such variations in the degree of participation can matter for the well-being of the people. In the countries in which at least half the electorate cast their votes, higher rate of electoral participation is associated with both faster growth of per capita income and higher share of income for the bottom quintile of the population. These results hold after controlling for differences in per capita income, which implies that among countries that are at similar levels of per capita income those with higher levels of electoral participation suffer from lower levels of absolute poverty.[17]

---

[17]   For evidence, see the literature reviewed in Przeworski (this volume).

Significantly, this relationship between the extent of electoral participation and poverty holds regardless of whether or not the elections are competitive, that is, regardless of whether elections are held under democratic or autocratic dispensations. Evidently, even though autocrats who allow elections do so without any fear of being forced out of office as a result, they tend to adopt more pro-poor policies in response to greater participation by the people in the electoral process, as do the democrats. This, along with the evidence on the pro-poor edge of democratic regimes discussed earlier, suggests that even the minimalist type of participation that is embodied in electoral participation at the national level can indeed be beneficial for the poor.

4. Participation in Decentralized Governance: The Efficiency Effect

Electing representatives for running the government at the national (or provincial) level is an essential part of people's participation in the conduct of public affairs. However it is an indirect and infrequent mode of participation. A much more continuous and engaged form of participation is possible in running the affairs at community and local levels. Both top-down decentralization of administration and bottom-up growth of community organizations, often occurring in tandem with each other, can open up such possibilities of engaged participation. A growing body of evidence shows that when this happens, participatory institutions managing service delivery and common property resources at the community level can perform better in terms of both efficiency and equity compared to alternative institutions such as market mechanism and bureaucratic management.[18]

Community participation has been known to have improved the efficiency of irrigation systems in many parts of the world by making use of local knowledge on soil conditions, water velocity and shifting water courses (e.g., Chambers, 1988; Ascher & Healy, 1990; Ostrom, Lam & Lee 1994); of water and sanitation projects, by ensuring that these are sited where they are most likely to be used (Manikutty 1997, 1998); and of public work projects, by utilizing local knowledge about safety hazards and vandalism (Adato *et al.*, 1999). The World Development Report 1994 on infrastructure reported that in a study of 121 completed rural water supply projects, financed by various agencies, projects with high degree of local participation in project selection and design were more likely to enjoy good maintenance subsequently than those with more centralized decision-making (World Bank, 1994).

---

[18]   Much of the evidence is discussed in Crook & Manor (1998), Manor (1999), Cooke & Kothari (2001), Ribot & Larson (2004), Mansuri & Rao (2004), World Bank (2004), Ahmad *et al.* (2005), Hickey & Mohan (2005) and Bardhan & Mookherjee (2006). See also Commins (2007).

Water Aid's work with communities around Hitosa in Ethiopia is a nice illustration of the efficiency-enhancing power of participation. The programme involved thirty-one communities that worked together to operate and maintain water tap stands and pipeline, with each community providing two representatives for the area Water Management Board. The standard of maintenance improved significantly as participation resulted in high community motivation, better design of solutions appropriate to community resources, and quick response to emerging problems (Silkin 1999). In the same vein, a study of water supply projects in Indonesia, India and Sri Lanka has found that community participation in designing and execution of projects led to higher level of community satisfaction with the project (Isham & Kähkönen 2002a, 2002b), thus confirming the results obtained by Katz and Sara (1997) based on a broader set of countries.

Participation can also improve efficiency by ensuring better monitoring and verification. The Education Guarantee Scheme (EGS) implemented in the Indian state of Madhya Pradesh is a shining example. Madhya Pradesh has long been one of the most backward states of India in terms of human development, with the literacy figure being appallingly low even by the low standard of the all-India average. In recognition of this problem, the State Government of Madhya Pradesh introduced in January 1997 the innovative Education Guarantee Scheme with a view to ensuring universal access to primary education in the shortest possible time. The scheme involved both a guarantee on the part of the government and a compact between the government and local communities for sharing the cost and managing the programme.

Under the Scheme, the government guaranteed the provision of a trained teacher, her/his salaries, training of teachers, teacher-training materials and contingencies to start a school within ninety days, wherever there was demand from a community without a primary schooling facility within one kilometre, and provided this demand came from at least twenty five learners in case of tribal areas and forty learners in case of non-tribal areas. The community in turn had to identify and put forward a teacher and also provide the space for teaching-learning. Local management committees were set up for taking responsibility for day-to-day management of schools, and in particular for ensuring regular attendance on the part of both teachers and students. By all accounts, the Scheme has proved to be an overwhelming success. In the first year of its operation, more than forty new schools opened each day, and after eighteen months, the State could boast universal access to primary education. A good deal of work remains to be done in terms of improving the quality of education offered by these schools, but at least in terms of ensuring access to education the Scheme clearly demonstrates the power of the participatory approach (GOMP 1998).

The efficiency effect of community participation in the provision of educational services is also evident in the Intensive District Approach to Education for All (IDEAL) project in Bangladesh. The project has institutionalized participation of the community in two crucial stages – namely, school catchment area mapping and school planning. At the mapping stage, the community helps in the identification of all primary age children in the catchment area, enrolled and otherwise. In the planning stage, the community takes part in all decisions related to creating conditions for better enrolment and retention, improving the quality of education, mobilizing local resources and allocating available resources. The outcome of this participatory approach has been a significant improvement in the enrolment and retention of students and in the quality of education (Mozumder & Halim 2006). Similarly, King and Ozler (1998) found in Nicaragua that students attending schools under community management achieved better test scores than students attending other schools.

Yet another way in which participation can enhance efficiency is by reducing costs and by augmenting resources in ways that are not available to outsiders. The cost-saving potential is demonstrated by the experience of Social Funds in Malawi. Communities operating these Funds were able to convince participants to accept lower wages than those officially sanctioned, with the savings being devoted to the construction of additional physical assets (Narayan 1998). This resource-augmenting potential is demonstrated by two studies in Nepal and Uganda. Participatory water management projects in Nepal have given the incentive to water users to contribute generously towards project costs (NSAC 1998). Nearly three-quarters of the beneficiaries contributed cash and/or labour for farmer managed irrigation projects. The Ugandan example comes from the Uganda Participatory Poverty Assessment Project (UPPAP) undertaken in the districts of Kumi and Kapchorwa (Owomugasho *et al.* 1999a, 1999b). The respondents of both districts felt that one of the greatest advantages of participatory management was the ease of mobilizing local resources for local use. Since people felt confident that locally mobilized resources would be used mainly for the benefit of local people, and according to the preferences of local people, they claimed to be more inclined to pay taxes to local governments than they otherwise would.

As for participatory management of common property resources by the users themselves, there are many examples of such institutions from around the world that have worked very well over a long period of time.[19] Their existence belies the notion popularized by a famous paper by Hardin (1968) that as a result of rapid economic growth and population pressure common property resources are inexorably being destroyed all over the world. This notion was misleading in an important sense. What is actually inexorable is the eventual disappearance of 'open access' commons, that is, those common

---

[19]   A small but rich sample of such studies includes McKay & Acheson (1987), Wade (1987), Ostrom (1990), Bromley (1992), Knudsen (1995), Baland & Platteau (1996) and Berkes (1998).

property resources to which access is not regulated one way or the other. But historically, most of the local commons (as distinct from global commons, such as the ozone layer) were subject to well-defined rules of access and use that evolved over many centuries of trial and error. There is no inevitability about the demise of these commons; it all depends on how well the age-old institutions can be adapted to the changed circumstances.

The possibility of creating and sustaining participatory institutions for managing local commons depends of course on the feasibility of co-operation among the users. Economists have traditionally been sceptical of the possibility of such co-operation in view of the scope for free-riding that is inherent in this situation. But recent advances in game theory have convinced them that it is possible for a group of self-interested individuals to find free-riding an unattractive option and to spontaneously devise institutions for co-operation, when they have to interact with each other repeatedly over a long period of time.[20] Such institutions are self-enforcing in nature, in the sense that once in place their rules are adhered to by the users out of self-interest – no external enforcement is needed. Many of the participatory institutions that exist in the real world are of this nature. But there are also other types that are based on mutual enforcement and peer monitoring, and still others that are based on hierarchical enforcement that is, those that are enforced by local leaders with the consent of all. In short, there are a variety of mechanisms - namely self-enforcement, peer monitoring, and hierarchical enforcement - through which users can in principle overcome the free-rider problem and devise viable participatory institutions.[21]

However, the important question is whether there is any reason to believe that these institutions are more efficient than alternative institutional arrangements, in particular bureaucratic management. At least one large-scale study suggests that it can be. In a comparison of a large number of community-managed and government-managed irrigation institutions in Nepal, the community-managed projects were found to be more efficient in terms of a number of criteria – such as crop yield, cropping intensity, and so on (Ostrom & Gardner 1993; Ostrom 1994).

The main reason for this difference lay in the superior ability of community-managed systems to resolve the tensions surrounding allocation of water among different users in the dry season. The study found that a higher percentage of community-managed systems were able to get abundant water to both the head and the tail of their systems across all the seasons. Since water availability may depend on a number of physical factors that have little to do with institutions, Ostrom and Gardner (1993) carried out a statistical analysis to isolate the effect of these factors and still found community man-

---

[20]   In the game-theory literature this proposition is known as the 'folk theorem'. The classic exposition can be found in Fudenberg & Maskin (1986).

[21]   The analytics of these mechanisms for institution-building have been discussed, among others, by Ostrom (1990, 1992) and Bardhan (1993).

agement to be the superior institutional framework. They concluded that 'farmer-managed systems are more likely to reach bargaining solutions about their own operational rules that more effectively take tailender interests into account.' (p. 104)

The value of participation for common property resource management is also highlighted by the experience of the Indian state of Madhya Pradesh and Nepal. Participatory management of forests instituted under the Joint Forest Management Scheme (JFM) initiated in the early 1990s has begun to yield hope of halting the age-old process of forest depletion. For a long time, the forest people themselves were partly responsible for resource depletion as they overexploited the forest resources for their immediate economic gain. JFM has sought to counter this tendency by vesting ownership of forest products to the local people so that they can perceive a stake in its long run preservation and by actively involving them in forest management. For this purpose, Village Forest Committees have been set up for rehabilitation of degraded forests, and Forest Protection Committees have been set up to protect the well-wooded forests. By all accounts, these efforts have begun to have a visible impact on the State's forest resources (GOMP 1998).

Something similar has happened in Nepal. In the early 1990s, the government undertook a project to hand over forest management to user groups within the framework of Community Forestry Projects. The Forest Act of 1993 recognized forest user groups as 'autonomous and corporate institutions with perpetual succession' with rights to acquire, sell or transfer forest products. A large number of user groups soon emerged being encouraged by this Act, and in 1995 the Federation of Community Forestry User Groups was founded with the purpose of mobilizing and articulating the interest of these groups. Evaluations have shown that this participatory approach to resource management has been much more successful than earlier top-down approaches in which the Forest Department had held supreme power, although the benefits may not have always been enjoyed equitably (NSAC 1998; Agrawal & Gupta 2005).

The preceding analysis suggests that there is no dearth of examples from around the world to support the hypothesis that community participation in development processes at the local level can improve efficiency in multiple ways. There, is, however, one methodological problem that often makes it difficult to draw any firm conclusions. When community participation is found to be associated with more efficient outcomes, it may not necessarily be right to conclude that participation contributed to higher efficiency, even if the association was found to hold after controlling for other possible influences on efficiency. The problem is that the observed positive association between participation and efficiency may reflect reverse causation – namely, that the communities chose to participate only in those cases where the projects were already known to be efficient or at least promised to be so. Technically, this is known as the endogeneity problem – community participation is said to be endogenous when the decision to participate is contingent on the community's evaluation of the likely outcome. In order to ascertain whether participation indeed contributed to efficiency, it is first necessary to know whether the problem of endogeneity existed in the particular case under investigation, and if it did, to isolate this effect. This is a technically demanding exercise, which is theoretically possible to do, but it requires additional information of a kind that does not always exist or is very difficult to obtain.

Fortunately, a recent study was able to deal with this problem while analyzing the effects of participation in public works programmes in South Africa (Adato *et al.* 2003).[22] Soon after South Africa's democratic transition in 1994, the new government launched a large-scale public works programme with multiple objectives: namely, to create jobs in response to extremely high levels of poverty and unemployment; to build or rehabilitate infrastructure in backward areas or to improve the natural environment; to provide job training that would enable workers subsequently to find formal sector employment; and finally to build the capacity of communities to control their own development through participation in public works projects. Although the projects were executed by government agencies with the help of private contractors, the community was involved in most of these projects at various stages – e.g., project design, project management and hiring of workers. Through careful econometric analysis that isolated the endogeneity effect, Adato *et al.* (2003) have found that participation indeed had an efficiency-enhancing effect. Higher levels of community participation were found to have a statistically significant, positive effect on the proportion of project budget spent on labour, the number of days of work created, the number of training days undertaken, and the percentage of employment going to women. It also reduced the cost of creating employment and the cost of transferring income to the poor.

Notwithstanding the evidence cited above, it should not be assumed that decentralized participation automatically and necessarily enhances efficiency. Participation may sometimes be injurious to technical efficiency, if people do not have the capacity to make informed judgments on technical matters. Thus, a study in Pakistan found that while greater community participation in non-technical decisions was associated with higher project outcomes, in technical decisions it actually led to worse outcomes (Khwaja 2004). Participation may also harm efficiency by diffusing control and authority in management. For example, in a study of water tanks in South India, Mosse (1997) observed that the tanks were not necessarily better managed in co-operative frameworks. In some areas, at least, management seemed to

---

[22]   See also Isham *et al.* (1995) on the question of establishing causality between participation and performance.

be better when order and discipline was imposed among users by a strong caste authority.

Participation may also fail to achieve allocative efficiency that is, to allocate resources in accordance with true preferences of the people, because there may be circumstances in which people, or those who claim to speak for them, have the incentive to distort information about preferences. This is especially true of donor-funded projects, in which the potential participants may deliberately express preferences which they think are more in line with the preferences of the donors rather than of their own, in the hope of improving their chance of receiving the funds, but there are also other circumstances in which such distortion may happen.[23]

Since these failures of participation occur due to factors that are endogenous to the logic of community participation rather than to exogenous forces, these have been described as examples of 'community imperfection', by analogy with the concepts of market imperfection and government imperfection (e.g. Platteau & Abraham 2002). The general point here is that just as both market and government may fail to function efficiently due to factors that are endogenous to their workings, so can community. The possibility of such community failure should warn us against entertaining the naïve view that all problems of governance would be solved simply by involving the community in decision-making processes. It is conceivable that some decisions are best taken in a non-participatory manner; and in any case, when communities do get involved certain complementary measures may have to be taken for them to function efficiently.[24]

5. Participation in Decentralized Governance: The Equity Effect

It was argued in section 3 that democracy at the national level is likely to be associated with more pro-poor policies compared to autocracies, and there is some evidence to suggest that this is indeed the case. A similar argument· applies at the local level as well. If allocative decisions at the local level are taken directly by people themselves or their democratically elected representatives, the weaker groups should be better able to influence allocations in their favour, compared to the mode of decision-making by unaccountable bureaucrats or traditional village elite. The argument rests on the presumption that in participatory decision-making processes, even the weaker groups would be able to express their preferences and hopefully make them count.

But this presumption may not hold in the presence of community imperfection, which is potentially an even more serious problem for equity

---

[23]   Platteau (this volume) offers an insightful analysis of the causes and consequences, as well as actual instances, of such information distortions in participatory activities.

[24]   Section VI is concerned with identifying the most important of these measures that are likely to have a general applicability.

than it is for efficiency. For understandable reasons, there is a great deal of skepticism about whether participation on its own can ensure an equitable outcome in an otherwise unequal world. There is also a good deal of evidence to support such skepticism.

For example, a recent study of the poverty alleviation effects of the Ecuadorian Social Fund found clear signs of unequal outcomes of participation in an unequal society (Araujo *et al.* 2006). The Fund offered a choice between two types of projects – local public goods (which were accessible to all) and excludable private goods meant mainly for the poor. The most important private good provided was latrines built in plots belonging to community members with no previous access to toilet facilities, that is, basically the poor. The choice between the two types of projects was made in a participatory manner. Rigorous statistical analysis of these choices showed that, after controlling for the effect of poverty, the more unequal communities opted more for local public goods than for the private good meant for the poor. Similar instances of mismatch between participatory outcomes and the preferences/needs of the weaker groups of the communities have been found in the case of the Peruvian Social Fund (Paxson & Schady 2002) and the Jamaican Social Investment Fund (Rao & Ibanez, 2001).

Despite these and other instances of so-called 'elite capture' of participatory activities[25], it would be wrong to suggest that the outcome of participation in unequal societies would inevitably be unequal.[26] A number of recent experiments in participation at local-level governance have attempted to overcome the natural disadvantage of the weaker groups with the help of innovative institutional design and supportive social action, and a few of them have met with spectacular success.[27]

Two such experiments have attracted widespread attention – namely participatory budgeting in Porto Alegre in Brazil and participatory planning for local development in the Kerala state of India. Though the success of these experiments may be difficult to replicate fully elsewhere in view of some special circumstances that have blessed them both[28], they still offer valuable lessons about the kind of actions that any exercise in participatory governance can take and implement to their benefit. For this reason, the workings and outcomes of these two projects are discussed at some length below.[29]

---

[25] For more on the phenomenon of 'elite capture', see Platteau (this volume).

[26] See Molinas (1998) for an empirical investigation of the relationship between inequality and co-operation at the community level.

[27] For a systematic analysis of some of the more important experiments, see Blair (this volume).

[28] Heller (2001) offers a perceptive analysis of the commonalities of circumstances that contributed to the success of Porto Alegre and Kerala.

[29] We focus on the workings and the outcomes of these experiments in this section; the lessons are discussed in the next.

The city of Porto Alegre, the capital of the industrialized and relatively wealthy state of Rio Grande do Sul, enjoys high social and economic indicators, with its life expectancy (72.6 years) and literacy rates (90 percent) well above the national average. However, at the same time, like much of the rest of Brazil, the city represents a highly unequal society. Until recently almost a third of its population lived in irregular housing – slums and illegal structures – which fanned outward from the city centre, with the poorest districts generally the farthest from downtown. The result was a segregated socio-geographic configuration, generating geographically distinct economic and social zones throughout the city.

Within this unequal setting has emerged one of the most successful experiments in participatory governance in the contemporary world. When an electoral alliance headed by the Workers Party (PT) achieved victory in the mayoral elections in 1989, one of its first actions was to respond to a longstanding demand of The Union of Neighborhood Associations of Porto Alegre (UAMPA) for a participatory structure involving the municipal budget. The new city administration developed a set of institutions that extended popular control over the municipal budget in a way that has by now become a classic in participatory budgeting.

The *Orçamento Participativo* (OP), or the participatory budget, has evolved over the years into a highly structured process in which citizens participate as individuals and as representatives of civil society groups at different stages of the budgetary process. They deliberate and decide on projects for specific districts and on municipal investment priorities, and then monitor the outcome of the projects. The process consists of a sequence of steps, beginning with regional assemblies in each of the city's sixteen districts, in which all residents of the district are invited to participate. These regional meetings have two functions: namely to elect delegates to represent specific neighborhoods in subsequent rounds of deliberations, and to review the previous year's projects and budget. The mayor and staff of the municipal council attend these meetings to reply to citizens' concerns about projects in the district.

In the next step, the delegates elected by regional assemblies join delegates elected by neighbourhood associations and other social groups in a series of meetings in each district. The objective of these meetings is first to learn about the technical issues involved in demanding projects and then to identify and prioritize the district's needs as well as to deliberate on projects that affect the city as a whole. At the end of this process, the regional delegates vote to ratify the district's demands and priorities and elect councilors to serve on the Municipal Council of the Budget. These elected councilors in conjunction with members of the administration finally reconcile the demands from each district with available resources and approve an agreed budget.[30]

This complex combination of direct and representative democracy has allowed citizen participation not only at all stages of the budgetary process – from preference revelation to monitoring and verification, it has also given participation a cutting edge by strengthening the channels of accountability. In the higher tier of the participatory structures, namely the Municipal Council of the Budget, the district representatives act as intermediaries between municipal government and regional activists, bringing the demands from districts to central government, and justifying government actions to regional activists, while themselves being accountable to the general citizenry through the regional assemblies.

There is both qualitative and quantitative evidence that the experiment has succeeded singularly in making urban improvements in the lowest-income areas.[31] The percentage of the public budget available for investment has increased to nearly 20 percent in 1994 from 2 percent in 1989, while the proportion of municipal expenses in service provision to expenses in administration has also improved. On the whole, investment in the poorer residential districts of the city has exceeded investment in wealthier areas as a result of these public policies. By the end of 2000, almost 98 percent of all residences in the city had running water, up from 75 percent in 1988; sewage coverage had risen to 98 percent from 46 percent; and the number of functioning public municipal schools had increased to 86 from 29. In the years between 1992 and 1995, housing assistance increased phenomenally, with the housing department offering housing assistance to 28,862 families as against just 1,714 families for the comparable period of 1986–88. In all these cases, investments have been redistributive in the sense that districts with higher levels of poverty have received significantly greater shares of investment.

This redistributive effect has been achieved through a careful institutional innovation that was designed to accord higher weight to the poorer districts. Investment allocation is guided by a pre-specified weighting system (also called a 'budget matrix'), which reconciles potentially conflicting preferences of residents from different districts by using 'statistically measured need' (the degree of previous access in relation to need, e.g., proportion of streets unpaved, housing units lacking sanitary water, etc.) and population size. The whole system is quite complex and requires a good deal of technical support from the municipal executive office to function properly.

---

[30]   In addition to preparing the budget, this group amends the scope and rules governing the process itself, e.g., increasing the range of activities covered by participatory budgeting, and changing the criteria for allocating resources among the districts.

[31]   For systematic analysis of the evidence, see Santos (1998), Baicochi (2003) and Koonings (2004).

This rule-based system of investment allocation, supported by strong accountability mechanisms, has successfully replaced the traditional patron-client structure in which citizen loyalty went upward and political largesse came downward, by a budget system based on neighborhood preferences and objective needs. In order to assess whether this reflects merely a change from the old type of patronage-based governance to a new one in which patronage is lavished on supporters of the ruling party, Baiocchi (2003) looked for statistical correlation between the distribution of Workers' Party's voting strength and geographical investment patterns, but could not find any.

The success of Porto Alegre has been impressive enough to encourage widespread emulation all over the world. In Brazil itself, over 100 municipalities as well as several states have taken up participatory budgeting practices. Similar experiments have been initiated in other Latin American countries such as Chile, Costa Rica, Guatemala and Mexico, as well as in such diverse countries as Ireland, Mauritius and Indonesia.

In terms of sheer scale and intensity of people's participation in the development process, there is perhaps no parallel to the 'People's Campaign for Decentralized Planning' – or just the Campaign, as it has come to be known – launched in the Indian state of Kerala in 1996. The left-wing government that came to power in that year took full advantage of the scope for deep decentralization and an unprecedented level of fiscal devolution that was permitted by the constitutional amendments of the preceding years. As much as 35-40% of the state development budget was devolved to elected local government institutions, conditional on the requirement that they must prepare local development plans based on extensive participation of the citizens. Every year since then, local governments throughout the state of Kerala have formulated and implemented their own development plans prepared through participatory democracy.[32]

As in the case of Porto Alegre, participation takes place through a multi-stage process of deliberation between elected representatives, local and higher-level government officials, civil society experts and activists, and ordinary citizens. The initial deliberation takes place in open local assemblies, called *grama sabhas*, in which participants discuss and identify development priorities. These assemblies then form so-called 'Development Seminars', which are entrusted with the task of developing more elaborate assessments of local problems and needs. These assessments form the basis of concrete projects prepared by a number of sectoral task forces, which are supported by technical experts. These projects are then submitted to local elected bodies (*panchayats*) that formulate and set budgets for local plans, which are presented back to *grama sabhas* for discussion and approval. The approved local plans are then integrated into higher-level plans (blocks and districts) during which all projects are scrutinized for technical and fiscal viability.

---

[32]   For authoritative accounts of the Kerala experiment, see Isaac (2000) and Isaac & Heller (2003).

As a participatory process of local-level planning, the Campaign was guided by two basic principles. The first was that instead of serving simply as a conduit of delivering services on behalf of state and national level governments, local governments should function as fully-fledged governing institutions with financial and administrative autonomy, based on the principle of subsidiarity: that is, what can best be done and decided at local level should be done there. The second principle was that the traditional structures of representative democracy should be complemented by more direct forms of democracy, so as to make elected representatives continuously, rather than just periodically, accountable to the citizens. A great deal of effort was put into social mobilization and institutional innovations so that ordinary citizens could play an active role in the selection, design, and implementation of local development plans.

Quite apart from making democracy a more immediate and meaningful experience for ordinary citizens, the Campaign has already begun to bear fruits in terms of furthering the cause of equity in Kerala, which was already famous for its welfarist and pro-poor policies. The equity impact has in fact improved with the passage of time. In the first year, financial devolution was based on a simple per capita formula that did not take levels of inter-regional poverty into account. Even this was an improvement, however, over the skewed patterns of patronage-driven allocation of the past (in which the relatively underdeveloped northern Kerala was systematically discriminated against). In subsequent years, the redistribute effect improved further as the devolution formula has progressively incorporated additional weights for poverty and underdevelopment.

Apart from regional distributions, other aspects of resource allocation also bear testimony to the redistributive potential of participatory planning. First, compared to the pre-Campaign experience, the plans prepared in the post-Campaign period have accorded much greater priority to basic needs such as housing, drinking water, and sanitation. At the same time, the pattern of expenditure on productive sectors has shifted discernibly toward activities undertaken mainly by the poor, e.g. animal husbandry, garden crops, and minor irrigation. Both these changes have redistributive implications favouring the poor. Second, in contrast to past patterns, priorities have been accorded to special plans for scheduled castes and tribes, traditionally the most disadvantaged groups in India.

Although special plans for these communities have existed in Kerala since the mid-1980s, they received a strong boost after the Campaign was launched. It has been estimated that as a result of the Campaign real resources earmarked for these plans have increased by 30 to 40 percent (Isaac & Heller 2003). Furthermore, in the post-Campaign period local bodies have emphasized projects that could be specifically targeted for individual beneficiaries from these communities such as housing, latrines, and income-producing animals. Similarly, the Campaign has grappled with the problem of entrenched gender discrimination, first by implementing the policy for reservation for women in local governments more rigorously than in any other state in India, and secondly by laying aside at least 10% of plan outlay for the Women's Component Plan designed specifically to benefit women.

While Porto Alegre and Kerala are special cases, the evidence for participation's ability to enhance equity is not confined to them. Several investigations of the *panchayat* system of decentralized democracy in the rest of India also offer corroborative evidence in this regard. In a well-known study, Rosenzweig and Foster (2003) formulated a model built on the idea that democracy would allow the numerical strength of the poorer groups to be reflected in favourable outcomes for them. A key prediction of the model is that in villages with democratic governance, an increase in the population share of the landless should result in outcomes that are more favourable to them – for example, there should be more expenditure on road construction or improvements (which are relatively labour-intensive) and less on public irrigation infrastructure (which benefits the landed households more). The prediction was vindicated by the analysis of a panel data set from 250 villages in rural India. It was found that increases in the population weight of the poor enhanced the likelihood of receiving pro-poor projects only in villages with elected village councils (*panchayats*). When more traditional leadership structures prevailed, no such effect was observed.

In another attempt to examine how local-level democracy affects the ability of the disadvantaged groups to implement their preferred options, Chattopadhyay and Duflo (2004) looked at the impact of reservation policy under the *panchayat* system in India. This policy stipulates that one-third of all positions of the chief of the village councils in India are to be reserved for women. An interesting question that arises in this context is whether participation of women as leaders in community affairs works to the advantage of the womenfolk in the community as a whole. Based on a survey in two states of India (West Bengal and Rajasthan), the authors found that it does. Women were found to be more likely to participate in the policymaking process if the leader of their village councils happened to be women, and women leaders of village councils tended to invest more in the kind of infrastructure that conformed better to the interests of women, e.g., drinking water, fuel, and roads, and so on.[33] Similarly, Pande (2003) has shown that when disadvantaged groups (lower castes, tribal groups and landless

---

[33]   A potential endogeneity problem, analogous to the one discussed in the context of efficiency, also exists here. It's conceivable that women's leadership is endogenous in the sense that women aim for leadership positions only in those communities where they are more likely to participate and to be assertive in community affairs. In that case, the positive association between women's leadership and favourable outcomes for women cannot necessarily be attributed to the fact that women happen to be in the position of power. However, this kind of endogeneity problem did not arise in the present case as the law requires that the village *panchayats* in which leadership is to be reserved for women are to be chosen on a random basis rather than on the basis of community characteristics.

people) in India are able to elect their own representatives at the local level where allocation decisions are made, a larger share of available governmental resources accrues to them.

These studies suggest that democracy at the local level can be beneficial for the poor and other disadvantaged groups, in the same way that democracy at the national level tends to be. However, one of the difficulties of rigorously assessing the equity impact of participation is that there is seldom any direct evidence on the distribution of costs and benefits at the household level. There are only a few studies that have been able to use household level information for this purpose. In one of them, Galasso and Ravallion (2005) examined the targeting impact of the participatory food-for-education programme in Bangladesh. In this programme, funds were allocated by the central government, but identification of beneficiary households within a community was typically made by local school management committee consisting of parents, teachers, education specialists and school donors. Using data from a nationally conducted household survey in 1995-96, the study found that poor households received benefit proportionately more than the non-poor. Moreover, the degree of intra-community equity achieved by participatory targeting was found to be higher compared to the inter-community equity achieved by central allocation of funds.

In a more recent study, Besley et al. (2005) examined the association between participation and equity in the functioning the *Panchayat* system in India. Under this system, village-level elected bodies known as *Gram Panchayats* have been entrusted with wide-ranging responsibilities, including selection of beneficiaries for the distribution of the BPL (below poverty line) card, which entitles a household to a number of benefits (e.g., subsidized food). The study sought to examine whether the quality of targeting was enhanced by regular holding of *gram sabha* or village meetings, in which village community get the opportunity to air their demands and to hold the elected officials to account. Using a large data set drawn from four southern states of India, the authors concluded that holding of *gram sabha* did have a significantly positive effect on equity in the sense that targeting of the disadvantaged groups was more intensive in villages that held the meeting. Thus, illiterate and landless people and individuals from the lowly scheduled castes and tribes were more likely to receive the BPL card in villages that held the meeting compared to their counterparts in villages that did not.

The evidence is thus quite clear that, contrary to the claims sometimes made, participation in unequal societies is not 'programmed to fail' to advance the goal of equity.[34] Nor is success guaranteed, however. Conditions of success must be created by conscious design. We now turn to a discussion of what those conditions are and how they might be created.

---

[34]   The characterization of participation as being 'programmed to fail' to deliver its lofty goals in an unequal society is due to Kumar & Corbridge (2002).

6. The Three-Gap Analysis of Effective Participation

While participation has great potential to be instrumentally valuable in promoting efficiency and equity, this potential is not always realized in the real world. Although there are some spectacularly successful examples of participatory governance in some parts of the world, they are far outnumbered by cases of failed and spurious participation. Even the successful cases are not uniform in terms of either the details of institutional design or in the degree of scope and intensity of participation. This lack of uniformity is often a consequence of contextual differences among participatory experiments, which makes it difficult to hold up any particular experiment, however successful, as the ideal model. What is important, however, from the point of view of learning from experience is that there are certain commonalities that bind the successful cases together and distinguish them from the failed ones. Careful analysis of the existing experiments in participatory governance suggests that success depends largely on how well a society can deal with three distinct but inter-related gaps that stand in the way of effective participation. These may be called the capacity gap, the incentive gap and the power gap.

The *capacity gap* arises from the fact that meaningful participation in the process of governance requires certain skills which common people, least of all the traditionally disadvantaged and marginalized segments of the society, do not typically possess. These include such general skills as the capacity to work in a team composed of people from different social strata and the ability to articulate one's views in a manner that would hopefully convince others, many of whom may view the world through a completely different lens, as well as more specific skills related to the tasks for which people are participating in a collaborative exercise. Some of these tasks – such as managing a local resource or delivering a community service – may be relatively simple and people may already have some experience in them. But others, more ambitious ones – such as budgeting for the local government or planning for local development – would often require a level of knowledge and skill that would be beyond even the educated elite.

This capacity gap must be bridged if participation is to be effective. General skills such as the ability to work in a team and to be able to articulate one's views rationally can only be developed through practice over a long period of time. In the real world, this practice typically happens through the intermediation of civil society organizations and social movements, which mobilize common people into groups for various purposes. This didactic aspect of social mobilization is of enormous importance for laying the foundations for participatory activities. It is no coincidence that the most successful experiments in participatory governance around the world have all been underpinned by years of social mobilization. In most cases, the actual motivation of such mobilizations was different from that of preparing people for the particular participatory experiment that followed. They each had their own agenda, but the didactic value of mobilization nonetheless acted as a positive externality to the benefit of the subsequent experiment.

As for the specific skills required for addressing the participatory enterprise, there is often no substitute for specialized training. What is needed for this purpose is imaginative institutional innovation that enables common people to receive knowledge from technocrats and experts, but without being beholden to them. If in the process of imparting knowledge the technocrats and experts come to acquire a dominant relationship vis-à-vis common people, the whole purpose of participation would be defeated. The transfer of knowledge must take place in a setting of fundamental equality and mutual respect between the providers and recipients of knowledge. In recognition of this imperative, the architects of both Kerala and Port Alegre experiments gave a lot of thought to designing institutions that would allow transfer of knowledge in a non-dominating mode. In particular, they ensured that at the end of the learning process the decisions of the common people rather than those of the experts would prevail. Institutional design for knowledge transfer was one of the crucial factors behind the success of these experiments.

The *incentive gap* stems from the fact that participation in public affairs is not costless and most people would not be keen to participate actively unless they perceive the potential gains to be large enough to outweigh the costs. The costs of participation are of various types. There is first the opportunity cost of the time and effort that people would have to put into participative activities. This cost is especially high for women, who are said to suffer from the 'triple burden' of devoting time to the conduct of public affairs in addition to the traditional double burden of engaging in productive as well as reproductive activities. It is not surprising that women are found to participate proportionately less even in the most progressive environment as in Porto Alegre or Kerala. There is also the psychological cost of speaking up in public, especially for those who are low in self-confidence, and the general hassle of having to deal with matters that many people feel officials are being paid to do anyway. Finally, for the subordinate groups living in hierarchical societies, there is the probable cost of retribution from the dominant classes who may not take kindly to the idea that the lower classes should come together to delve into matters that have traditionally been the preserve of social superiors.

In suggesting that people would weigh these costs against potential benefits in deciding whether or not to participate, we are not imputing a narrowly utilitarian calculus to them. Most people would surely value participation for its own sake, whatever additional value they may attach to the tangible instrumental benefits of participation that might accrue to them. What is being claimed here, however, is that consideration of this intrinsic value alone may not suffice to override the consideration of costs in all cases. In that event, the instrumental value will also have to be factored in. The incentive to participate will exist only if the totality of intrinsic and instrumental value exceeds the costs of participation in the judgment of an individual. This argument implies that in situations where the costs of participation are especially high, the instrumental value may well be the decisive factor.

The force of this argument has been recognized both by theorists and successful practitioners of participatory governance. In formulating the theoretical construct of Empowered Participatory Governance, Fung & Wright (2003) have enunciated three general principles, one of which is 'practical rientation' - that is, a focus on specific, tangible problems.[35] Underlying this principle is the recognition that participation in the abstract may not be a terribly attractive idea. People would be more inclined to participate if they focus on a problem they can all identify with as being important for their day-to-day lives. Since the solution of a tangible problem will yield tangible benefits, participation is more likely to occur when it has a 'practical orientation'.

When the problem in question relates to allocation of budgetary expenditure as in Porto Alegre or formulation of a local development plan as in Kerala, it helps if the resource base is large enough so that large tangible benefits can accrue to the participants as an outcome of their efforts. It has indeed been suggested that one of the reasons for the spectacular success of Porto Alegre is that it happens to be one of the most resourceful cities in Brazil. When the same practice of participatory budgeting has been applied to other, poorer cities of Brazil and elsewhere, it has not been equally successful. In the case of Kerala, it has been argued that a very substantial fiscal devolution at the very outset of the process of participatory decentralization has played a key role in its success (Isaac & Heller 2003). Normally, fiscal devolution occurs at a late stage of the decentralization process on the grounds that until the structures of administrative decentralization are firmly established, entrusting local governments with large fiscal resources might lead to wastage, mismanagement or out-and-out corruption. This conventional wisdom was stood on its head in Kerala, where the state government deliberately transferred unprecedented amount of resources into the coffers of local governments up front, even before the practice of participatory planning had taken firm roots. The intention was clearly to close the incentive gap for the potential participants, by raising the expected pay-off from participation though a pre-commitment of large fiscal devolution. By all accounts, the device worked wonderfully well.

Of the three gaps mentioned above, the *power gap* is perhaps the most pernicious of all. It arises from systematic asymmetries of power that is inherent in unequal societies. In a society where there exists a wide gulf between the rich and the poor, where entrenched social hierarchies have led to a rigid demarcation between the elite and the commoners, and where age-old norms

---

[35]   The other two principles are bottom-up participation and deliberative solution generation.

of discrimination against specific social groups – defined in terms of gender, ethnicity, religion, and so on – have long been internalized by the oppressors and the oppressed alike, it is very likely that the dominant groups will use participation merely as a ruse to further their own ends. Participation in such unequal societies is likely to be unequal too, with members of dominant groups wielding superior power to further their own narrow interests.

The subordinate groups in these societies suffer from a 'power gap' relative to the dominant groups, and one way or the other this gap must be closed or at least narrowed down substantially, if they are to participate on an equal footing. This can only be done by creating some countervailing power in favour of the subordinate groups so as to compensate for the power gap they otherwise face.[36] Theory and practice suggest a number of ways in which this countervailing power can be created.

The theory of deliberative democracy, conceived as an approach to collective decision-making, offers one such way. Any participatory enterprise must follow some rules of collective decision-making. Furthermore, if participation is not to degenerate into a way of simply legitimizing the exercise of unequal power by the dominant groups, these rules must ensure that the preferences and interests of the weaker segments receive due consideration. In other words, the rules must have the property that the very adherence to them would afford some countervailing power to the weak and the disadvantaged groups, so that their preferences and interests cannot be trumped by those of the dominant groups simply by virtue of their superior power. The idea of deliberative democracy is concerned with devising such rules of collective decision-making. It seeks to do so by positing the power of 'reason' as a counterweight to the traditional sources of power.

There are several alternative ways in which collective decisions may be taken in a participatory enterprise. One possibility is that the participants come to the table with their respective preferences and bargain with each other with a view to achieving the best possible outcomes for themselves. Since the distribution of pay-offs of this process would depend on the relative bargaining strengths of the parties concerned, this procedure is almost certain to be detrimental to the interests of the weaker groups. It might be supposed that the alternative procedure of democratic decision-making based on the majority rule would serve them better, but this is not necessarily so. As is well known from the experience of democracy in grossly unequal societies based on patron-client relationships, the minority of patrons may easily manipulate the majority of clients by using their traditional leverages of power. If for some reason, they cannot manipulate and override the majority, the powerful groups at least have the option of 'exiting' that is, refusing to participate in the collaboration, which might then jeopardize the whole

---

[36]   For an excellent discussion of the need for and forms of countervailing power relevant for participatory governance, see Fung & Wright (2003b).

participatory enterprise. So, while democracy is certainly essential, the rules of decision-making must be such that neither can the weaker groups be easily manipulated nor are the powerful groups easily attracted to the option of 'exit'. The issue of institutional design is crucial in this context. As discussed in Section 2, there is no unique formula for institutional design that would be applicable under all circumstances – the details of design will have to vary depending on the specificity of the context. The objective must be the same, however – to ensure a fair and equitable decision-making process.

This is precisely what deliberative democracy seeks to achieve. It requires that the participants come to the table not primarily to engage in strategic bargaining, nor merely to place their preferences on the table to be aggregated by some mechanical formula (such as majority voting), but to present the reasons for the views they hold and for the actions they suggest. As Cohen and Rogers (2003) explain: 'Briefly, to deliberate means to debate alternatives on the basis of considerations that all take to be relevant; it is a matter of offering reasons for alternatives, rather than merely stating a preference for one or another, with such preferences then subject to some rule of aggregation or submitted to bargaining. The exchange of reasons that a deliberative democracy puts at the center of collective decision-making is not to be confused with simple discussion, or the revelation and exchange of private information. Any view of intelligent political decision-making sees such discussion and exchange as important, if only because of initial asymmetries in the possession of relevant information. What is distinctive about a deliberative view is that the processing of this information is disciplined by the claims of reason – that arguments must be offered on behalf of proposals, and be supported by considerations that are acknowledged to provide relevant reasons, even though there may be disagreements about the weight and precise content of those considerations.'

It is the requirement of offering a generally acceptable reason for what one proposes that acts as a countervailing force against the manipulative and coercive methods that the powerful groups might otherwise adopt in order to pursue their narrow self-interest.[37] However, the critiques of deliberative democracy have questioned, quite plausibly, whether the exchange of reason is potent enough to safeguard the interests of the weaker groups in the face of entrenched social inequalities. Some have worried, for example, that the

---

[37] Using reason as a force to offset the asymmetry of entrenched power is not the only rationale of deliberative democracy, although it is the most relevant one in the present context. Political theorists who have expounded the theory of deliberative democracy have done so from several different perspectives. In the Aristotelian tradition, reasoned deliberation as a means of reaching collective decisions is seen as an intrinsic good. From a consequentialist perspective, Habermas (1987) justifies it as a necessary tool for discovering rational laws that will promote justice and the common good, while Rawls (1993) finds it necessary for giving legitimacy to political institutions. For an illuminating discussion of alternative perspectives, see, among others, Freeman (2000).

emphasis on the articulation of reason implies that the process may work to the advantage of the 'laryingically gifted', and there is no reason to suppose that the socially disadvantaged groups are especially well endowed with this gift. On the contrary, there is reason to fear that in a hierarchically divided society people at the bottom rungs would not have the confidence and courage to articulate their reasons forcefully in the presence of social superiors, even if they had a good understanding of the reasons behind their views and were articulate enough to express them in their own way.

While these fears are entirely reasonable on *a priori* grounds, only empirical evidence can show how well grounded they are in reality. In this regard, the experience of the actual practice of deliberative democracy is quite encouraging. We have already mentioned two classic cases of deliberative democracy in the contemporary world – namely, the Porto Alegre experiment in participatory budgeting in Brazil and the Kerala experiment in participatory planning in India. In both these cases, citizens at large engage in reasoned deliberation – both directly and through elected representatives – at several stages in the decision-making process. In both cases, there is ample evidence that the traditionally voiceless people have been able in engage in meaningful deliberation, undeterred by pre-existing asymmetries of power.

The experience of Port Alegre is described thus by Baiocchi (2003): 'There is no evidence, however, that lack of education or gender pose insurmountable barriers to effective participation … Ethnographic evidence from district-level meetings did not show any pattern of women or the less educated speaking less often or conceding authority to educated men. A survey question about how often a person spoke at meetings painted a similar picture. Responses to the question: 'Do you speak at meetings?' (Always, almost always, sometimes, never) showed that there was parity between the poor and non-poor, and between the less educated and the rest.' Moreover, we have already seen that all this was not mere empty talk, because these deliberations led to a decisive shift towards redistributive measures in favour of the poor.

The Indian experience of decentralized governance (*panchayat*) is also instructive in this regard. The *panchayat* system of representative democracy at the local level has existed in India for many decades, but without being terribly effective, however. It was only when local-level elections were supplemented by the holding of effective village assemblies (*grama sabha*) in states like Kerala and West Bengal that the system began to yield benefits for the poor and for disadvantaged social groups such as women, and scheduled castes and tribes. The scope for deliberation offered by these village assemblies enabled these groups to press their case and to hold the elected officials accountable in a way that was not possible before, resulting in a systematic move towards redistributive measures. It is significant that in Besley *et al*'s (2005) study of local governance in the southern states of India, policies were found to be more pro-poor in those villages where *grama sabha* was regularly held, compared to villages where it was not, which clearly suggests that deliberations in village assemblies empowered marginalized groups to influence decisions in their favour.

It is clear, however, that creating the institutions for deliberative democracy by itself will not be enough to generate all the countervailing force that is necessary to make participation effective. Other types of countervailing force must be created at the same time to complement the power of reason so that people from all strata of society can deliberate on a more equal footing.

The first and the most basic of these complementary forms of countervailing power consists in the self-confidence that comes with education and economic security. Poor illiterate people, whose livelihoods are insecure and whose very survival depends on maintaining an obsequious humility in the context of patron-client relationships, are not very likely to participate independently or assertively in the conduct of public affairs. To the extent that they do participate, they will do so mainly to lend their numerical strength in support of their patron's interests. This type of participation will only help reproduce existing social inequalities instead of redressing them. If participation is to act as part of a transformative process designed to fundamentally alter the balance of power in the society, then the poor and the weaker groups must be able to participate in support of their own cause, even if it goes against the interests of their patrons. But lack of education and economic security prevents them from doing so. Any programme for deepening democracy through participatory approaches must, therefore, accompany simultaneous efforts to spread basic education and to ensure at least a minimum level of economic security so that the weaker groups do not have to fear that independent participation might cost them their livelihoods (Osmani 2001).

A second and broader way of creating complementary countervailing force is to empower the poor and the weak by implementing the full range of human rights, including both civil-political and socio-economic rights. The fulfillment of basic socio-economic rights (such as right to food, right to education, etc.) will create the countervailing force in the manner describe above, by giving the weaker groups the self-confidence to assert their independence. But this needs to be supplemented by the fulfillment of civil-political rights as well - because without them assertion of independence in the participatory process will be either impossible or pernicious for the weaker groups.

It is obvious that for participatory deliberation to be possible, people at large must enjoy the rights to free speech and rights of association and free assembly. At the same time, the right to information must be fulfilled so that people can access the information necessary for making informed decisions and also for holding the officials (elected or otherwise) accountable for their actions. Without relevant information, accountability will be impossible to achieve, which of course gives the officials every incentive to withhold information whenever possible; but without accountability participation will be an exercise in futility. It is, therefore, essential to establish the right to information, which can be used by the people to pierce the veil of secrecy with which officials tend to shield relevant information from the public arena. Finally, people must enjoy the right of equal access to justice, so that the weaker groups may protect themselves from any attempt by the powerful members of society to intimidate and victimize them. Without the confidence that the justice system of the state machinery can be relied upon for protection against vengeful retribution, the weaker segments of the society may not have the courage to assert their independence in any participatory enterprise.

Finally, countervailing power may be generated through social mobilization. It has not escaped attention of careful observers of successful participatory experiments, such as those of Porto Alegre, South Africa, Kerala and West Bengal, that in all these cases the ground for effective participation was created by years of social and political activism by progressive political parties aimed at mobilizing the weaker segments of the society in a wider enterprise in social transformation. Although creation of participatory democracy was not necessarily the initial objective of such activism, the act of social mobilization that the political parties performed nonetheless created positive externalities in favour of the participatory enterprise they eventually embarked upon.

Two such externalities are worthy of note. First, social mobilization helped resolve the problem of collective action that stems from the possibility of free riding by self-interested individuals. It did so by creating and strengthening 'bonding' social capital among the weaker segments, which in turn engendered the mutual trust and confidence that is the foundation of any participatory enterprise.

Second, the act of mobilization endowed the weaker segments with a countervailing power against the dominant groups of the society. This was partly the power that comes from unity and partly the power that comes from the knowledge of being backed by a larger social force. Whatever the source, the consequence of possessing this power was that the participatory enterprise that was built on the foundation of previous social mobilization was resilient enough not to fall prey to the all-too-common phenomenon of 'elite capture'.

7. Concluding Observations: Fostering the Synergies

Creating conditions for effective participation by common people in the conduct of public affairs is a complex task. It requires the adoption of a multi-pronged strategy involving state, civil society, and the common people. The state in particular must play a very important role on a number of fronts – by ensuring free and fair electoral participation for governance at the national level; by creating a legal framework that devolves and decentralizes decision-making power at local levels, where the scope for direct participation by the people is the greatest; by providing basic education, guaranteeing minimum economic security and implementing the whole range of human rights so that the weaker segments of the society can participate confidently and independently in the presence of entrenched asymmetries of power; and by providing the space for civil society and social movements to mobilize and educate common people for participatory enterprises.[38]

The existence of strong political will and competent leadership is essential for this purpose. The civil society too must play an important role. On the one hand, it must engage with the state to ensure that the latter actually does what it needs to do for effective participation to be possible, and engage with the common people on the other to gain their trust and confidence and to mobilize them into a potent force for participatory governance. The common people for their part must be willing to devote the time and energy needed to take control of the development process in their own hands instead of leaving it completely to others.

The inter-relatedness of these multi-dimensional conditions may seem to make the task too daunting for the goal of participatory governance to be anything other than an abstract utopia. Effective participation cannot occur without committed state support, but given the tradition of centralized decision-making processes in most parts of the world, the state's commitment to diffuse power through people's participation in governance is unlikely to be forthcoming without persistent and overwhelming pressure emanating from civil society and social movements; yet civil society and social movements can only function if the state creates the enabling conditions for them to operate in the first place. Similar cyclicity as opposed to linearity of causal connections exists in other spheres as well. For instance, one of the objectives of participation in the development process is to ensure efficient and equitable delivery of basic services to all, but it has been argued at the same time that the poor are unlikely to be able to participate effectively without prior access to basic education and a minimum level of economic security. Similarly, participatory governance is expected to empower people and yet is it clear that certain amount of empowerment must exist to begin with for the weaker segments of the society not to be overwhelmed by the dominant groups in the conduct of deliberative democracy.

This kind of cyclicity of causal connections may at first sight seem like a reason for despair, but it need not be. For cyclical causality also implies the existence of synergies – between different pre-conditions for effective participation and also between pre-conditions and practice of participation. Existence of these synergies implies that the practice of participation can be self-reinforcing in nature. Once a participatory process is set in motion, even

---

[38]   Manor (2007) gives a cogent explanation of why government must play the most critical role in promoting effective participation.

if imperfectly, the very practice of participation will help improve some of the pre-conditions; the resulting improvement in one set of pre-conditions may then induce improvement in others, which turn will enhance the effectiveness of participation, thereby unleashing a virtuous cycle.[39]

Evidence for the existence of these synergies does exist in the real world. In Kerala, for instance, the participation of scheduled castes, scheduled tribes and women was below their population share in the first year of the Campaign, but the percentages increased in subsequent years, as the confidence and the knowledge that came with practice emboldened them to come forward more (Isaac & Heller 2003). Porto Alegre has had a similar experience. In the initial years, women and less educated men participated less in the various rounds of deliberation compared to educated men, but this difference disappeared with accumulation of experience over time. Once the years of experience crossed a minimum threshold, there remained no significant difference between men and women reporting participation, or between persons with or without formal schooling (Bairocchi 2003). In their study of the targeting performance of the participatory food-for-education programme in Bangladesh, Galasso and Ravallion (2005) found some evidence for elite capture in the early years of the programme, in so far as targeting was found to be worse in villages with larger land inequality and in remote locations. However, targeting improved as the programme expanded, suggesting that the programme itself shifted the balance of power in favour of the poor. All this points to the existence of a mutually reinforcing relationship between empowerment and the practice of participation.

Similar synergy is found between participation and social capital. It is generally recognized that the existence of social capital facilitates the emergence and sustainability of participatory institutions (e.g., Krishna 2002). It is equally true, however, that the very practice of participation can contribute to the strengthening of social capital. One example is the emergence of Neighbourhood Groups in Kerala below the tier of village assemblies (*grama sabha*), which is formally the lowest tier of participatory process devised by the Campaign. These new Groups have emerged as the *grama sabha* turned out to be too large and too distant an entity for most people given the dispersed nature of habitats in rural Kerala. These Groups have begun to function as mini-*grama sabhas* that discuss local issues and priorities, review plan implementation, and select beneficiaries. They have also taken up other activities such as conflict resolution, after school educational programs, health clinics, cultural activities and thrift schemes. As Isaac and Heller (2003) note, 'The crowding-in effect that the Campaign appears to be having on associational

---

[39]   Dreze & Sen (2002) make a similar point in the specific context of Indian democracy. After noting that many of the deficiencies of India's democracy stem from its deep-rooted social inequalities, they go on to argue that the very practice of democracy would help offset some of the effects of those inequalities, thereby rendering democracy a self-reinforcing process.

life in Kerala is also manifest in the proliferation of a variety of self-help groups, particularly women's micro-credit schemes.'

In Porto Alegre, Baiocchi (2003) has noted that as people became deeply involved in negotiations and became acquainted with other persons in the district through the process of participatory budgeting, they developed lasting bonds with activists from other districts and developed solidarities. Through this process, many new associations in civil society have emerged, which has added a new zeal and vibrancy to the civil society in Porto Alegre. This catalytic effect has been so strong that some have even described the Porto Alegre experiment as a 'school of deliberative democracy'. 'Observers of the process, such as Gildo Lima, one of the architects of the participatory structures in the first administration, argue that civil society has indeed become less locally focused as a result of the PB, and that a new form of mobilization has emerged.' (Baiocchi 2003).

Another kind of synergy – one between local participation and broader political changes – can be seen in places as diverse as Rajasthan (India) and Bolivia. In one of the poorest regions in the Indian state of Rajasthan, ordinary rural people engaged in a participatory exercise in social auditing to check whether the local government (*panchayat*) expenditures were made according to the plan. The leading actor was a mass-based organization called *Mazdoor Kishan Shakti Sangathan* (MKSS; translated as Movement for the Empowerment of Peasants and Workers), which mobilized the common people against severe odds, as the exercise was going to expose corruption of powerful people. One of the main problems MKSS faced in this task was in eliciting relevant information from official records, which was necessary to hold the corrupt people accountable on the basis of solid evidence. It took nearly seven years to prepare the documentation that made a prima facie case that corruption was widespread. This experience inspired MKSS to launch a broader campaign for the fulfillment of people's right to information. As the campaign gathered momentum, other organizations joined forces both within and outside Rajasthan, and eventually forced the Indian government to legally recognize the right to information.[40]

Bolivia launched its Popular Participation Law in 1994 mainly to give opportunities for democratic participation to the indigenous people whose rights had long been neglected. A large-scale reform at administrative and fiscal decentralization allowed these people to take part in governance and developmental activities for the first time through a number of channels.[41] These channels also became avenues for expressing local grievances, and as the practice of expressing grievances became widespread it led first to small movements, which soon snowballed into larger ones. Thus, local grievances

---

[40]   For perceptive analyses of the Rajasthan movement, see Jenkins & Goetz (1999) and Goetz & Jenkins (2001).

[41]   See, among others, Blair (2000 & this volume) and Grindle (2000) for insightful analyses of the Bolivian experience.

among *cocoleros* (coca growers) in the *Chapare* region led to a small grass-roots party winning control of 11 municipalities in the 1995 elections. Evo Morales, an indigenous leader, transformed this movement into a nation-wide campaign against privatization of water provision and energy resource policies, which set in motion a series of political events that eventually led Morales to assume the office of the Presidency of Bolivia in 1995. As Blair (2007) rightly observes: 'It would not be too great a stretch to say that the Popular Participation Law of 1994, intended to stimulate grassroots participation among a long neglected indigenous population, quickly became so successful that an indigenous movement gained control of the national government itself.'

These examples of synergy between local-level participation and larger political changes help address one worry that is sometimes expressed about the fall-out of excessive emphasis on decentralized participation. Questions have been asked as to whether success in community participation at local levels might not jeopardize efforts to make the state function better at all levels. For example, there is a fear that deep engagement of people in local level democracy might create apathy towards democracy at the national level, or that emphasis on accountability at the local level might weaken accountability mechanisms at the national level (sometimes expressed as the trade-off between the short route and the long route to accountability[42]), or that the spirit of collaboration between different social strata imbibed by community participation at local levels might sap the force of adversarial social movements (such as trade unions) that seek to combat social inequalities on a larger scale, and so on. In short, the fear is that success of participation in the local arena might create negative externalities for the larger arena.

Examples can be found where one or other of these fears has indeed come true, but the examples of synergy we have discussed above (and many more that we haven't) clearly indicate that there is no inevitability about them. Nor is it a matter of chance whether the relationship between local and larger arenas turns out to be one of synergy or one of negative externalities. It is the nature of human agency that makes the difference. Just as the success or failure of participation itself depends on human agency – namely, how well various actors like the state, civil society and people themselves take measures to bridge the capacity gap, the incentive gap and the power gap, the relationship between local and larger arenas also depends on human agency – namely, how conscientiously these same actors try to foster potential synergies. It should not come as a surprise that the role of human agency should be pre-eminent in determining the success or failure of what is after all a social institution.

---

[42]   On this and other issues related to accountability, see Goetz & Jenkins (2004).

References

Adato, M, Haddad, L, Horner, D, Ravjee, N & Haywood, R 1999, *From Works to Public Works: The Performance of Labour-Intensive Public Works in Western Cape Province, South Africa*, Final Report, International Food Policy Research Institute, Washington, DC.

Adato, M, Hoddinott, J & Haddad, L 1993, *Power, Politics and Performance. Community Participation in South African Public Works Program*, Research Report No. 143, International Food Policy Research Institute, Washington, DC.

Agrawal, A & Gupta, K 2005, Decentralization and Participation: The Governance of Common Pool Resources in Nepal's Terai, *World Development,* vol. 33(7).

Ahmad, J, Devarajan, S, Khemani, J & Shah, S 2005, 'Decentralization and Service Delivery', Policy Research Working Paper No. 3603, World Bank, Washington, DC.

Araujo, MC, Ferreira, FHG, Lanjouw, P & Özler, B 2006, 'Local Inequality and Project Choice: Theory and Evidence from Ecuador', Working Paper, World Bank, Washington DC.

Ascher, W & Healy, R 1990, *Natural Resource Policymaking in Developing Countries,* Duke University Press, Durham NC.

Baiocchi, G 2003, 'Participation, Activism and Politics: The Porto Alegre Experiment', in Fung & Wright 2003a.

Baland, JM & Platteau, JP 1996, *Halting Degradation of Natural Resources. Is There a Role for Rural Communities?* Clarendon Press, Oxford.

Bardhan, P 1993, 'Analytics of the Institutions of Informal Cooperation in Rural Development', *World Development,* vol. 21(4).

Bardhan, P 2002, 'Decentralization of Governance and Development', *Journal of Economic Perspectives*, vol. 16(4).

Bardhan, P & Mookherjee, D 2006, *Decentralization and Local Governance in Developing Countries – A Comparative Perspective,* MIT Press, Cambridge, Mass.

Berkes, F (ed.) 1998, *Common Property Resources: Ecology and Community-Based Sustainable Development*, Belhaven Press, London.

Besley, T, Pande, R & Rao, V 2005, 'Participatory Democracy in Action: Survey Evidence from South India', *Journal of European Economic Association,* vol. 3(2-3).

Blair, H 2000, 'Participation and Accountability at the Periphery: Democratic Local Governance in Six Countries', *World Development,* vol. 28(1).

Bohman, J & Rehg, W (eds.) 1997, *Deliberative Democracy, Essays on Reason and Politics*, MIT Press, Cambridge, Mass.

Bromley, DW 1992, *Making the Commons Work: Theory, Practice and Policy,* Institute for Contemporary Press, San Francisco.

Brown, K (ed.) 2006, *Transacting Transition: The Micropolitics of Democracy Assistance in the Former Yugoslavia*, Kumarian Press, Bloomfield, CT.

Chambers, R 1988, *Managing Canal Irrigation: Practical Analysis from South Asia*, Oxford University Press, Delhi.

Chattopadhyay, R & Duflo, E 2004, 'Women as Policy-Makers: Evidence from a Randomized Policy Experiment in India', *Econometrica*, vol. 72(5).

Cohen, J & Rogers, J 2003, 'Power and Reason', in Fung & Wright 2003a.

Commins, S 2007, 'Community Participation in Service Delivery and Accountability', (mimeo), Background paper written for the World *Public Sector Report 2007*, United Nations Department for Economic and Social Affairs, New York.

Conover, PJ, Searing, DD & Crewe, IM 2002, 'The Deliberative Potential of Political Discussion', *British Journal of Political Science*, vol. 32.

Cooke, B & Kothari, U (eds.) 2001, *Participation: The New Tyranny?* Zed Books, London and New York.

Crook, RC & Manor, J 1998, *Democracy and Decentralisation in South Asia and West Africa: Participation, Accountability and Performance*, Cambridge University Press, Cambridge.

Dreze, J & Sen, A 1989, *Hunger and Public Action*, Clarendon Press, Oxford.

Dreze, J & Sen, A 1995 *India: Economic Development and Social Opportunity*, Clarendon Press, Oxford.

Dreze, J & Sen, A 2002 'Democratic Practice and Social Inequality in India', *Journal of Asian and African Studies*, vol. 37(2).

Elster, J (ed.) 1998, *Deliberative Democracy*, Cambridge University Press, Cambridge,

Freeman, S 2000, 'Deliberative Democracy: A Sympathetic Comment', *Philosophy and Public Affairs*, vol. 29(4).

Fudenberg, D & Maskin, E 1986, 'The Folk Theorem in Repeated Games with Discounting or with Incomplete Information', *Economterica* vol. 54(3).

Fung, A & Wright, EO 2003b, 'Countervailing Power in Empowered Participatory Governance', in Fung & Wright 2003a.

Fung, A & Wright, EO (eds.) 2003a, *Deepening Democracy: Institutional Innovations in Empowered Participatory Governance*, Verso Books, London and New York.

Galasso, E & Ravallion, M 2005, 'Decentralized Targeting of an Anti-Poverty Program', *Journal of Public Economics*, 89(4).

Goetz, AM & Jenkins, R 2001, 'Hybrid Forms of Accountability: Citizen Engagement in Institutions of Public-Sector Oversight in India', *Public Management Review*, vol. 3(3).

Goetz, AM & Jenkins, R 2004, *Reinventing Accountability: Making Democracy Work for the Poor*, Macmillan/Palgrave, London.

GOMP 1998, *The Madhya Pradesh Human Development Report, 1998*, Government of Madhya Pradesh (India), Bhopal.

Grindle, MS 2000, *Audacious Reforms: Institutional Innovation in Latin America and Africa*, Johns Hopkins University Press, Baltimore, MD and London.

Grindle, MS 2004, 'Good Enough Governance: Poverty Reduction and Reforms in Developing Countries', *Governance*, vol. 17(4).

Habermas, J 1987, *The Theory of Communicative Action*, 2 vols. (translated by Thomas A. McCarthy), Beacon Press, Boston, Mass.

Hardin, GJ 1968, 'The Tragedy of the Commons', *Science*, vol. 162.

Heller, P 2001, Moving the State: 'The Politics of Democratic Decentralization in Kerala, South Africa, and Porto Alegre', *Politics and Society*, vol. 29(1).

Hickey, S & Mohan, G (eds.) 2005, *Participation: From Tyranny to Transformation? Exploring New Approaches to Participation in Development*, Zed Books, London.

Isaac, TMT 2000, *Local Democracy and Development: People's Campaign for Decentralized Planning*, New Left Books, New Delhi.

Isaac, TMT & Heller, P 2003, 'Democracy and Development: Decentralized Planning' in Kerala, in Fung & Wright 2003a.

Isham, J & Kähkönen, S 2000a, 'Institutional Determinants of the Impact of Community-Based Water Services: Evidence from Sri Lanka and India', *Economic Development and Cultural Change,* vol. 50(3).

Isham, J & Kähkönen, S 2000b, 'How Do Participation and Social Capital Affect Community-Based Water Projects? Evidence from Central Java, Indonesia', in C. Grootaert, & T. van Batselaer (eds.), *The Role of Social Capital in Development: An Empirical Assessment*, Cambridge University Press, Cambridge.

Isham, J, Narayan, D & Pritchett, L 1995, 'Does Participation Improve Performance? Establishing Causality with Subjective Data', *The World Bank Economic Review,* vol. 9(2).

Jenkins, R & Goetz, A-M 1999, 'Accounts and Accountability: Theoretical Implications of the Right-to-Information Movement in India', *Third World Quarterly*, vol. 20(3).

Katz, T & Sara, J 1997, 'Making Rural Water Supply Sustainable: Recommendations from a Global Study, UNDP-World Bank Water and Sanitation Program', World Bank, Washington DC.

Keefer, P & Khemani, S 2005, 'Democracy, Public Expenditures and the Poor', *World Bank Research Observer,* vol. 20(1).

Khwaja, AI 2004, 'Is Increasing Community Participation Always a Good Thing?', *Journal of the European Economic Association*, vol. 2(2-3).

King, E & Ozler, B 1998, 'What's Decentralization Got to do with Learning? The Case of Nicaragua's School Autonomy Reform', Development Research Group Working Paper, World Bank, Washington, DC.

Knudsen, AJ 1995, *Living with the Commons: Local Institutions for Natural Resource Management*, Christian Michelsen Institute, Bergen.

Koonings, K 2004, 'Strengthening Citizenship in Brazil's Democracy: Local Participatory Governance in Porto Alegre', *Bulletin of Latin American Research* vol. 23(1).

Krishna, A 2002, 'Enhancing Political Participation in Democracies: What is the Role of Social Capital?' *Comparative Political Studies*, vol. 35(4).

Kumar, S & Corbridge, S 2002, 'Programmed to Fail? Development Projects and the Politics of Participation', *Journal of Development Studies*, vol. 39(2).

Lee, W 2003, 'Is Democracy More Expropriative than Dictatorship? Tocquevillian Wisdom Revisited', *Journal of Development Economics*, vol. 71.

Manikutty, S 1997, 'Community Participation: So What? Evidence From a Comparative Study of Two Rural Water and Supply Projects in India', *Development Policy Review*, vol. 15.

Manikutty, S 1998, 'Community Participation: Lessons from Experiences in Five Water and Sanitation Projects in India', *Development Policy Review*, vol. 16(3).

Manor, J 1999, *The Political Economy of Democratic Decentralization*, World Bank, Washington, DC.

Manor, J 2007, 'Strategies to Promote Effective Participation' (mimeo), Background paper written for the World *Public Sector Report 2007*, United Nations Department for Economic and Social Affairs, New York.

Mansuri, G & Rao, V 2004, 'Community-Based and Driven Development: A Critical Review', *World Bank Research Observer*, vol. 19(1).

McCay, BJ & Acheson, JM 1987, *The Question of the Commons: The Culture and Ecology of Communal Resources*, University of Arizona Press, Tucson.

Molinas, JR 1998, 'The Impact of Inequality, Gender and External Assistance and Social Capital on Local-Level Cooperation', *World Development*, vol. 26(3).

Mosse, D 1997, 'The Symbolic Making of a Common Property Resource: History, Ecology and Locality in a Tank-irrigated Landscape in South India', *Development and Change*, vol. 28(3).

Mozumder, P & Halim, N 2006, 'Social Capital Fostering Human Capital: The Role of Community Participation in Primary School Management in Bangladesh', *Journal of International Development*, vol. 18(2).

Narayan, D 1998, 'Participatory Rural Development', in E. Lutz with H. Binswanger, P. Hazell, & A. McCalla (eds.) *Agriculture and the Environment*, World Bank, Washington, DC.

Navia, P & Zweifel, TD 2003, 'Democracy, Dictatorship and Infant Mortality Revisited', *Journal of Democracy*, vol. 14(3).

NSAC 1998, *Nepal Human Development Report, 1998*, Nepal South Asia Centre, Kathmandu.

Osmani, SR 2001, 'Participatory Governance and Poverty Reduction', in A. Grinspun (ed.) *Choices for the Poor: Lessons from National Poverty Strategies*, UNDP, New York.

Osmani, SR 2002, 'Expanding Voice and Accountability through the Budgetary Process', *Journal of Human Development*, vol. 3(2).

Ostrom, E 1990, *Governing the Commons: The Evolution of the Institutions for Collective Action*, Cambridge University Press, New York.

Ostrom, E 1992, *Crafting Institutions for Self-Governing Irrigation Systems*, Institute for Contemporary Press, San Francisco.

Ostrom, E 1994, *Neither Market nor State: Governance of Common-Pool Resources in the Twenty-First Century*, Lecture Series No. 2, International Food Policy Research Institute, Washington DC.

Ostrom, E & Gardner, R 1993, 'Coping with Asymmetries in the Commons: Self-Governing Irrigation Systems Can Work', *Journal of Economic Perspectives,* vol. 7(4).

Ostrom, E, Lam, W & Lee, M 1994, 'The Performance of Self-Governing Irrigation Systems in Nepal', *Human Systems Management,* vol. 13(3).

Owomugasho, D *et al.* 1999a, 'Kapchorwa District Report', (mimeo) Uganda Participatory Poverty Assessment Project, Ministry of Finance, Government of Uganda, Kampala.

Owomugasho, D *et al.* 1999b, 'Kumi District Report' (mimeo), Uganda Participatory Poverty Assessment Project, Ministry of Finance, Government of Uganda, Kampala.

Pande, R 2003, 'Can Mandated Political Representation Increase Political Influence for Disadvantaged Minorities? Theory and Evidence from India', *American Economic Review* (forthcoming).

Paxson, C & Schady, N 2002, 'The Allocation and Impact of Social Funds: Spending on School Infrastructure in Peru', *The World Bank Economic Review,* vol. 16(2).

Persson, T & Tabellini, G 2006, 'Democracy and Development: The Devil in the Details', Working Paper 11993, National Bureau of Economic Research, Cambridge, Mass.

Platteau, JP 2004, 'Community-Based Development in the Context of within Group Heterogeneity' in Bourguignon, F. & B. Pleskovic (eds.), *Proceedings of the Annual World Bank Conference on Development Economics 2004,* World Bank, Washington DC.

Platteau, JP & Abraham, A 2002, 'Participatory Development in the Presence of Endogenous Community Imperfections', *Journal of Development Studies,* vol. 39(2).

Przeworski, A, Alvarez, ME, Cheibub, JA & Limongi, F 2000, *Democracy and Development: Political Institutions and Well-being in the World, 1950-1990,* Cambridge University Press, New York.

Przeworski, A, & Limongi, F 1993, 'Political Regimes and Economic Growth', *Journal of Economic Perspectives,* vol. 7.

Rao, V & Ibanez, AM 2001, 'The Social Impact of Social Funds in Jamaica: A Mixed-Methods Analysis of Participation, Targeting and Collective Action in Community Driven Development', DECRG, World Bank, Washington, DC.

Rawls, J 1993, *Political Liberalism*, Columbia University Press, New York.

Ribot, J & Larson, AM (eds.) 2004, *Democratic Decentralisation through a Natural Resource Lens*, Routledge, New York and London.

Rosenzweig, MR & Foster, AD 2003, 'Democratization, Decentralization and the Distribution of Local Public Goods in a Poor Rural Economy', BREAD Working Paper No. 10.

Ross, M 2006, 'Is Democracy Good for the Poor?' *American Journal of Political Science*, vol 50.

Santos, BS 1998, 'Participatory Budgeting in Porto Alegre: Toward a Redistributive Democracy', *Politics and Society*, vol. 26(4).

Sen, A 1983, 'Development: Which Way Now?' *Economic Journal*, vol. 93.

Sen, A 1999, *Development as Freedom*, Alfred Knopf, New York.

Sen, A 2002, 'Opportunities and Freedom', in A. Sen, *Rationality and Freedom*, The Belknap Press of the Harvard University Press, Cambridge, Mass.

Silkin, T 1998, 'Hitosa Water Supply: A People's Project', Water Aid.

Sinmazdemir, NT 2006, 'Political Regimes, Redistribution, and Poverty: An Empirical Investigation', Paper presented at the Workshop on Democracy and Poverty, Duke University.

Sirowy, L & Inkeles, A 1990, The Effects of Democracy on Economic Growth and Inequality: A Review', *Studies in International Development*, vol. 25.

Tavares, J & Wacziarg, R 2001, 'How Democracy Affects Growth', *European Economic Review,* vol. 45.

United Nations 1986, *The Declaration on the Right to Development*, General Assembly Resolution No. 41/128, UN GAOR, 41st Session. UN Doc. A.Res/41/128 Annex 1987, New York.

Varshney, A 2002, 'Poverty Eradication and Democracy in the Developing World', Background Paper for Human Development Report, United Nations Development Programme, New York.

Wade, R 1987, *Village Republics: Economic Conditions for Collective Action in South India*, Cambridge University Press, Cambridge.

World Bank 2004, *World Development Report 2004: Making Services Work for Poor People*, World Bank, Washington, DC.

Formalizing a Connection between Trust in Government and Civic Engagement and the Community of NGOs: Institutionalizing Openness and Accessibility

Herrington J. Bryce

Notwithstanding the espousal of civic engagement, the growth of the civil society, and the need for trust in government[43], there is no existing conceptual link among the three concepts although there is outstanding work on the role of groups in economics, politics and lobbying.[44]   The aim of this paper is to conceptually link the public's trust in government to civic engagement via the involvement of nonprofit organizations (NGOs) as players in the public policy process. Through what logic may trust in government follow from civic engagement through the operation of NGOs?

This paper does not presume that trust in government is necessarily good, that NGOs are necessarily trustworthy or representative, that civic engagement in the process of governance is necessarily without limits or that increased civic engagement leads to greater trust in government. Rather, this paper seeks to specify certain definitions, limits, conditions, connections, and processes that are conducive to enhancing trust in government through civic engagement and specifically through NGOs.

---

[43]   Joseph Nye, Philip D. Zelikow and David C. King, eds, <u>Why People Don't Trust Governments</u> (Cambridge, MA: Harvard University Press, 1997). David G. Carnevale, <u>Trustworthy Government: Leadership and Management Strategies for Building Trust and High Performance,</u> (San Francisco: CA: Jossey-Bass, 1995). Peter D. Behn, "Government Performance and the Conundrum of Public Trust," in John D. Donahue and Joseph S. Nye, Jr. eds, <u>Market-Based Government</u> (Washington, DC: Brookings Institution Press), pp. 325-348; Joseph E. Stiglitz, "Participation and Development : Perspective from the Comprehensive Development Paradigm," Review of Development Economics, 2002, Vol. 6, No. 2, pp. 163-182.

[44]   Frank Baumgartner and B. L. Leach, <u>Basic Interest: The Importance of Groups in Politics and Political Science </u>(Princeton NJ: Princeton, 1998); Larry Diamond, "Rethinking Civil Society"<u> Journal of Democracy,</u> 1994, Vol. 5, pp 5-17; Gary S. Becker, "Public Policies, Pressure Groups, and Dead Weight Costs," in George Stigler, ed. <u>Chicago Studies in Political Economy</u>, (Chicago, IL: The University of Chicago Press, 1988), pp. 85-105; Andreas Dur and Dirk de Bievre, "The Question of Interest Group Influence," Journal of Public Policy, January 2007, Vol. 27, Issue 1, pp. 1-12.

This paper assumes that governments, no matter how open, are exposed to the risk of loss of public trust; that the deepening of distrust is a sequential and consequential process in which corrective intervention by NGOs is possible. Therefore, the management of citizen trust in government can be treated as a risk management problem in which the NGO, operating in its own self-interest, might be an instrument for modifying the public's trust in government. In this way, it is hoped that this paper will contribute to the construction of a conceptual framework to advance real-world propensities and practices in incorporating NGOs in creating and maintaining trustworthy processes of governance where trustworthiness is based upon actual government performance. This paper concludes with a summary statement incorporating the arguments developed in the body of the paper. It represents the theoretical logic contributed by this paper.

The Basic Theoretical Challenge

In a recent empirical study, Hill and Matsubayahsi[45] found that "…. membership in bridging social–capital civic associations is unrelated to democratic responsiveness of leaders to the mass public but that bonding social–capital membership is negatively associated with such responsiveness." (p.215) In addition, "…. bonding social–capital civic engagement weakens the democratic linkage processes inherent in elections." (p. 215) Bonding social capital tightens in-group solidarity. Bridging social capital facilitates inter-group connections--networking.

These findings imply that in order for theory to move forward about the role of NGOs in the public policy process, we must (a) identify systemic limits to their performing in that process, and (b) provide a logic through which we may expect NGOs to have any impact on the process especially as bridging social capital (connecting to government, and to other nonprofits). This paper addresses both challenges.

Uslander and Brown[46] observed that in the literature on trust, social capital, and civic engagement, trust is treated both as a facilitator of engagement--the greater the trust the greater and more successful the engagement; and as the product of engagement--the greater the engagement the greater the probability for trust to develop. They found that the stronger of the two

---

[45]   Kim Quaile Hill and Tetsuya Matsubayahsi "Civic Engagement and Mass Elite Policy Agenda Agreement in American Communities," American Political Science Review, Vol. 99 No. 2 2005, pp. 215-224.

[46]   Eric Uslander and Mitchell Brown, "Inequality, Trust and Civic Engagement," American Politics Research, 2005, Vol. 33, No. 6, pp. 868-894.

directions is that trust encourages civic engagement--especially in community as differentiated from political organizations.[47]

These two empirical studies imply a significant feedback loop: Trust leads to increased civic engagement, and civic engagement in turn leads to greater trust even if the feedback is weaker. Furthermore, these findings imply that NGOs of the community type are not only significant for incubating and expressing trust, but that they are potential bridges and links to civic engagement in governance. Thus the key task of this paper is to delineate the definitions and conditions that, in general, could make civic engagement and NGOs contribute meaningfully to trust in government.

Placing Trust in Gorvernment into Perspectice

Since trust in government is a stated objective, we must first define what is meant by trust in government, the limits of that trust, and the stages through which that trust declines and corrective NGO intervention may be effective:

A Meaning and Significance of Trust in Government

Hardin[48], a political scientist, argues that what motivates civic participation in government is distrust, not trust. Citizens are motivated to act because they believe that government may be oppressive, self-serving, or unable to administer to the particular needs of individuals or groups as well as the citizens themselves individually or as collectives. It is commonly held that the enduring foundation of the United States is distrust of government.

As Rousseau long noted[49], distrust is a risk that is endemic to governments and institutions because they restrain natural expression. Aside from Arrow's Impossibility Theorem showing how impossible it might be to have a unanimous choice among voters with different preferences, governance implies choosing within multiple constraints.[50] The imperfection of compromise and the inability to satisfy all parties equally and simultaneously sow the

---

[47] They also find that inequality in income distribution is a significant determinant of trust. The greater the income inequality the less trust is felt across the general population. Thus, the larger the income disparity, the less the trust and the harder it is to cultivate. This is instructive in all countries, but probably more so in underdeveloped countries with severer inequalities.

[48] Russell Hardin, Trust and Trustworthiness (New York: Russell Sage Foundation, 2003), and Russell Hardin, "Trust in Government," in Valerie Braithwaite and Margaret Levi, Trust & Governance (New York: Russell Sage Foundation, 1998) pp. 10-11.

[49] Jean Jacque Rousseau , Social Contract: Principles of Political Rights, (1792).

[50] Harold Lasswell, Politics: Who Gets What, When and How, (New York: (McGraw-Hill, Meridian Books, (1936).

seeds of dissatisfaction, disgruntlement, and distrust. But the imperfection of choices may be because the government lacks information, provides no channel for it to be communicated, and may be administratively comfortable due to its ignorance (or arrogance) even as citizens become restless, resentful, and distrustful. This latter distrust is clearly "unhealthy" and is of the type that concerns this paper.

On the other extreme, complete trust in government may dampen civic engagement if it leads to apathy and indifference. This type of complete trust may express itself in resignation, disinterest, or uncritical acceptance. Citizens acquiesce. This form of trust may not be in itself a cause of bad government because government, operating in this mode, could be benevolent. But this dampened civic involvement does lead to government that may be uninformed, misguided and one acting without or indifferent to the preferences of its citizens. This too can lead to disgruntlement, to distrust and desires of dismantlement.

But what does trust mean? Social scientists have many concepts of trust.[51] The definition of trust used in this paper is trust as the reciprocity of expectations. As political scientist Hardin[52] puts it, A expects B to perform in a specific way other than in B's own self-interest. Applied to this paper, the citizens (A) expect that the government (B) will perform in the interest of the citizens as they were promised.

Within this definition, the decline in trust of the government would derive from the latter's failure to live up to the expectations of its citizens based on its promises to them whether constitutional or electoral. The keys to managing this trust, therefore, are managing citizens' expectations and managing government performance so that they mesh. This approach, upon which this paper is based, is supported by a recent empirical finding that public participation helps trust in government particularly as it relates to "administrative integrity" and "service competence" (performance).[53] In at least one developing country, the Dominican Republic[54], trust of citizen shows a high, significant, and positive link to government "political and economic performance" and in the United States empirical results show a similar link to "economic performance and the public's assessment of the political process"[55].

---

[51]   See Pior Sztompka, Trust: A Sociological Theory (Cambridge University Press, 1999) and Diego Gambetta (ed) Trust: Making and Breaking Cooperative Relationships (Oxford University, UK Basil Blackwell, 1988).

[52]   Hardin, (2003), Ibid.

[53]   XiaoHu Wang and Montgomery Wan Warf, "When Public Participation in Administration Leads to Trust: An Empirical Assessment of Managers' Perceptions," Public Administration Review, Vol. 67, Issue 2, pp. 265-278.

[54]   Rosario Espinal, Jonathan Hartlyn and Jana Morgan Kelly, "Performance Still Matters: Explaining Trust in Government in the Dominican Republic" Comparative Political Studies. March 2006 Vol. 39. Number 2, pp. 200-223.

[55]   Luke J Keele, "Macro Measures and Mechanics of Social Capital," Political Analysis, 2005, Vol. 3, Issue No 2, pp. 139-156.

Stages of Distrust in Government and Opportunities for NGO Intervention

Arguably, the chronic loss of trust in government is not instantaneous. Table 1 depicts likely steps in the movement toward distrust in government and its aftermath when government performance continues to be inconsistent with citizen expectation. It also describes how intervention by NGOs might arrest the deterioration of the process and also restore trust in government. Later we shall argue that this intervention occurs not because the NGO is benevolent toward government, but because it aims to satisfy its own self-interest and that which it represents. The NGOs contribution to trust in government is mostly an unintended consequence of its exercise of its own self-interest.

Table 1 posits that there is first deep or extended dissatisfaction or disappointment in the government's performance based on public expectations. If this stage is left unattended and allowed to fester it may lead to disgruntlement; which if unattended, leads to distrust. Distrust, left unattended, may generate reactions ranging from citizen disengagement and alienation (the passive citizens) to cries and actions for dismantlement by others (the activists).

Table 1: Stages to Distrust in Governemnt and its Aftermath: Themes of Curative or Restorative Intervention by NGOs

Stages to Distrust and Its Aftermath	What Occurs	Aim of Some Curative or Restorative Actions by NGOs that May Increase Trust in Government
Dissatisfaction	Meaningful citizen expectations are not met	Avoiding deterioration to disgruntlement partly by explication, mollification, reasoning, making new or altered promises, getting alterations in government performance and/or citizen expectations. Dissatisfaction of some NGOs is matched by satisfaction by others. Increase trust by celebration of government performance consistent with victor's expectations.
Disgruntlement	Dissatisfaction is left unattended and allowed to fester.	Avoiding deterioration to distrust partly by doing all of the above but emphasizing and nurturing hope and purpose. People may still be dissatisfied but can be made to "understand."
Distrust	Disgruntlement turns to lack of trust in government's intent, or capability to be satisfactorily responsive to those who are disgruntled.	Arresting deterioration by all of the above, by assisting improved government performance to match expectations on a demonstrable and sustainable basis. "Show me that we can rely on the government to adequately respond to our needs and our exposure to natural or human risks." "What am I going to get out of my efforts?" "Why bother?" "What can the NGO do?"
Disengagement	Citizens become disinterested, indifferent, alienated; find no value in engagement with government and in the public policy process.	Restoration of trust aimed to energize citizens by demonstrating not only change in government performance but also the benefits that can accrue to civic involvement; thus, affecting expectations. "Engagement and involvement are worth it." "There is hope." "The system needs you to participate." "You can make a difference." "Let your voice be heard." "Your vote counts."
Dismantlement	Citizens seek change because engagement with government is felt to have failed, been thwarted, not rewarded, and access is unavailable.	Restoration of trust principally by advocating and accomplishing change in incumbency, the system, and/or its processes. Restoring and heightening expectations of "better" government performance through change. "Let's get rid of them." "Lets fix the system where it is broken." "Let's replace it."

"Dismantlement" may range from structural or procedural changes in the system of governance or in who governs how or for how long.[56] In the very extreme, dismantlement could lead to the replacement of one despot with another as much as to the installation of a democracy. As Tilly[57] has argued, the dismantlement of an undemocratic government is no assurance that a democratic one will replace it.

To assure a specific outcome, then, dismantlement and the distrust upon which it is based must be managed because even the most dramatic democratic change can lead to disappointment and possible distrust if there is a severe disconnect between what citizens are made to expect and what can realistically be achieved.[58] Hence, the larger task is to manage the risk of this cycle--disappointment, disgruntlement, distrust, disengagement, and dismantlement by (as we shall argue) the effective employment of NGOs (as we shall describe) as instruments for civic engagement in shaping, monitoring, implementing and in making in-process policy modifications so that expectations and performance are better matched and that distrust is healthy and dismantlement orderly even when extensive.[59]

---

[56]   The American Revolution of 1776 dismantled the relationship with England and was followed by the writing (1787) of the U.S. Constitution. The latter did not precede or occur simultaneously with the former. Similarly, the French in 1789 overthrew the system of Louis the XVI, but it took another two years before a draft constitution was completed and many more years (1799) before it had any meaningful force. For the purposes of this paper, what is particularly noteworthy about these two revolutions (as examples of extreme dismantlement) is that they both were encapsulated in a rich philosophical setting about good governance as in the Federalist Papers and the motto: "Liberty, Equality, and Fraternity."

[57]   Charles Tilly, Trust and Rule, (New York: Cambridge University Press, 2005).

[58]   See, for example, the experience of the former Soviet Union and its country components, Herrington J. Bryce, "The Unintended Budgetary Consequences of Devolution: Capacity Enhancing Potentials within the Current Russian Constitutional Framework" in Bryane Michael, Rainer Kattel and Wolgang Drechsler, (eds.) Enhancing the Capacity to Govern: Challenges Facing the CEE Countries, (Braislava: NISPAcee, 2004), pp. 180-192, and in Zeljko Sevic (ed), Fiscal Decentralization and Grant Transfers in Transition Countries: A Critical Perspective (Braislava: NISPAcee, 2005), pp. 336-349. These two volumes among many others, document various transitional problems in Central and Eastern European countries. NISPAcee (the Network of Schools in Public Administration in Central Eastern Europe) was specifically created in assisting current and future government officials in carrying out their duties in the post-Soviet transition. See also Gabriel Badescu and Eric Uslander (eds.), Social Capital and Democratic Transition, (London: Policy Press, 2003).

[59]   The sequence in described fits my understanding of history. See footnote 5. The reader may want to begin with the classic work of Charles Tilly, Social Movements 1768-2004 (University of British Columbia Press, 2005). As Charles Tilly notes, various types of networks of trust (including organizations and families) have confronted unfavorable leadership with a variety of techniques and outcomes--not always leading to democracy. See Charles Tilly, Trust and Rule, (New York: Cambridge University Press, 2005).

<u>The Focal Point of Curative or Restorative Intervention</u>
To avoid or cure distrust, or to restore trust, or even to nurture distrust when
that is the political objective, we must locate where in the governance process
such opportunities, occurrences and events are most likely to arise and at
the same time be susceptible to the impact of NGO action or intervention.
Hence, Table 2 distinguishes trust in government as in its integrity—its
proneness to deceit and corruption--from trust in government as in its
capacity or capability to manage the bureaucracy during the normal course
of events or in crisis. It distinguishes trust in the way the government is managed from trust in its judicial and legislatives systems. It also distinguishes
trust in government in the public policy from the electoral process--its openness, fairness, and inclusiveness in leadership choices--from trust in its management and performance in the public policy process—the government's
making and implementing decisions affecting the welfare of the public. This
paper points to the last--the public policy process-- as the principal locus of
the risk that the government will lose the public's trust due to performance
inconsistent with citizen expectations.

Table 2: The Objects of Trust in Government

Object of Trust	Some Questions We Ask in Deciding on Trustworthiness
Integrity	Is it corrupt? Is it deceitful?
Administrative Competence Judicial Legislative	Does it operate efficiently? How does it manage the bureaucracy? Is it fair, arbitrary, consistent, and obedient to the rule of law? Is it representative, transparent, open, reasonable?
Electoral Process	Is it fair? Is it inclusive? Is it transparent?
Public Policy Process	How does it make and implement policy?

The rationale is as follows. All NGOs can operate in the public policy
process, but few can or elect engagement in the administrative or electoral[60].
At least in countries using the United Kingdom and Wales[61] or the United
States model of nonprofit law, the involvement of NGOs in the political
process (defined in law as the influencing of elections) is prohibited; but

---

[60]   The theory and evidence of this are provided in Herrington J. Bryce, <u>Players
in the Public Policy Process: Nonprofits as Social Capital and Agents</u>, (Palgrave
Macmillan, 2005).
[61]   Based on the Charities Act of 1993, which is based on the Preamble to
Charities Uses Act of 1601.

lobbying (affecting the design and implementation of law and regulations) is not [62]. Section 501 (c) of the Internal Revenue Code prohibits political activities by NGOs except for Section 527 organizations—political parties and action committees.[63]

Furthermore, campaigns often highlight flaws as well as exploit and sow disappointment and discontent in the incumbent government as a way of attracting voters often making the electoral process an incubator of distrust more so than trust. In the public policy process distrust may also be imbued, but in that process policy is debated (information), decided upon (lobbying), designed (planning and drafting), implemented (doing), continued or amended (evaluation and lobbying), or discarded.

The public policy process is also the venue in which promises as policy, policy as expectations, and policy as performance occur--making it a natural basis of Hardin's definition of trust as described earlier. In addition, the public policy process continuously links citizens and their governments--unlike the periodic intervention of the electoral process. The public policy process gives meaning to the electoral process. Once elected, the citizens judge whether performance matches expectations and promises. The public policy process is therefore philosophically and pragmatically a natural breeding ground for distrust in government through the inconsistency of its performance with citizen expectations.

But, the public policy process can also be a scapegoat. To illustrate, a government agency that is seen as inefficient may be the victim of resource diversion--never getting the resources it needs to meet the expectations of citizens. Yet, it is the agency's lack of performance that disappoints and causes distrust and distress. Similarly, distrust in the public process may result, not from the process as from the ability of some individuals to legally, even "ethically", exploit it. In this case, changing the public policy or its process is not the solution, but changing or equalizing effective access to it (e.g., through NGOs) may be.

The Static and Dynamics Aspects of Trust in Government

Table 3 reflects that trust in government as it relates specifically to the public policy process connotes a flow of positive and negative sentiments that increases or decreases the stock of trust people have accumulated in their governments. These flows of sentiments change the size, intensity, fragility (placing it on the brink of being destroyed), and depth of this accumulated stock of trust.

---

[62]   See Herrington J. Bryce, Financial and Strategic Management for Nonprofit Organizations: A Comprehensive Reference to Legal, Financial, Management and Operations Rules and Guidelines for Nonprofits, 3rd ed (San Diego: Jossey Bass 2000), esp. pp. 49-61. The only exceptions to this are Section 527 organizations.

[63]   This distinction is the basis of the charges made against Speaker Gingrich in 1997; See a lengthy analysis in Herrington J. Bryce, "For the Speaker, It's Not Over Till the IRS Agent Sings," Outlook, The Washington Post, Sunday January 26, 1997 C3.

Table 3: The Risk Exposure of Government to the Loss of Public Trust, and a Role for NGOs in Managing that Risk in the Public Policy Process

Exposure to Loss of Trust by Government	Manifestation of Distrust by Citizens	Trust-anagement Strategies of NGOs
To hear and understand all citizens with diverse views, sentiments, and dispersed over a wide space.	Expression of loss of trust that the government listens or understands and that involvement matters.	The NGO as a channel for communicating interests, explaining and conciliating.
To formulate policies reflecting not merely power, but costs and benefits and minimizing the extent and depth of dissatisfaction and disgruntlement leading to distrust.	Expression of loss of trust that the government can deliberate expediently and decide fairly and clearly.	NGOs as screening bodies: ideas tested, preferences (positive and negative) and acceptability of policy revealed in early warning.
To finance and to provide adequate resources to meet policy requirements and aims on a timely basis.	Expression of loss of trust that the government can and will adequately finance or deliver over time as government priorities change for whatever reason.	NGO's commitment, use of voluntary and private resources, and substitution of deductions and exemptions for direct government expenditures.
To receive and act upon complaints in a timely and satisfactory manner even when project is being done by outside contractors.	Expression of loss of trust that the government cares, represents the best interests of citizens, is not corrupt.	NGO as monitor, contractor, advocate.
To mollify, satisfy, reason, and to timely and orderly change incumbency and policies and to provide for orderly change.	Expression of loss of trust that government cares, is responsive, amenable to change. Expressions of alienation: "Nothing matters."	The NGO as partner, social agent, creator of social capital--facilitating civic participation and so increasing trust in government if public process allows.

Since the public policy process is on going, the government's exposure to the loss of trust is on going. But the nature of the exposure differs from stage to stage in the public policy process; i.e., trust that the government will listen, but distrust that it will respond appropriately; or trust that it may initially be responsive but not sufficiently supportive, sustaining or self-correcting.

Thus, in Table 3, intervention by NGOs is more than gathering and providing information. The availability of information is not sufficient to trust that the government will receive it, assess it with due diligence, fairly, apolitically,[64] and accurately. Hence, trust in government through the public policy process is based not only on the government's willingness to obtain information, but in its wisdom to judge credibility, urgency and significance; to weigh the consequences of various options and to follow this with an appropriate program of funding and implementation; to harness the citizen involvement that is necessary to co-produce the results (not just support it) and the willingness or capability of the government to amend policy as required. This is the sequence of Table 3 showing the role of the NGO in each step of the sequence. Moreover, effective intervention requires trust by government in the NGOs because NGOs are not always apolitical.[65] To some extent a political alignment is positive because each change in government incumbency is supplied with a set of NGOs that shares its ideology and therefore is available to its ideological position.

Civic Engagement as a Srategic Tool to Manage Trust in Government

The literature well argues the pros and cons of civic engagement[66]. Here we are concerned with the pragmatic limitations on civic engagement from the point of view of governance and the governed--what are its useful and

---

[64]   "Prevailing political relationships play a significant role in how policy needs are perceived." Clarence Stone, "Rethinking the Policy-Politics Connection," Policy Studies, Sept/Dec 2005, Vol. 26, Issue 3-4, p. 241.

[65]   For example, policy evaluations by NGOs are not always purely scientific and apolitical in its conduct or in its motivation. See David Taylor, "Governing Through Evidence: Participation and Power in Policy Evaluation," Journal of Social Policy, Vol. 34, Part 4, pp. 601-619, October 2005 for a recent summary of that literature. Nor is it unbiased culturally, Iris Geva-May "Cultural Theory: The Neglected Variable in the Craft of Policy Analysis," Journal of Comparative Policy Analysis, 2002, Vol. 4, Issue. 3, pp. 243-263; and Robert Hoppe, "Culture of Public Policy Problems," Journal of Comparative Policy Analysis, Vol. 4, Issue 3, pp. 305-327 Ibid.

[66]   Kathe Callahan, Elements of Effective Governance: Measurement, Accountability and Participation, (Taylor and Francis, 2007) offers the most recent assessment of the literature on the pros and cons of citizen as it relates to governance.

practical limits even in an open democratic system--therefore, its limits on contributing to trust in government? We have described a relevant concept of trust in government and identified the public policy process as an arena where that trust plays--the government's performance as it aligns with citizen expectations.   We now turn to civic engagement as a strategic method to managing the risk of loss of trust in government in that arena.

The Limitations of Civic Engagement Even in the Ideal Democracy

"In all the countries where political associations are prohibited, civil associations are rare. It is hardly probable that this is the result of accident... there is a natural and perhaps a necessary connection between these two kinds of associations…Civil associations…facilitate political association…political association singularly strengthens and improves associations for civil purposes."

Alexis de Tocqueville, "Relation of Civil to Political Associations" Democracy in America, Volume 2, Section 2.

In today's world, there are some pragmatic limitations to civic engagement even through civic associations or NGOs. By noting them, we tame expectations of what civil engagement might yield or when it is not pragmatic and therefore diminish the likelihood that civic engagement will be a source of disappointment and distrust:

1. In many matters of state, open and unconstrained civic engagement is not desirable. These are matters including prosecutorial affairs, personal or corporate privacy, diplomacy, espionage, some technical matters[67], subversion, military movements, and security.
2. Civic engagement is a process apart from its content[68], and the process may yield the victor. Victory may come through power as it may through both corrupt and legitimate strategies[69] or through the abuse of a flawed process.

---

[67]   The word "technical" is, of course, quite elastic. There are some technical matters that citizens can and should influence. Dorothy M. Daley, "Citizen Groups and Scientific Decision-making: Does Public Participation Influence Environmental Outcomes," Journal of Policy Analysis and Management, Spring 2007, Vol. 26, Issue 2, p. 349, finds empirical evidence that citizens do influence Superfund environmental decisions.

[68]   Justin Fox, "Government Transparency and Policymaking," Public Choice, April 2007, Vol. 131, Issue 1-2, pp. 23-25. Holds that given the electoral process, some candidates may choose not to fully disclose their intent or policy preferences in order to win. Therefore, in the context of this paper, the public policy process, rather than the electoral one, is where intent may most likely be revealed. We point this out here to make the point that the "facts" of the civil discourse may itself be distorted.

[69]   Johann Graf Lambsdorff, "Corruption and Rent-Seeking," Public Choice, Vol. 113, Issue, 1-2, pp 97, October 2002. Public choice theory actually held that the social cost of corruption could be less than the social welfare cost of rent seeking. Graf finds that the reverse is true. We point this out here to be fair to corruption as a cost of doing business.

3. Civic engagement does encourage disparate views, preferences, urgencies, and sentiments. Therefore what an undiscerning government may hear is discordance that encourages indecision or hastens a decision improperly vetted.

4. Civic engagement can be captured by special interests just as these interests may form, transform or influence others to do their private (group or corporate) bidding. These interests though legitimate, are not necessarily consistent with the best interest of the wider community--if the "best" interest is at all ascertainable.[70]

5. Civic engagement can be inconvenient or inopportune to the government given its outlook, its promises, its philosophies, and its ability or willingness to perform.

6. Civic engagement can be costly to governments. [71] This includes cost of delay, modification and cancellation of projects.

7. Civic engagement, though often low cost, is rarely a zero opportunity cost activity to individual citizens. People must choose to engage. The level of civic engagement is often a consequence of a choice of citizens not to do so.

8. Many obstacles to citizen engagement have little to do with repressive behavior on the part of governments. They are legislated with good intentions—such as the age limit on voting, residency requirements, and the need for permits to demonstrate. But some result purely from vengeance, discrimination, and to preserve power status and positions.

---

[70]   The reader should note that the one question that is not raised anywhere in this essay is whether or not the organization is single-interest, self-promoting, or promoting only of its interests or of those it represents. These are irrelevant questions. As Bryce explains these are precisely the reasons these organizations are formed; i.e., it is stated in their mission statements and also precisely why they may be effective. A good public policy space is replete with competitive and contrary ideas. In the end, it is the policy maker who is sworn to choose the best interest of the public giving the competing ideas. Herrington J. Bryce, Players in the Public Policy Process: Nonprofits as Social Capital and Agents, (New York: Palgrave Macmillan, 2005) Chapter 8.

[71]   For a discussion of some costs, see Renee A. Irvin and John Stansbury, "Citizen Participation in Decision Making: Is It Worth the Effort?" Public Administration Review, February 2000, Vol. 64, Issue 1, pp. 55-65. See also Becker, op. cit. and," Martha S. Feldman and Anne M Khademian "The Role of Public Manager in Inclusion: Creating Communities of Participation" Governance, April 2007 Special Issue, pp. 305- 324.

9. A significant limitation to civic participation is the structure of government and the attitude of public administrators.[72]

10. The more numerous and diversified the civic engagement, the more democratic the system may be, but also the greater the probability of redundancy and stalemates. Number or diversity does not reduce the possibilities of dissatisfaction. They could increase it as the exposure to being denied is increased and the cost of failure having participated is internalized.

Within the constraints of these and other limitations[73] to civic engagement or participation, how can NGOs affect the management of the risk of loss of trust in government as reflected in the public policy process?[74]What are the inherent capabilities of NGOs to exercise influence over trust in government?

The NGO as an AGgent for Civic Engagement Aimed at Reducing the Risk of Loss of the Public's Trust in Government Via the Public Policy Process

This section deals with some inherent capabilities, legitimacy, and network power that NGOs may bring to the public policy process and how in the exercise of these they may aid in the management of the loss of trust in government through the public policy process. The Organizations for Economic Cooperation and Development (OECD) and the United Nations (UN) have

---

[72] It has been found, again in the United States, that the greatest impediment to civic participation in local governance is the lack of facilitation--even encouragement--by government administrators. Kaifeng Yang and Kathe Callahan "Citizen Involvement Efforts and Bureaucratic Responsiveness: Participatory Values, Stakeholder Pressures, and Administrative Practicality" Public Administration Review, March/ April 2007, Issue 2, Vol. 7 'pp. 249-264 and Xiaho-Hu Wang and Montgomery Van Ward, "When Public Participation in Administration Leads to Trust: An Empirical Assessment of Managers' Perceptions," Public Administration Review, March/April 2007, Vol. 7, Issue 2, pp. 265-278.

[73] The conditions for effective citizen participation are discussed in John Clayton Thomas, "Citizen Participation and Effective Governance: Designing a Better Partnership," paper presented at the conference "Governance Crisis in Comparative Perspective, 2007 Conference of SOG, Korea University, Seoul, Korea, October 10-13. See also Peri K. Blind, "Building Trust in Government in the Twenty-First Century: A Review of the Literature and Emerging Issues," 7th Global Forum on Reinventing Government, Building Trust in Government, Vienna Austria June 27-29.

[74] We are not confusing this with acting as a nation-state. At least one author writes interestingly about the extent to which NGOs may or may not conform to the covenants of Westphalia, generally recognized as giving policy formation and implementing authority to nation-states. See Robert Christensen, "International Nongovernmental Organizations: Globalization, Policy, Learning and the Nation-State," International Journal of Public Administration, April 2006, Issue 4-6, p. 281

both noted the rise of NGOs throughout the world and their intervention in all aspects of society. The need for civic engagement is also increasingly necessary because of the need for *cross-sector* cooperation[75], co-production and citizen collaboration[76] in issues including national security.

The Inherent Capabilities that NGOs May Apply in the Public Policy Process to Influence Trust in Government

NGOs have capabilities that transcend size, resources, scope, mission, political power or information (some distorting or self-serving)[77] that they can apply the public policy process--reducing government exposure to citizen dissatisfaction, and distrust. These capabilities are inherent in being an NGO. These capabilities are not resource or otherwise dependent for their existence, although these factors may influence the effectiveness with which these capabilities are exercised.

---

[75]   John M. Bryson, Barbara C. Crosby, and Melissa Middleton Stone "The Design and Implementation of Cross-Sector Collaborations", <u>Public Administration Review</u>, December 2006, Vol. 66. pp 44-55.

[76]   For a history of collaborative efforts involving citizens and citizen organizations and various models for how collaboration may work, their antecedents, constraints see John Bryson, Barbara Crosby and Melissa Stone, "The Design and Implementation of Cross-sector Collaborations: Propositions from the Literature," <u>Public Administration Review</u>, Vol. 66, December 2006, pp. 44-56 and Terry L Cooper, Thomas A. Bryer, Jack W. Meek, "Citizen-Centered Collaborative Public Management," <u>Public Administration Review</u>, December 2006, pp. 76-89, Vol. 66. See Chris Skelcher, Navdeep Mathur, Mike Smith (2005) The Public Governance of Collaborative Spaces: Discourse, Design and Democracy <u>Public Administration</u> 83 (3), 573–596 for a discussion of the nature of institutional collaborative relationship including nonprofits.

[77]   Indeed as Verba and Nie argue, civic engagement in the political process can cause distortions--such that the politician responds to those who most likely will vote. But, if we are allowed an extension of their concept of civic engagement yielding information, we may conclude that civic engagement is important in the public policy process by providing information for the formation, implementation, and modification of policy. Sidney Verba and Norman Nie, <u>Participation in America</u> (New York: NY Harper and Row 1972).

Table 4: Capabilities NGOs Bring to the Public Policy Process

Function	Description
Information:	Gathering of information from needs to innovative research
Diffusion:	Disseminate information, aims, values, political and other philosophies
Evaluation:	Judging and monitoring the efficacy of policy
Signaling:	Calling attention to needs, problems, opportunities, and giving early warning
Organization:	Organize groups and persons for or against a position, action, or regime
Contention:	Opposing policy, policymaking, or policy makers
Screening:	Locus of discourse, refinement, sanctioning and selecting of options and reactions
Intermediation:	Facilitating access of the people through government processes and agencies
Brokering:	Working with both people and government to make things happen between them
Representation:	Advocating, defending, and rationalizing positions or purposes
Collaboration:	Working with governments and other entities toward a public product
Provider:	Provider of output or service using governmental and nongovernmental finance
Regulation:	Sanction behavior or performance

Table 4 shows the range of capabilities, observable in common practice that the community of NGOs can bring to the public policy process. NGOs can be providers of products or services independently or in collaboration with governments, firms, and other NGOs. They can attract resources that may not be available to the government (even by confiscation since some come from abroad) yet are needed to improve the welfare of its citizens (food and medical services); and in so doing, reduce dissatisfaction with government. They can assume portions of certain social risks (caring for the poor)--reducing a source of dissatisfaction. They can be intermediaries that facilitate access by the public and they can be brokers[78] that work to make things happen by bringing parties together without favoring one or the other (conflict resolution, peace). Of course, they can represent a particular interest, party or policy-related point of view (unions, cooperatives, business and other interest groups). In addition, they can gather information and disseminate it through public and private channels. They can be contentious (pro this or anti that). They can organize on behalf of or against a cause (leagues and associations). They can screen and refine information through discourse and signal preferred options (educational and informational organizations). They can certify, sanction, and thereby control or signal appropriate behavior and also advance conformity with public policy to promote the best interest of citizens (medical, law, trade and other professional boards).[79]

The *Empowerment* of the NGOs to Function as Described, Influencing Trust in Government

How is the NGO empowered to use these inherent capabilities on behalf of the public or subgroup in the public policy process? Pierre-Joseph Produhan, General Idea of the Revolution in the Nineteenth Century (1851) noted the increasing role of institutions as representatives of people in the governance process in lieu of individuals representing themselves. In more recent years, it has been said that NGOs can be intermediaries between the people and their government[80] or that they may substitute, complement or be adversaries to government, partners to government[81] and as providers of goods or services that are unattractive to profit-makers[82]. Reacting to

---

[78]   For a description of the brokerage function in social movements, see Mario Dani, "Leaders or Brokers: Positions and Influence in Social Movement Networks" in Mario Diani and Doug McAdams (eds) Social Movememt and Networks: Relational Approaches to Collective Action, (Oxford University Press), pp. 105-122.

[79]   For a policy-related classification of NGOs, See Bryce (2005) , pp 232-234.

[80]   Peter Berger and Richard Neuhaus, To Empower People: The role of Mediating structures in Public Policy (Washington, D.C., American Enterprise Institute for Public Policy Research, 1977) and Peter Berger, Richard Neuhaus, and Robert Novak, eds., To Empower People: From State to Civil Society (Washington, DC: The American Enterprise Institute, 1996).

[81]   Dennis R. Young, "Complementary, Supplementary, or Adversarial? A Theoretical and Historical Examination of Nonprofit-Government Relationship the United States," in Elizabeth T. Boris and C. Eugene Steuerle, Nonprofits & Government (Washington, DC: The Urban Institute, 1998), pp. 31-67. Lester M. Salamon, Partners in Public Service: Government-Nonprofit Relations in the Modern Welfare State (Baltimore, MD: Johns Hopkins University Press, 1995).

[82]   To see a review of these theories specifically as they may relate to the content of this paper, see Herrington J. Bryce, Players in the Public Policy Process: Nonprofits as Social Capital and Agents (New York: Palgrave Macmillan 2005), Chapter 2, pp. 11-33.

the work of Putnam[83], there is a growing literature concerning the role of NGOs in the formation of social capital for the furtherance of civic engagement. For our purposes, we need a more formal expression of the relationship between the NGO and the public,[84] and the basis of its empowerment and legitimacy. The empowerment of the NGO is based on the following. NGOs are organizations voluntarily formed by citizens on the basis of their commitment to serve a specific purpose or mission. The government's granting of a charter to the NGO is tantamount to its giving it a license of empowerment to function in the carrying out of that mission. The government's giving of tax exemption to the NGO is tantamount to its concluding that the mission is of sufficient public import to be publicly financed. This is the legal basis for the NGO's empowerment[85] to function as described. The government formally grants and certifies it in a charter in which its powers to act, as specified, are enumerated.[86]

Therefore, the engagement of the NGO by the government in the public policy process is not based on a palliative motive, but on its prior empowerment of the organization, its legitimacy and a mutuality of interests. All three parties in this triangular relationship (the citizens, the NGO, and the government) share a common motive. The triangular trust among them is based on the expectation of performance each of the other; but the common interest they share is the motivation for their performance and collaboration.

---

[83]   Robert Putnam, Bowling Alone: The Collapse and Revival of American Community (New York: Simon Schuster, 2000).

[84]   In policy formulation, the network can be an intermediary, but it can also be in a sequence: (a) a creator or molder of a policy idea, (b) an intermediary for moving that idea forward, and (c) an instrument of the policy outcome. See Ben Kisby, "Analyzing Policy Networks: Toward and Ideational Approach," Policy Studies, March 2007, Vol. 28, Issue 1, p. 7.

[85]   Section 501 (c) grants federal tax exemption to nonprofits--whether they are charities or not--only to provide (thus "in exchange for") specific public or social benefits. Private (nonpublic-intended) and political (electoral) benefits are prohibited. States follow the same rule. Hence, the following language in a report by attorneys general of several states..."society confers upon nonprofit organizations, including charities, such special privileges as tax exemptions in return for the performance of services providing socially desirable objectives which benefit the community." What's in a Nonprofit's Name: Public Trust, Profits and the Potential for Public Deception," (California Attorney General's Office, April, 1999). For an extensive discussion of the legal application of this principles, see Herrington J. Bryce, Financial and Strategic Management for Nonprofit Organizations, 3rd edition, (San Diego, Jossey Bass 2000), esp. pp 23-84; and in establishing the nonprofit as an agent of the public principal, See Herrington J. Bryce, Players in the Public Policy Process: Nonprofits as Social Capital and Agents (New York: Palgrave Macmillan, 2005) esp. pp. 59-80.

[86]   For a further development of this point as it appears in charters and in law, see Bryce (2000) and Bryce (2005), Ibid.

What is the common interest? The common interest is the advancement of the community and country of which each is by location and loyalty a member. Failure simultaneously places all three--the citizens, the NGO, and the government--at risk.

The *Legitimacy* of NGOs to Function as Described, Influencing Trust in Government

To be effective, to be taken seriously in the public policy process, it is not enough for the NGO to be empowered but it must have legitimacy--policy makers must feel that they represent a constituency to which or about which they are answerable or vulnerable. Legitimacy relates to the NGO's being a true representative of an issue or citizens.[87] Legitimacy affects the acceptance by the government of the NGO's intrusion as an agent of citizens or interests in the public policy process. Legitimacy is a narrow concept because the public policy maker does not ask if the organization represents the citizen in general, but whether it represents a specific segment with respect to the specific issue at hand. The legitimacy of a labor union is with respect to its representing its members on issues related to their work and profession and reflected in the votes of members.

The lack of legitimacy of an NGO in the public policy process is likely to be short-lived if its members or members of the public are informed of its representations and capable of voluntary action. They can refuse to support the organization. Where the NGO is a membership organization such as a cooperative, a union, or an association, the members may quit. Citizens may also support or join rival organizations. Furthermore, to the extent that the organization continues not to comply with its mission, its charter can be revoked by the state. Hence, the continued intrusion of an NGO in the public policy process is reasonable prima facie evidence of its legitimacy to some collection of citizens.

Networking as Multiplier of NGOs Power to Affect Trust in Government

Beyond its legitimacy to act, the NGO's influence is related to its ability to draw upon networks and coalitions held together by strongly shared val-

---

[87]   For a discussion of other concepts of legitimacy and forms of civic participation see, Anchon Fung, "Varieties of Participation in a Complex Governance," Public Administration Review, December 2006, Vol. 66, pp. 10-20.

ues.[88] Each NGO can be considered to be part of a complex web of partially intersecting sets of NGOs. The more dense and differentiated the NGOs in a country space (given its fixed borders) the less likely the probability of complete uniqueness or unrelated interest to others in that space. On any issue, therefore, there are other NGOs within the same space with whom an NGO finds common cause even if the primary mission is different.[89] Thus the producers of spirits may finance NGO programs against driving under the influence of alcohol because of a common interest in avoiding the probable consequences of such behavior.

Within any fixed country space there is constant rearranging of networks in response to changes in public policy considerations. These rearrangements and intersections also occur because, as public choice teaches about lobbying and rent seeking, NGOs can trade support: "We'll support and get others to support you on this one if you will do the same for us on our issue." With this latter behavior, networking can occur even when the interests in a policy issue are not identical.[90] Thus, the diversity and large number of NGOs even covering a single subject such as the environment can connect associated interests into a network of common and shared interests, knowledge, and other resources [91] (bridging social capital). Hence, networks (some cross-

---

[88]   Bryce (2005), pp. 163-182 argues, for example, that business coalitions, although having sizeable resources, depend heavily upon cohesive networks—many reaching into every congressional district for their power. The strength of many coalitions lies in the singularity, depth, and extensive reach. For empirical support of shared values holding together coalitions, see Joanne Sobeck, "Comparing Policy Process Frameworks, What Do They Tell Us about Group Membership and Participation for Policy Development?" Administration and Society, 2003, Vol. 35, No. 3; pp. 350-374; Edella Schager, "Policy Making and Collective Action, Defining Coalitions with the Advocacy Coalition Framework," Policy Sciences, 1995, Vol. 28, pp. 242-270, and Edella Schlager and William Blomquist, "A Comparison of Three Emerging Theories of the Policy Process," Political Research Quarterly, 1996, Vol. 49, pp. 651-672.

[89]   In administrative space, organizations have at least five boundaries: mission, accountability, resources, capacity and responsibility. Donald F. Kettl, "Managing Boundaries in American Administration, the Collective Imperative," Public Administration Review, December 2006, Vol. 66, pp. 10-20.

[90]   See the discussions in footnotes 6 and 7.

[91]   Networks are also an important source of resources to apply to public policy purposes. Margaret Mikkelson, "Policy Network Analysis as a Strategic Tool for the Voluntary Sector," Policy Studies, March 2006, Vol. 27, issue 1, pg. 17.

border)[92] can dramatically magnify the potential resources NGOs bring to the public policy process[93] on specific issues.[94]

Networks, First and Second Order Legitimacy. Special problems arise when through networks or other means NGOs form coalitions or federations for the purpose of having an impact on the public policy process; for example, through negotiation or lobbying. This introduces what may be called first and second order problems of legitimacy. First, each NGO has to be legitimatised by those it represents--that is--first order legitimacy. Then the coalition it enters into with others must, as a collective body, be legitimatised by each NGO in the coalition--second order legitimacy. And the moral hazard and risk of loss of trust can be as great for the NGO and its coalition as it is for the government; for they too must perform to meet the expectations for which they were formed. Hence, normally there is a disincentive for the NGO or coalition (even if rent-seeking with respect to the government) to deviate from its path just to increase trust in government.

Points of Orderly Intervention of NGOs in the Public Policy Process Impacting Citizen Expextations and/or Government Performance

The preceding discussion can be most useful if there are institutionalized, predictable and orderly points of NGO intervention in the public policy process. In this section, we identify and describe specific points in the public policy process where NGO intervention may be useful in shaping a policy product that is consistent with public expectations and therefore trust in government. At each point, the NGO is acting in its own self-interest or that of the citizens with an impact on government performance and/or citizen expectations influencing trust in government.

---

[92]   Sidney Tarrow, The New Transnational Activism (Cambridge Studies in Contentious Politics) (Cambridge, NY, 2005) notes the growing importance of transnational networks and links in activism, but notes that the power of each, actor such as an NGO, is grounded in its local space while its transnational linkages are based on rules of relationships.

[93]   Unlike other activities, such as local economic development, civic networks increase political participation along class lines. Ronald Smith, Discerning Differences in Social Capital: The Significance of Interpersonal Network and Neighborhood, Dissertation, the University of Indiana, 2006, UMI 3206874, Proquest Information and Learning Co, Ann Arbor, Michigan. And, social networks in turn facilitate political participation of all types, Maria Elena Sandovici, Social Capital and Political Action, Dissertation, State University of New York at Binghamton, 2005, UMI 932371601, Proquest Information and Learning Co., Ann Arbor, Michigan.

[94]   Many writers before me have asked this question; therefore, I do not pretend to suggest a general theory of why they work—only as it applies to this paper. See for example, Chapter 2 of Charles Tilly, Trust and Rule, op. cit. for his version and Roger V. Gould, " Why Do Networks Matter: Relational and Structural Interpretations," in Diani and Mc Adams, op. cit.

Table 5: Points and Forms of Civic Intervention of NGOs in the Public Policy Process

Points of Intervention	Forms of Intervention
Initial Policy Formulation	Information gathering, group formation, discussion, taking of group position, cooperative action, lobbying, commenting, information dissemination, influencing legislative drafting and voting.
Implementation	Financing, facilitating and carrying out policy.
Monitoring and Evaluation	Information gathering and sharing, judging impact
Experimentation and Innovation	Technical and sentimental information gathering, influencing and advancing new policy initiatives and modifications of extant policies.
Policy Revision	Information gathering, discussion, advocacy, lobbying, commenting, information dissemination, influencing legislative drafting and voting-- helping government to chart course and to win acceptance of revision

Table 5 notes that in the formulation of policy, civic engagement by NGOs for example through representative public hearing, can be an important source of information for defining need, expected involvement, and specifying the expectations of government performance. Another strategy an NGO may use at this stage is lowering expectations from government policy (partly to protect its own image) or heightening it so as to put pressure on the government. In either case, citizen *expectation* is being managed and so too government *performance* (policy product or service design).

In the second stage, the NGO may impact how the policy is implemented. It may help in rule making, and it might implement policy. One of the effects of civic involvement in the design as well as in the implementation stage is to potentially shift some of the risks and responsibility of failure (and therefore a cause of disappointment leading to distrust) away from the government and to those NGOs that participated in the design, neglected to do so but should have, or participated in the implementation of the policy. In the implementation phase, the NGO is focused on *performance*.

A third stage of intervention relates to continuous experimentation, innovation and in-process adjustments and modifications to how the policy is applied as partly through NGO monitoring. Trust in government at this stage is derived from the speed as well as the direction of government response. But the monitoring and the public insistence on modifications by the NGO would invariably impact trust in government. Whether this is positive or negative would depend upon how the government reacts. In this phase, the NGO directs its energies to both *performance* (i.e., better product and delivery systems) and *expectations*.

Finally, in Table 5 we note that the public policy process involves an end period of evaluation provided for by sunset rules, and required reauthorization. At this point, public trust depends upon the ability or willingness of the government to listen, to discard bad policy, and to modify the offending ones (or parts). NGOs can record and communicate common public experiences and suggest appropriate modifications based on actual experience and expectations. Importantly, this is tied to the belief that the government will learn, adjust, and continue a policy that has been successful and still needed. At this stage the NGOs can influence both *performance* and *expectations*.

Throughout, civic engagement is meaningless if there is no demonstrable government commitment to initiate, to modify or to (dis) continue bad policy and adopt good ones. Non-commitment likely breeds disappointment in its revelation, followed eventually by distrust, call for disengagement (among the passive citizens) and dismantlement among the activists.

Finally, at each point of intervention in Table 5, there is need for triangular trust: (a) The public's trust of the NGO[95], (b) the government's trust

---

[95]   There is a considerable amount of theorizing and research concerning trust in organizations. See for example, Roderick Kramer and Tom Tyler, <u>Trust in Organization: Frontiers of Theory and Research</u> (Thousand Oaks: CA Sage Publications, 1996) and Elinor Ostrom and James Walker, <u>Trust and Reciprocity</u> (NY. Russell Sage 2003). I have specifically addressed the public trust in nonprofit organization, see Herrington J. Bryce, "The Publics Trust in Nonprofit Organizations: The Role of Relationship Marketing and Management" <u>California Management Review</u>, Vol. 49, Issue 4, Summer, 2007, pp. 112-13.

in the legitimacy of the NGO[96] and (c) the NGO's trust that its engagement is a meaningful part of the public policy process are important. Also note that at each point, the NGO is acting on behalf of its mission to serve its clients, its donors, its community, and itself--revenues, reputation and survival. They need not be servants of or in the employ of the government itself to shield it (to various extent) from the diminution of trust.

Recirpocal and Tripartite Trust

Finally, at each point of intervention in Table 5, there is need for reciprocal and tripartite trust:

1. The public's trust in the NGO must be *reciprocated* by the NGO's trust in the particular public or subgroup that it represents. It must trust that at net, this public will be forthcoming with support and will not at net dissociate from the NGO as a result of its performance in the public policy process. In short, the NGO does not put itself at risk of its own loss of trust, dissociation and dismantlement (including the dismissal of its management) by its supporters, directors, or members.

2. The government's trust in the legitimacy of the NGO must be *reciprocated* by the NGO's trust in the government to act in a way that is not continuously injurious to the NGO and its public. This is the trust that the government will be responsive in its performance and at worst be benign in its opposition to the NGO.

3. The people's trust in the government must be *reciprocated* by the government's trust in them; i.e., their loyalty as citizens, their commitment to the rules and regulations, the expectation that they will comply with rules, regulations, law, and common community norms and expectations, etc.

Also note that at each point in Table 5, the NGO is acting on behalf of its mission to serve its clients, its donors, its community, or itself in the form of revenues, reputation and survival. The NGOs need not be servants of, affiliated with, or in the employ of the government to shield the latter (as described in this paper) from the diminution of public trust or to increase the level of public distrust by affecting citizen expectations and/or government performance (as described in this section).

A Summary Statement Theoretically Linking NGOs, Civic Enagement, and Building Trust in Government

---

[96]   It has been argued that while civic engagement broadens the plane of involvement and may increase efficiency and flexibility, it raises questions of equity, accountability and democratic legitimacy. See Peter Bogason, Juliet A. Musso, "The Democratic Prospects of Network Governance," American Review of Public Administration, March 1, 2006; Vol. 36, Issue 1, pp. 3.

Every government has a store of trust (no matter how small or fragile) that is subject to a flow of citizen sentiments that may increase or decrease that store. In the public policy process, the diminution of the size of that store is always at risk because all citizens cannot be equally satisfied at the same and at all times. Choices must be made. Given the propensity of citizens to form groups to express and carryout their interests, the success of these organizations (NGOs) depends on their inherent capabilities, triangular trust, identifiable points for their intervention in the political process, and the responsiveness of government to them. All of this occurs within pragmatic operational constraints on the utility of civic engagement in the public policy process.

In this framework, NGOs can influence the flow of sentiments and therefore the overall stock of trust in government by influencing the coherence between citizen expectations and government performance or the performance of those with whom the government contracts--given that in modern societies governments perform many of their duties through third parties. Since under outsourcing, the government remains ultimately responsible to the citizens, governments remain the citizens' final recourse and target of disappointment that can lead to distrust; i.e. due to its failure to act expeditiously against its contractors.

By influencing citizen expectations and performance, the NGO may minimize the exposure of a government to the loss of trust by its citizenry. This risk reduction is not necessarily a direct objective of the NGO. Rather, it is most often an indirect consequence of the NGO's pursuing its own self-interest or the interest of those it represents and serves in the fulfillment of its promise to them. Accordingly, the more successful the NGO in its own mission, the less exposed might the government be to the loss of trust by its citizenry. A watchdog NGO in its threat of revealing wrong doing, increases the trust in government by reducing the temptation to abuse its powers and the confidence it gives the citizenry that someone is watching. Alternatively, the more successful the watchdog agency in uncovering wrongdoing, the less trust individuals may have in government due to the uncovering, for example, of ingrain incompetence, corruption, and misinformation. But the NGO is also susceptible to the loss of trust and its own dismantlement. So too are its coalitions or networks if its or their performance disappoints expectations. Members can disassociate-- and eventually completely dismantle (dissolve) the NGO, the network or coalition. Hence, in the end the ability of the NGO to build trust in government through civic engagement will depend upon its ability to build and sustain trust in itself and it in its network or coalition through performance consistent with its own promises that led to citizen expectations.

Developing Capacity: The Reasonable Conversation of Representative Democratic Politics

Patrick Bishop

Governments have committed to community engagement for a number of reasons. These include overt political reasons, such as the need for electoral success or the need to placate interest groups, as well as commitments to greater efficiency and in response to community interests. At the most simple level, bureaucrats engage because they need to know and communities engage because they want to be heard. How can these efforts lead to genuine and sustainable conversations between citizens and government? In this paper, I reflect on the barriers and opportunities to developing a conversation between governments and citizens in the context of representative democratic structures and traditional models of the role of citizens and public servants in that conversation.

This paper considers a political and an administrative innovation in the Australian state of Queensland as potential mechanisms for enhanced community engagement and trust-building at the regional level. The 'enhancement' occurs in their potential to develop genuine governance conversations between government and community.

In using the analogy of a 'conversation' to describe what is often a multi-faceted and certainly multi-vocal exchange between government and citizens, I am drawing out the kinds of rules that underpin a successful conversation. These would include the capacities to listen and to articulate a point of view, empathy and a willingness to resolve conflict and the equality of participants – no one is shouting! An allied challenge to this particular conversational space is the way in which government structures impede these conversational rules.

The Ministerial Regional Community Forum (MRCF) has been in operation for some seven years. It was the initiative of the Hon. Terry Mackenroth, the then Minister for Communication and Information, Local Government and Planning and his Department. Its genesis was intensely political,[97] a direct response to a close election result where the Labor government only held power through the support of an Independent, and the high voter support in the regions of the populist One Nation Party in the 1998 election. The politics was clear. What constituted 'the regions' matched closely the areas of high One Nation support. The perception was that One

---

[97]   A comment at the time from one of the public servants involved in the process was that "the initiative will be a success if the government gets re-elected."

Nation had capitalised on a failure of government to respond to the changed economic environment in the regions and to a growing level of fear and uncertainty about the future in those electorates.

The Forum goals are simple. They aim to explore what the State Government can do in the regions. The process began in February 1999 with a series of regional conferences. These generated considerable public support. The conferences produced many issues that were forwarded to the relevant Departments for comment. (Only the vague, unspecific, or racist requests were culled.) Responses were published at the February 2000 Forum. From the conference process, ongoing membership of the Ministerial Regional Community Forum was selected. A novel selection process was used. Conference attendees were asked to identify five 'undisputed' community leaders. These leaders were then asked to nominate representatives across eleven 'sectors'. From this group, representatives were then selected, taking into account geographic location to ensure wide representation. The process was chosen to avoid calls of political bias and to achieve broad community support.

The stated aim of the Forums is to 'provide regional communities with the mechanism to identify priority issues, needs and strategies and present them directly to State Government Ministers.' Each forum is attended by Cabinet Ministers and Parliamentary Secretaries who meet with regional representatives. The forum process provides a range of opportunities for forum members to raise regional issues or make comment on behalf of the region and present proposals designed to address priority regional needs. In turn, Cabinet Ministers can use the forum to ask members for a regional perspective on government policies, programs and initiatives. The ministerial representation is provided on a rotation basis, with each Minister attending two MRCF meetings before moving on to a new region.

This initiative has been joined by a shift to encourage collaboration among managers and officers in state government regional offices. The aim has been to strengthen regional coordination through the creation of the Regional Managers' Coordination Networks (RMCN). The stated aim of the network is to assist agencies to achieve their outcomes 'through better regional engagement and coordination'. Primarily comprised of regional managers of Queensland Government departments and agencies, the networks also include and are open to representatives from other spheres of government and non-government organisations.

According to the government website, these Regional Managers' Coordination Networks aim to:

- achieve economic, social and environmental benefits for Queensland regions through coordinating priority, cross-agency initiatives at the regional level; and
- ensure that services align with government priorities and community needs by supporting collaboration across state government agencies and with local government, business and communities.

There is a further expectation that these networks will "work closely with Forum Members in providing advice and identifying local solutions and, where possible, in resolving issues and implementing solutions at the local level."

(see http://www.communities.qld.gov.au/community/regional/index.html).

The particular political environment that led to the formation of the MRCF has changed dramatically. The Labor government now enjoys a health majority. Nonetheless, along with the Community Cabinet process, (Bishop and Chalmers 1999, Bishop 2004) the Forum has remained a feature of an administration that has emphasised its consultative character. The more recent development of RMCN can be read as an indication of a genuine desire on the part of the government to meet its obligations to the regions.

A feature of both of these initiatives is to increase engagement between the community and government. Initially aimed squarely at rebuilding trust in a government on a 'knife edge', the forums were a response to charges of 'elitism' and 'dissociation' from the 'real people' made by populists. These governance mechanisms have since evolved and become a feature of the regional political and administrative landscape.

While the term 'engagement' has recently reenergised thinking about a number of governance techniques previously labelled 'community consultation', in many instances what is being talked about is the same thing. The 'engagement' policy brief from the OECD (2001)[98] specifically outlines a familiar continuum or series of techniques, ranging from one-way information to two-way communication to full partnership and identifies that *spectrum* as 'community engagement'. Nonetheless, the term community engagement has borne considerable aspirational hope that governments who adopt this terminology are somehow developing more sincere forms of citizen participation in government – in some instances that their advocacy heralds 'strong democracy' or 'genuine participation'.[99]

The claims made by the OECD are not so strong. Nonetheless, these techniques are expected to pay considerable dividends in terms of better policy, governance and, significantly for the participatory enthusiasts, 'representative democracy'.

---

[98]   This document was very influential in the formulation of the Community Engagement policy that underpinned the formation of the Community Engagement Division of the Department of the Premier and Cabinet (since relocated to the Department of Communities).

[99]   I have noted in conversation with a number of bureaucrats in the Queensland administration that there is a real belief that this change of term has heralded a significant qualitative change.

Strengthening relations with citizens is a sound investment in better policy-making and a core element of good
governance. It allows government to tap new sources of
policy-relevant ideas, information and resources when
making decisions. Equally important, it contributes to
building public trust in government, raising the quality
of democracy and strengthening civic capacity. Such
efforts help strengthen representative democracy, in
which parliaments play a central role. (OECD 2001)

Most engagement (or consultation practices) carried out by governments has these instrumental goals. The consultative or engaged government of the early 21st century in the UK, Australia, the US or Canada has
much more to do with building the credibility of elected representatives and
the outcomes of the public sector reform process than they do with the
adoption of Carole Pateman's, (1970) Benjamin Barber's (1984) or even
Sherry Arnstein's (1969) demands from the late sixties (Bishop and Davis
2002). When governments do consult, it is still often as a result of the adoption of market techniques where 'citizens' are subsumed into 'customers' and
'stakeholders' (Bishop 2000, Cooper 2000). Simply put, there has been no
revolution of democracy. What we see in 'engagement' is the application of
a series of government-led techniques, usually for clear political motives.

This paper is not critical of the failure of these techniques to deliver a
more participatory democracy. Rather I look at engagement mechanisms
as techniques that can be utilized specifically at the regional level to build
a reasonable conversation between government and community and also
to consider how some of these techniques may stumble on conventions of
representation and a resistant bureaucracy.

Language is significant here. Noted above is the shift from 'consultation'
to 'engagement' as a mechanism for driving reform or refocusing attention.
Here, adding to the word 'engagement', are other terms that drive discussions regarding coordination of the massive enterprise of government. Terms
such as: 'joined-up'; 'seamless'; 'horizontalism'; and even the term 'whole-of-
government' itself. Each term attempts to evoke an idea of how government
could be made more directly responsive to the community. They are often
juxtaposed to words such as 'silo'; 'hierarchy'; 'bureaucracy' and so on.

In a recent speech to the Institute of Public Administration Australia, Dr.
Peter Shergold, Secretary of the Australian Department of the Prime Minister
and Cabinet, saw this as a demand from citizens, saying: "Australian's rightly
demand the delivery of government programmes and services in a seamless
way." (Shergold 2004:5). He further pointed out that

A whole-of-government perspective does not just
depend upon the development of policy in a 'joined-
up' way or the delivery of policy in a 'seamless' man-

ner. More importantly, it depends upon the integration of the two. Operational issues matter, the development of policy and the planning of its delivery are two sides of the same coin. Both are the currency of political decision–making. (Shergold 2004:8)

This 'demand', to the extent that it actually comes from the community, is more of an unstated expectation, and an expectation built on a lack of knowledge of, or interest in inter and intra-governmental power sharing arrangements or agency turf disputes.

'The community' in negotiations between community and government can have a range of characteristics. A recent panel discussion at Harvard University brought this home. The topic was the 9/11 Commission, an inquiry reluctantly agreed to by the Bush administration, following 'community pressure' from a group known as The Families of the Victims of 9/11. The representative from the victims group reported that the group was never more than fifteen families and by the time the report came down there were only two people in that group to read and comment on the report on behalf of the victims. Nonetheless, Commissioner Slade Gorton, a former US Senator on the panel noted that this group had been the most effective lobby group he had ever encountered in a long career in Washington. The group worked because it saw its goal as working through all levels of the government, of understanding the system and recognising where pressure could be best applied. In this instance 'the community' was informed, and prepared to become more informed, to the extent that they became savvy players within the politics of the administration.[100] This 'elite community' becomes well adapted to negotiating with the multiple layers of government. It may even derive strategic benefit from it. Community activists, over time, become relatively adept at picking their way through the 'small p' politics of government agencies. (If one department won't help maybe another will. If one level of government is unresponsive try another and so on.)

There are other 'communities'. The political push to reengage (in response to 'populist' criticism) with disaffected citizens, or more importantly, voters, leads governments to attempt to engage a broader community, not just sectional interests. These groups know little of the political system, little of the institutions of government, of federalism. These people already see government as a seamless entity. To this community, whose capacity to 'engage' is limited, the term whole-of-government is almost tautological. Citizens are not interested in which portfolio has relevant authority, interagency rivalries, or even, in a three-tiered federal system, what level of government has the responsibility.[101] Their input into engagement arrives

---

[100]   Carie Lemack, the spokesperson for the group is currently undertaking an MPA at the Kennedy School of Government, Harvard.
(For a video of the forum see: http://www.iop.harvard.edu/events_forum_archive.html).
[101]   Much of the work of a diligent electorate secretary at any level government is to redirect requests to their correct level of government. (The response of 'not my problem' offers little kudos to the representative).

as a problem for government, not as a discrete problem for specific agencies. For them government is the government and it is there to solve problems, deliver services and, more often than not, be the object of blame for a range of current economic or social maladies. My point is, to this 'community', the push for a 'whole-of-government' approach is an issue entirely within government. Any 'demand', therefore, is coming, not from the community, but from governments and is being made of bureaucracies to get them to be responsive to political direction.

It is important that these issues play out at the local or regional level. Place, identity and interests are all vital components for encouraging citizen engagement. The 'region' may be the largest unit within a modern complex state where issues have enough local significance to potentially attract broad community participation. The region also brings the different agencies of government into closer relationship with communities and with each other. Work in the regions also exposes central decisions to the test of implementation. It is usually at the regional level that decisions will need to be taken to shape the implementation of policy or the delivery of services and to meet the needs of local communities.

If, as I have argued, decisions to engage, how to engage and what to expect from engagement are ultimately political decisions, how might engagement techniques be utilised to develop governance capacity through engagement? While skilled activists remain a part of the landscape, a conscious effort needs to be made to engage the broader community in a manner congruent with their expectations of government. The MRCF seeks to make a direct political connection between the heart of representative democratic decision-making – the Cabinet – and the regions. Community engagement techniques adopted by the bureaucracy at the regional level, given the advantages of proximity to the people they serve and to the development of the RMCN, should apply the outsider's single view of government to the multi-agency bureaucracy. This source of community information may be one way of shifting internal organisational cultures to consider the work of government as a single destination.

There are, however, organisational barriers to this approach. Despite considerable public sector reform, public managers still report within agencies and to a hierarchical structure. The active interagency 'collaborator' may well receive little acknowledgment of his or her efforts if they are not seen to directly benefit their agency goals. The developing coordination mechanisms at the regional level, such as the RMCN, should concentrate their efforts on the way in which agencies relate to communities so that community information is both received and processed as 'whole-of-government' information. Building community capacity should not be a code for creating the capacity to meet with government on its multi-agency terms but rather encouraging the articulation of community's expectation of a coordinated government response.

The MRCF faces a different potential problem but one that is instructive of the structural problem in the relationship between ministerial authority and bureaucracy. The tradition of Cabinet solidarity, where ministers are bound to support the decision of Cabinet is the strongest *political* instrument of ensuring whole-of-government policy. It is the point where *the* government position is developed and agreed. Another ministerial convention is that Ministers should not speak on matters outside their portfolio. While there is an effort to align topics to portfolio responsibility, the rotation of ministers in the MRCF means that Ministers will be speaking outside their portfolio in some instances. At an early forum in Ipswich the two ministers present, Hon. David Hamill and Hon. Dean Wells, actually commented on this point in a rather bemused manner. While this has not yet been an issue (there have been no controversies reported), it shows how a new engagement technique can cut across conventions of representative government and in, this case, one related to the traditional protocols of how whole-of-government positions are established and maintained.

The first problem is far more significant than the second in terms of the likely impact on improving engagement strategies. The MRCF works well. It works best as an engagement mechanism when completing communication loops: *"At the last meeting this course of action was determined and this is what we have done."* From observation, even when the news is bad, there is a sense of respect for being treated honestly and explanations being given. In the bureaucracy, the RMCN endorses the espoused benefits of collaboration but there has been little work done in actually quantifying the benefits. Accordingly, successful careers are more often built by placing agency goals ahead of collaboration. In short, there is little direct incentive to build the kinds of community relationships outlined above. From a career perspective engaging with an 'elite community' would still deliver a greater dividend.

Both problems are significant in that they highlight that administering government has multiple objectives. While there is a need to present *the* government position, it is also true that there are good reasons for specialisation – efficient use of people with expertise in a particular area – but if this is not integrated with the broader governmental picture, agencies with different areas and skill sets may well routinely and systematically work against one another. The benefits of specialisation, both bureaucratic and ministerial, need to be brought into line with government priorities. In a conventional Westminster system, this is done in Cabinet. My argument here is that appropriate community engagement strategies might also be used to develop a capacity on the community side of the conversation that becomes a 'bottom-up' coordination strategy.

To attempt to bring some clarity to the emerging complex environment and to relate it to democratic outcomes, Chris Skelcher, following work by Hooge and Marks, makes the following distinction between two types of governance.

Table 1: Typology of Governance Systems

Type I	Type II
Multi-purpose policy domains	Single-purpose policy domains
Mutually exclusive spatial domains	Territorially overlapping spatial domains
Limited number of jurisdictional tiers	Many jurisdictional tiers
Relatively permanent jurisdictional system	Flexible and changing jurisdictional system

Source: Skelcher 2005, p. 94

Type I, or 'traditional' governance is still the predominant mode within national polities. Type II or 'emergent', is 'likely to flourish specifically where there is a need for a tailored governmental body to address an issue that is not susceptible to policy action by a Type I organization, in the international arena and where there are particular functional policy problems.' Further, Type II governance bodies have been developed in new cross-cutting policy area such as "sustainability, community safety, and neighbourhood revital-ization" (2005:94). Increasingly, governments are attempting to deliver ser-vices in a way that reflects these broader cross-cutting policy agendas. Thus Main Roads departments no longer just build roads, but 'connect citizens' and do so in a manner that considers a much broader range of social and environmental consequences. These new policy formulations have also led to the emergence of 'whole of government' strategy, on the governmental side (Shergold 2004) and extensive consultation with communities, (Bishop and Davis 2002) both drivers for a more reasonable governance conversation. As Skelcher says:

The emergent governance of the public realm presents challenging yet exciting possibilities for institutional design. The challenge is to enable subtle but effective processes for collective action that also recognize the integrity of jurisdictions and maintain the principle of segmental authority (subsidiarity) whether this is expressed in terms of spatial or policy boundary conditions, or both. The challenge is accentuated by the changes in societies that reflect the emergence of polities around established beliefs and locales (2005:106).

It is significant to reflect on why 'emergent' governance comes into being and the consequent need for institutional redesign. It emerges because traditional modes lack capacity due to policy problems that governments are now choosing to address. Citizens are also now demanding that governments address these policy problems that are framed in ways that do not neatly fit into traditional spatial and institutional considerations. Traditional under-standings of 'legitimacy' and 'accountability' – developed along with notions of responsible government; of cabinet; of the functional separation of departments – are more readily understood and implemented in their traditional forms but now need considerable reinterpretation and reformulation in the light of emerging areas of policy interest and governance modes. It is also important to see that the challenge emergent (Type II) governance poses for institutional design also represents a challenge for those who inhabit these institutions and are charged with making them work. In fact leadership techniques within the new institutions need to be just as subtle if they are to be effective.

On a traditional account, leadership is a quality expected of the head of an organization. The expectation is that the singular 'leader' has a group who they lead and, in a hierarchical system, they acquire that power through their perceived capacities and retain it, in terms of the quality of their leadership. Like the classical military leader, they 'lead from the front'. In the traditional legitimating accounts of responsible government and bureaucracy the public official sits within a fixed a hierarchy, may be very powerful and influential but is never the titular leader. Even the CEO is subject to ministerial authority. Therefore, the expressions of leadership by the public officials have to gain authority through something other than the mere fact of being 'in charge.' The public official also has a very complex relationship with those they lead. As already noted, not only can they not lead from the head, but those who are to be led are always in some sense their superior – ministers through departmental hierarchy and citizens who can be said to ultimately hold them to account through the notion of responsible government. While the term 'public manager' is now more frequently applied in many ways 'public servant' remains apt.

It is only in the differentiated polity, or network society, (Rhodes 1997) that the notion of public sector leadership can gain any real purchase, outside of any immediate organisational hierarchy that the public official might find themselves the nominal 'head'. The diffusion created in the differentiated polity means that leadership relationships are not tied to status or hierarchy but to relevance, knowledge coherence, but also power, politics and even popularity. While the subsequent policy discourse can, as Torgerson, says inaugurate new forms of democratic practice (2003:138), it can also lead to more malign outcomes.

If, as Ian Shapiro argues, our allegiance to democracy relies on it being 'the best available system for managing power relations among people who disagree about the nature of the common good, among many other things, but who nonetheless are bound to live together' (2003:146). We also arrive at a suitably 'thin' theory of the common good that allows for both democratic interplay and an assessment of the democratic merits of networked government and service delivery, not by a simple numerical calculus – how many belong to a network – but by how effectively they diffuse power.

Shapiro claims that it is the possibility of diminishing – if not eradicating – domination that is often what draws people to democracy. (2003:146)

For the public manager it becomes crucial that they both realise their position vis-à-vis the power of the state and the power present in civil society and
continue to negotiate that interface in a manner that ensures the bridging
between the two. There is a crucial insight here. The breadth of the network
alone is not a measure of its democratic quality – small networks that work
efficiently in the community's interest and that do not reproduce dominant
power relationships may be far more democratic than large populist movements in support of policies and practices that oppress or marginalise some
community members.

Robert Putnam's seminal study of social capital in the United States maps
the decline of informal social networks, (2000) a social form that Putnam
argues, based on this and previous studies (1993), is essential to the health
of democracy. Leaving aside the many criticisms that Putnam's claims about
the relationship between group membership and democracy have attracted,
(Goldberg 1996; Sabetti 1996) his thinking has been very influential on
governments. Indeed on his speaking tour of Australia in 2001, he was billed
as 'the most influential academic in the world today'. His influence can now
be seen, for example, in that the Australian Bureau of Statistics now reports
a social capital index (www.abs.gov.au). Thus part of the role of the public
management leader in building a governance conversation could be seen as
replacing or revivifying the more organic and spontaneous networks shown
to be in decline, or rather freefall, in civil society. Paradoxically, almost by
definition governments cannot directly build social capital. In fact government activity often has negative impacts on social capital. The urban decay
and subsequent loss of communities in large cities in the US, and elsewhere,
in the 1960s, for example, were the direct result of ill considered freeway
development. In the same way that development applications are now subject
to environmental impact statements, so should impacts on social capital be
considered. As the Putnam study makes clear, it is important that social capital is developed by 'social' networks, not bureaucratic impost. The solution to
the decline in the number of picnics cannot be government initiated picnics!

While some government initiated networks have the appearance of
building or creating social capital, it is significant that many are a function of
funding arrangements. If, for example, a portion of the public housing budget is distributed to community-based housing co-operatives, such organisations will emerge. If funding to improve land care in rural communities
is distributed to 'the community', again community bodies will be created
to meet that requirement. In effect you have government created, non-
government organisations. These will be, following Putnam, more effective
if they are built on already existing social capital rich networks but they can
also emerge, like mushrooms after rain, in response to the funding stimulus,
only to wither once fiscal capital dries up.

One aspect of these relationships that is consistent with Robert Putman's
typology of social capital creation is the distinction he makes between bridg-

ing and bonding social capital. Where "some forms of social capital are… inward looking and tend to reinforce exclusive identities, and homogenous groups…Other networks are outward looking and encompass people across diverse social cleavages" (2000: 22).

This distinction can have significant social and democratic effects. Bonding social capital, according to Putnam, is "good for undergirding specific reciprocity and mobilizing solidarity" (2000:22). If, however, the solidarity generated is not 'mobilized' the 'capital' developed in bonding group does not develop social (as in society wide) capital at all. The 'capital' remains in its 'enclave' and is only beneficial to the social subset of group membership. This is not necessarily malevolent; it may as Putnam says "provide crucial social and psychological support for less fortunate members of the community" (2000:22). It also has the potential to be malevolent and Putnam (2000:350-366) and others have written on this problem of social capital. The 'Hell's Angels problem' (Rothstein 2004) can be applied to groups as diverse as the Mafia and exclusive religious charities where church membership or adherence to certain moral codes are prerequisites to receiving benefits. In such examples, the problem is that strong bonding links between group members work against the broader society. Such networks always run the risk of generating as much social enmity as social capital.

On the other hand, bridging social capital networks are "outward looking and encompass people across the diverse social cleavages". As such they "generate broader identities and reciprocity" (Putnam 2000:22-23) and it is this feature of social capital formation that also provides insights for how and in what directions networks should be led by public managers. In some instances, as seen above, a network might ensure the dominance of a particular view and become a closed system creating a very strong bonding network. Far from reaching out in democratic 'inclusion', they exclude and keep tight dominant positions. A bridging network on the other hand can be a vehicle for bringing in the excluded, diversify the policy mix, enhancing policy learning and so on. Putnam, in his more popular Bowling Alone, uses two household products as analogies: superglue for bonding and WD40 for bridging (2000:23). Of course all networks and conversations require some level of glue to hold them together but the 'lubricant' is crucial for the outcome to be democratic, in the sense of diffusing power and managing domination.

As Considine points out (2002), the driving force behind the shift in the public sector has been the push for real performance. To the extent that networks have become a 'fad' any test of their success has to be based on its capacity to deliver and perform, not only on its mere existence. Its effectiveness, however, cannot rest only on whether it 'gets the job done'. It has to do so in a manner that allows the expression of democratic public values.

To achieve this, its effectiveness has to be balanced against its capacity to include all relevant players. If networks become the site of policy capture and result in the systematic exclusion of significant actors – either of 'stakeholders' or broader community interest – they work against rather than contribute to democratic governance. As a locus of diffused power in a differentiated polity, a network should work in the interests of the community it serves rather than only the sectional interests of its membership. While bonding relationships offer a bedrock of solidarity, especially among oppressed or minority groups, in a democratic polity the wider aim of networks should be to develop connections across society not to solidify in a manner that disconnects them from society.

The kind of leadership capacities required of the contemporary public service manager can be brought together under the term 'nodal leadership'. Here leadership (or 'leading from where you are') is expressed across the horizontal rather than up and down the hierarchical plain. The network itself, built around either common interests or functions, can be seen as a flat plain where people, with different levels of formal and informal authority, operate across the network at the same level. Leading within the network becomes a collective exercise. While the public manager operates across that plane and at that level they need to always be aware of the other dimensions, in particular 'public' and 'service', of their role. The particular 'node' they inhabit intersects with hierarchical leadership structures. While in terms of accountability, this hierarchical structure has the higher formal status this does not mean that they are not also accountable to their network.

Putnam's earlier Italian study distinguishes between vertical and horizontal networks and sees that the horizontal networks, those "involving the organization of individuals of equal status and resources as generating the kind of social capital for institutional success" (Putnam 1993:173-175). While in public service delivery networks formal authority may differ, the functioning dynamic of the network attempts the same kind of equality, not through equal power, but shared interest. Network accountability then is expressed as a function of keeping the network meaningfully and democrati¬cally connected. It is here that the successful public manager's 'navigation' becomes crucial to both the network and their own careers. To further complicate the process some actors, such as ministers, appear on both the horizontal and vertical plains. The relationships into and out of the public servant's 'node' then may be best expressed as two functions of 'responsiveness' ; responsive to ministerial formal authority, through which traditional democratic accountability is established, but also responsive to the network to ensure the transfer of knowledge and power across the network to achieve desired policy goals. A further distinction to keep in mind is that there is not a direct conduit between the two kinds of accountability because their organisational structures are ultimately incompatible. Ideally they 'lead' through becoming capacitors.

The governance conversation is always multidimensional. If you are looking at the delivery of public services, for example, they are political in the Laswellian sense of 'who gets what when and how?' While Harold Laswell's definition pointed to an elite theory of politics, service delivery programs and policies developed through a conversation between government and community might devolve, diffuse or fragment power. In some instances, political power rests with the government or the service deliverer, in others, for example in community-based and administered housing co-operatives, power is devolved back to the community itself.

The conversation also remains highly political in the sense of negotiating interests and conflict. The dimensions of this sense of the political are not fully covered here, but they include, negotiation between new and old accountability structures, between government and community relationships, distinguishing between bridging and bonding social capital, negotiating intra- and intergovernmental relations in response to a 'whole of government' agendas and also, as I have argued here, between competing, legitimating narratives. This multidimensional political terrain requires skilled performance, not only in delivering services but in negotiating its politics. Mark Considine calls this "the appropriate exercise of a navigational competence: that is, the proper use of authority to range freely across a multi relationship terrain in search of the most advantageous path to success" (2002:22). The nautical metaphor is apt but the task is made even harder by there being fewer fixed points to navigate by. 'Proper authority', for example, can differ politically depending on whether that authority is derived from horizontal networks or vertical governmental hierarchies; or whether they derive from the functional and political fragments of the changed and changing policy terrain, all matters for the reasonable conversation of democratic politics.

References

Arnstein, S. (1969) 'A Ladder of Citizen Participation', *Journal of the American Institute of Planners*, vol. 35, no. 4, pp. 216-24.

Barber, B. (1984) *Strong Democracy: Participatory Politics in a New Age*, University of California Press, Berkeley.

Bishop, P (2004) (Net) working the Electorate' in *Griffith Review* February vol.3

Bishop, P. Carmel, C. (2003), The New Public Sector: Changing Management, Organisation and Ethics, in: Bishop, P. Connors, C. and Sampford, C. (eds.), Management, Organisation, and Ethics in the Public Sector, Ashgate, UK, pp. 3 -18

Bishop, P and G Davis (2002) 'Mapping Participation in Policy Choices' in *Australian Journal of Public Administration* March pp. 14-29

Bishop, P (2000) 'Customers, Citizens and Consultation' in *Local Government, Public Enterprise & Ethics*, P. Bishop and N. Preston eds. Federation Press, pp. 23-36

Bishop, P and J Chalmers (1999) 'A Response to Populism: Community Cabinets in Queensland' *Published proceedings of the Australasian Political Science Association Conference* pp 39-46

Considine, M. (2002) The End of the Line? Accountable Governance in the Age of Networks, Partnerships, and Joined-up Services, in: Governance, Vol. 15, pp. 21 -40

Cooper, T L.(2000) 'Ethics and Local Community Politics: The US Experience'; in Patrick Bishop and Noel Preston eds. Local Government, Public Enterprise, and Ethics. Leichardt, NSW, Australia: The Federation Press, pp. 64-78

Englestad, F. Østerid, Ø. (eds.) (2004) Power and Democracy, Critical Interventions, Aldershot: Ashgate

Fox, C. Miller, H. (1995) Postmodern Public Administration, Towards Discourse, London: Sage

Goldberg, E. (1996) Thinking about How Democracy Works, in: Politics and Society, Vol. 24, pp. 7-18

Hajer, M. A. Wagenaar, H. (2003) Deliberative Policy Analysis, Understanding Governance in the Network Society, Cambridge: Cambridge University Press

Hooge, L. Marks, G. (2003) Unravelling the central State but How? Types of Multi-level Governance, in: American Political Science Review, Vol. 97, pp. 233 -243

OECD (2001) Policy Brief No.10 Public Management Policy Brief Engaging Citizens in Policy-making:Information, Consultation and Public Participation

Pateman, C. (1970) *Participation and Democratic Theory*, Cambridge University Press, Cambridge.

Pollitt, C. Bouckaert, G. (2000) Public Management Reform, A Comparative Analysis, Oxford: Oxford University Press

Putman, R. D. (1993) Making Democracy Work, Civic Traditions in Modern Italy, Princeton: Princeton University Press

Putman, R. D. (2000) Bowling Alone, The Collapse and Revival of American Community, New York: Simon & Schuster

Queensland Government *http://www.communities.qld.gov.au/community/regional/index.html*

Rhodes, R. (1997) Understanding Governance, Policy Networks, Governance, Reflexivity and Accountability, Buckingham: Open University Press

Sabetti, F. (1996) Path Dependency and Civic Culture: Some Lessons from Italy about Interpreting Social Experiments, in: Politics and Society, Vol. 24, pp. 19-44

Shapiro, I. (2003) The State of Democratic Theory, Princeton: Princeton University Press

Shergold, P (2004) 'Connecting Government: Whole of Government Approaches to Australia's Priority Challenges' *Occasional Paper Institute of Public Administration Australia, Queensland*, 22 September

Skelcher, C. (2005), Jurisdictional Integrity, Polycentrism and the Design of Democratic Governance, in: Governance, Vol. 18, No.1, pp. 89-110

Torgerson, D. (2003) Democracy through Policy Discourse, in: Hajer, M. A./ Wagenaar, H. (eds.), Deliberative Policy Analysis Understanding Governance in the Network Society, Cambridge: Cambridge University Press, pp. 113-138

Part Two

Building Trust through Civic Engagement - the Austrian Example

Andreas Henkel

Reinventing Government has been the core issue of government as well as social partners after the Second World War. The result was a so called double coalition, on the one hand, of conservative and social-democratic parties, and on the other hand, of the large representative organisations of employers and employees. Their joint efforts facilitated the catching up of Austria in economic terms, but also provided a stable basis for democratic development.

But there had to be some prerequisites for providing the "civic basis" of that success story.

Austria enjoys a particularly well-developed system of co-operation between the major economic interest groups and between them and the government. This system of co-operation on economic and social issues, commonly referred to as "social partnership", is a voluntary arrangement, mostly of an informal nature and not regulated by law. This means that there is no common formal organisation like in many European countries, for instance in the form of national Economic and Social Councils, no formal address and no common budget. All common work is guided by goodwill.

The social partnership does not deal with industrial relations alone (collective agreements), but it extends to practically all areas of economic and social policy. The four large representative organisations – i) Trade Union Federation (ÖGB); ii) Federal Economic Chamber (WKÖ); iii) Federal Chamber of Labour (BAK); and iv) the Chamber of Agriculture are not merely interest groups in the narrow sense, but well established institutions anchored in Austria's political system. A unique feature is the mandatory membership of Economic, Workers and Agriculture Chambers in Austria.

The essence of the social partnership is the commitment of these four interest groups to pursuing long-term economic and social policy aims and their shared conviction that such aims are better achieved through dialogue leading to co-operation and co-ordinated action than through open conflict. These conflicts are not denied or ignored, but the partners try to balance contradictory economic and social interests by seeking solutions that benefit all participants and maintain a willingness to compromise to achieve this end.

Example: 5 Price-Wages-Agreements after the war (1947-1951). Production facilities had been destroyed, consumption started to soar, but supply could not catch up: A spiral of rising prices and rising wages started to build up. The agreements provided for a soft landing of this situation.

In the Sixties, Seventies and Eighties, we see a continuing development of expertise and influence of Austrian Social Partners on politics, backed by the phenomenon of double coalition including strong personal links. There is value-added in the co-operation of social partners: As they did not have to compete in the daily political contest, they were able to concentrate on common issues and interests while keeping political differences out of the discussion.

Since 1957, the co-operation of social partners has taken place mainly through the institution of the Parity Commission, consisting of representatives of the government and the four major interest groups. This commission also has four subcommittees: the Advisory Council for Economic and Social Affairs, the Subcommittee on International Issues, the Subcommittee on Wages and the Subcommittee on Competition and Prices.

Whereas the Parity Commission formerly dealt mainly with price controls and fighting inflation, the Commission has become today an institutionalised forum for dialogue between the social partners and the government. Here, matters of particular importance, common strategies and concerted actions as well as any arising conflicts are discussed and the recommendations of the Advisory Council for Economic and Social Affairs are considered.

In addition, the social partners are well-established in Austria's political system in many ways:

- Legislation: The representative organisations have the right to evaluate proposed legislation, to make recommendations to law-making bodies, and to draft texts for legislation directly related to the interests of the social partners (social welfare and labour law, etc.).

- Administration: The social partners are represented on numerous commissions, advisory boards and committees and thus exert influence in matters of, for example, the apprenticeship system, inspection of working conditions, issuance of certificates of origin, competition and anti-trust policy, labour market policy and public promotion and funding programmes.

- The organisations play an important role in the social security system by maintaining representatives in the social insurance institutions, which are organised as self-administrating entities under public law.

- The social partners' responsibilities also include informal negotiating and problem solving in their special areas of expertise, such as labour law and social welfare issues, but also trade regulations and family law, where agreement between the social partners is often a prerequisite for an appropriate solution at the political level.

The aims of the social partnership have been defined in several agreements. The Social Partnership Agreement of 23 November 1992 sets out the current activities and, most importantly, has considerably broadened the aims of the partnership. The social partners are no longer concerned solely with full employment, price stability and growth, but also with securing the competitiveness of the Austrian economy in the international markets, full participation in international and especially European integration, increasing the internationalisation of the Austrian economy, promoting human talent and skills, maintaining and improving humane labour conditions, and meeting environmental challenges.

Through their deep involvement, the interest groups have developed a strong sense of responsibility for their political decisions, for they are aware that they influence not only their members but also the economy and society as a whole. The social partners strive to promote social stability as a comparative advantage in the international market and, through their co-operation, to stabilise economic policy and the expectations of the economic players in the medium term, thereby contributing to a balanced economic development.

Eighties and Nineties: Austria opened itself to the world, became a member of the European Union (EU) and experienced a new drive global competition. We see an emancipation of political parties; social partners are not anymore the only political think tanks, and expertise can additionally be bought on the markets. The influence of social partners, but also NGOs now rely on their ability to offer sound solutions to political problems, taking into account the global developments and having the backing of large parts of civil society (employers and employees). They have to be better, quicker and more down to earth, to exert influence on politics than before. At the same time, they rely on the good management of their stakeholders, especially also NGOs.

Examples: There are several areas, in which co-operation of the Economic Chamber with Amnesty International was successful for example in the case of conflict diamonds, and with Clean Clothes, especially around occasions like the incoming European Football Championships 2008 in Austria and Switzerland.

A cautious review on the development of current Austrian politics allows the following picture: Austrian Social Partners gave serious input for the coalition treaty of the government. This input is being worked on at the moment, leading to a new law on working time flexibility, on opening hours for shops, and hopefully leading to a basic paper on Lifelong Learning, which should seriously influence the Austrian system of education and training, only to give a few examples.

New developments are being discussed, as globalisation leads to intense discussions about fair treatment of workers, fair sharing of revenues, and in the end about common, mutually benefiting development goals for a globalised world. This leads also to new initiatives in the direction of a "Global Social Dialogue."

During the visit of the United Nations Secretary-General Ban Ki-Moon to Austria, a working meeting with Presidents Leitl (Federal Economic Chamber) and Hundstorfer (Trade Union Federation) dealt with these issues. The special Austrian problem in this respect is that because of its mandatory membership, it cannot be a member of the European or International Employers Federations which are normally entitled to deal with these questions within the International Labour Organization (ILO) or other international bodies. And the Global Compact of the UN is influenced by the International Chamber of Commerce (ICC) and not by the Global Chamber Platform, which is linked to the Eurochambers. This leads to ideas to just "set up" a project with the Global Chamber Platform and the International Trade Union Confederation, focusing on labour conditions in a certain emerging market and trying to jointly improve them. We will see in the future if these ideas can lead to some real benefits for people concerned.

This special Austrian model of a social partnership increasingly attracts international interest. Academic research in the US as well as emerging social partnership structures in South Korea seek to understand the main features of the Austrian model and build on this experience. Being aware that any political model cannot just be exported and used like any product or software or reproduced, there are nevertheless unique qualities within this system, which can be copied. The most important features are independence, mutual trust, having common goals and achieving a fair balance of interests. And the successful method is analysing facts, agreeing on facts, caring for a common interpretation of facts, setting common mid-term and long-term goals and developing common recommendations based on these facts and goals.

The so-called Bad Ischl Declaration (2006) of the Austrian Social Partners summarizes the values and achievements of this successful partnership as follows:

"60 years of social partnership in Austria have made a decisive contribution to the success of our country. 60 years of co-operative action have made Austria one of the most prosperous and stable countries in the world today."

EU expansion and globalisation, new technologies and new methods of communication present new challenges to our society. On the one hand, there are new opportunities; at the same time, the need to adapt creates new uncertainties. The most important task of the social partners in the next ten years will be to support those people affected by the inevitable changes, to minimise the risks they face as much as possible, and to take advantage of the great opportunities presented.

Austria cannot compete on the basis of price. Our strengths are rather to be found in our talent, creativity and innovation. These are enhanced by our peaceful social order and security, well-developed infrastructure, excellent educational system, high productivity and stability. Austria's success in the future will thus depend upon our promoting and making optimal use of these strengths. Exploiting this potential in the best possible way to create opportunities for all players, and inspiring confidence, courage and optimism in a world of uncertainty, will be the task of the social partners in the coming decade.

The social partners stand for involvement in all aspects of economic and social policy through fair co-operation and partnership with all responsible decision-makers. They see themselves as co-architects of the future and, as such, will strengthen their expertise, practical orientation and ability to act in such important areas as education and continuing education, economic policy, the labour market, and social security. The social partners are fully aware of their special responsibility towards those people affected by the process and speed of change. Therefore, in addition to the promotion of economic growth and sustainable competitiveness of the Austrian economy, high priority is assigned to solidarity and ensuring social cohesion.

Beyond these aims, the social partnership should work to facilitate a linking of the various decision-making structures, whether within enterprises or on a regional, European or international level and to ensure sustainable development.

The central objective of the Austrian social partnership is to secure and enhance the prosperity of all levels of the population by strengthening Austria's competitive position as a location for business. A sustainable growth policy should ensure full employment by the year 2016.

All this seems to be quite convincing, but they can be supported by hard facts that lead to a real business case for social partnership:

- GNP per capita (based on purchasing power) has risen considerably, especially compared to the US and the EU;

- The jobless rate stays at a very low level copared to the EU average and the US;

- Productivity and wages have risen especially since the EU-accession; productivity has risen quicker than in the EU or even the US. Labour costs per product are steadily declining – faster than in most competing markets;

- The annual growth of wages per working hour since 1995 has been around 1.6 per cent, compared to the EU (2.6 per cent) and the US (4.9 per cent);

- Inflation has remained very low; and

- There are virtually no strikes in Austria, except in the public sectors.

But there are also costs for this system-relatively high taxes and social contributions. These social contributions are tied to wages which makes gross wages rather expensive and leaves employees with rather low net wages. But summarizing these facts, we believe in a competitive advantage for Austria made by the social partnership.

Civic Engagement in Policy Development at the Local Government Level: The Experience of Naga City, Philippines

Jesse Manalastas Robredo[102]

Introduction and Setting

This paper seeks to describe how the city of Naga made civic engagement a cornerstone of its policy development processes through its homegrown participatory governance model.

As such, it will describe sequentially how that governance model came about, how it was formalized, and how it continues to inform current efforts to institutionalize innovations on participatory governance. Specifically, it will cover the following topics and phases:

- *Confidence building*, carried out under the Kaantabay sa Kauswagan social housing program;
- *Institution building*, which centers on how the Naga City People's Council was built up and formalized;
- *Continuous improvement*, which describes how Naga Governance Model informs current initiatives built around civic engagement mechanisms; and
- *Insights,* conclusions that can be drawn from our experience in participatory governance and civic engagement.

Naga, a city of more than 150,000 in central Philippines, is noted for its participatory governance processes and mechanisms that have empowered communities and individual citizens alike. Its effort towards continuous improvement has insured the development and deployment of new ways to engage ordinary residents in governance.

When I first became mayor of Naga in 1988, my administration had to deal with formidable social, economic and political problems. But underpinning them is the bigger challenge that faces democratically elected governments all throughout the world: *how to encourage and sustain citizen engagement in the business of governing.*

Confidence Building: The Kaantabay program

That challenge is illustrated by the plight of the urban poor sector in Naga, which at the time accounted for a quarter of the city population.

---

[102]   Jesse Manalastas Robredo is Mayor of the City Government of Naga, Philippines.

Notwithstanding the magnitude of the problem, informal settlers were largely ignored by previous administrations, making them vulnerable to forcible ejection and harassment by powerful interests.

But the new administration adopted a more open approach in dealing with the problem, choosing to work with, instead of against, the marginalized sector and their NGO partners. In the process, the city government sent a strong message that (1) it is serious about governance, (2) it is willing to explore new approaches to long standing problems, and (3) it is ready to work with local communities and interest groups in resolving these problems.

This collaborative effort yielded the Kaantabay sa Kauswagan program in 1989. This secure-tenure social housing program is built around organizing urban poor communities, giving them a voice in government decision-making processes, and crafting local laws that institutionalized these reforms.

Mechanics. At the core of Kaantabay is securing tenurial rights for urban poor beneficiaries. This is accomplished by acquiring the landholding they are occupying through various innovative schemes, with the city government playing a critical facilitative and mediating role. When negotiations are completed, beneficiaries then amortize their homelots under very affordable terms through community mortgage. When the landholding is fully paid up, property rights to individual homelots are transferred to beneficiaries, thereby facilitating asset building by the poor.

Strategies. Participation and civic engagement are operationalized through the following:

- *Community organizing.* Putting together a group of potential urban poor beneficiaries is a critical requirement under the Kaantabay program. A policy of dealing only with urban poor organizations compels applicants to take the initiative in organizing themselves. Recognizing that community organizing is not its core competence, the non-government sector (through the Community Organizers of the Philippines Enterprises or COPE) has played the lead role in social preparation

- *Tripartism.* The program's effectiveness also stems from a tripartite approach to problem resolution at the project level, involving (1) the city government and other national government agencies; (2) urban poor associations, aided by NGOs and POs; and (3) private landowners. This mechanism enables the involved parties to sit down and cooperate in solving their disputes.

- *Policymaking.* The program's success impelled the city to ensure its sustainability, which came in the form of the Kaantabay sa Kauswagan Ordinance (Ordinance No. 1998-033). Among others, the ordinance secured funding support for the program and reconstituted the

Housing and Urban Development Board, the city's lead policymaking body on urban development issues. Under the ordinance, half of this 20-man body comes from the Naga City Urban Poor Federation and its civil society partners.

Institution building: The Naga City People's Council

That highly successful initiative spurred the city government to work with local civil society in areas beyond housing.

In 1993, the NGO-PO-Council was established to explore other areas of collaborative work, mainly by bringing together elected officials and key staff of the city government and their counterparts in the local civil society in a series of continuing dialogue.

The Empowerment Ordinance

In 1996, Ordinance No. 95-092, more popularly known as the Empowerment Ordinance of Naga City, was enacted. This legislation formalizes a system of partnership between the city government and the NGO community under the auspices of the Naga City People's Council (NCPC), the federation of around 100 civil society organizations in Naga.

The ordinance established the structure to achieve active partnership between the city government and the people of Naga in the formulation, implementation and evaluation of government policies, projects and activities. Today, this partnership already went beyond traditional policy making and is now effectively co-managing the city in certain mutually identified areas.

Among others, the ordinance expressly declared that the city government is open to a partnership with duly accredited NGOs and POs; it laid out a clear process of accreditation; provided for their organization into an autonomous council, now named as the Naga City People's Council (NCPC); and gave such organization the right to be represented in the different bodies within the city government including those which may be created in the future.

The Naga City People's Council

From that time on, the NCPC identifies its own representatives, which account for at least 25 per cent of the total membership, to all local special bodies and standing committees of the city government. They participate in the various phases of program and project development, from conceptualization, implementation up to monitoring and evaluation. And they can propose legislation and vote up to the committee level.

Thus, the NCPC representatives are now the ones sitting in the Local Government Code-mandated special bodies which are the Development Council, the Health Board, the Peace and Order Council, the School

Board and the Bids and Awards Committee (BAC). These special bodies are charged with formulating programs and policies relating to developare charged with formulating programs and policies relating to development, health, peace and order, and education. The BAC, on the other hand, ensures that the bidding of projects requiring private contractors are done in a transparent and above board manner. In addition, these special bodies monitor and evaluate how the city implements these programs and policies. Membership in these special bodies therefore is already a potent tool to influence local governance.

The NCPC further sits in 31 standing committees of the city legislature positioning it to influence local laws and policy. As we all know, the nitty-gritty of legislative work happens at the committee level. This is where laws are hammered out to their near-final version before being passed upon by the legislature in plenary session. Membership in committees therefore placed the NCPC right where they could influence lawmaking the most.

NCPC representatives likewise sit in the Naga City Investment Board not only making up half of its total membership but also occupying its vice-chairmanship. This is based on the principle that an investment incentive code's primary goal is to generate jobs and income for the people. The NCPC is also present in the Housing and Urban Development Board and indeed, in most other task forces, committees and other bodies created by the city government in the course of planning, implementing and evaluating its development programs.

CONTINUOUS IMPROVEMENT: THE NAGA GOVERNANCE MODEL AND ITS APPLICATIONS

Buoyed by the city's positive experience with Kaantabay and the NCPC, in particular, and civic engagement in general, there was clearly a need to distill and crystallize that emerging experience into something that will guide the local government in the business of governing. The Naga Governance Model (NGM) was therefore conceived in 2000 in response to this need.

The NGM framework

The NGM is our own unique approach to public management that builds on Naga City's participative traditions and practices to redefine local governance. Over the last two decades, this homegrown model has anchored all innovative programs and projects that the city government pioneered, most of which were eventually recognized nationally and internationally.

People participation is the defining feature of the model. As such, it directly addresses the very problem I described at the outset. The framework depicts good governance as a triangle whose points represent three fundamental elements – progressive perspective (leadership), partnerships and participation – that shaped the Naga experience since 1988, beginning with the Kaantabay program. (See the Naga Governance Framework figure below.) To date, this framework continues to inform new initiatives being undertaken by the city.

The Naga Governance Framework

In this framework, three elements form the foundation of good urban governance:

* **Progressive perspective** In the model, it lies at the apex of the triangle because it is a function of leadership which the local administration must provide. Among others, a progressive perspective seeks to build prosperity for the community at large. But the goal of prosperity building is tempered by an enlightened perception of the poor, whose upliftment is an end to governance.
* **Functional partnerships** These are vehicles that enable the city to tap community resources for priority undertakings, in the process multiplying its capacity and enabling it to overcome resource constraints that usually hamper government.
* **Participation** These are mechanisms that ensure long-term sustainability by generating broad-based stakeholdership and community ownership over local undertakings. Partnerships and participation lie at the base of the triangle because they are the elements that provide its sustainability.

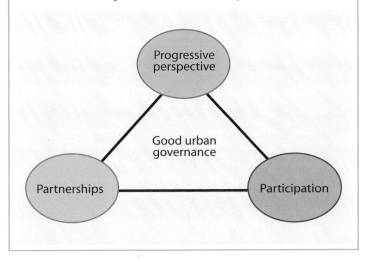

i-Governance Program

Its most important recent iteration is the i-Governance program. This initiative was driven by the need to create new engagement mechanisms that will enable ordinary citizens to participate more actively in local governance. Making full use of both analog and digital tools in reaching out to these key stakeholders, it further strengthened the participative tradition of which Naga has become known for in the Philippines and abroad. These tools consist of locally developed citizen guidebooks, an interactive website that promotes transparency, accountability and participation by even natives residing outside the Philippines, and weblogs chronicling local life and issues in the city.

i-Governance was conceptualized in 2001. Fresh from a fellowship at the Kennedy School of Government in Harvard, I challenged city staff to find new ways of improving existing programs and practices. One of the responses is a concept paper arguing for a need to expand people participation by bringing existing mechanisms to the next level. At the time, the city was preoccupied with engaging civil society through the NCPC.

The paper identified ordinary citizens and households as the logical focus of this expansion thrust. It also outlined two initial strategies that can make this possible, which have been strengthened and expanded over time:

(1) reengineering the existing city government website (http://www.naga.gov.ph) as a means of citizen empowerment under a more pervasive information openness policy; and
(2) documenting the city's frontline services as a means of improving transparency and accountability in public service delivery (which later yielded the Naga City Citizen's Charter, a guidebook on 140 frontline government services.).

Other complementary strategies, including the innovative use of SMS messaging or texting, were later developed to widen engagement options available to ordinary citizens.

Development of MDG-aligned local plans

Lately, these efforts are being systematized by the ongoing effort to revitalize the city's planning processes – seeking to engage sectors in crafting Naga's long-term plans that will guide resource allocation, aided by a public governance scorecard system that puts primacy on civic engagement.

Beginning in September 2006, the city government, through its local planning office, has begun updating Naga's development and land use plans, providing it an opportunity to further institutionalize participative approaches in local governance processes. In so doing, the following innovations were adopted:

1. *Using the Millennium Development Goals (MDGs) and the Public Governance Scorecard (PGS)* outputs as planning targets. By adopting the MDGs and the PGS vision-mission statement and scorecards, the city will no longer need to reinvent the wheel and go through a time-consuming visioning process. This also means that it will be updating the local land use and development plans with a 9-year time horizon. The planning process will therefore focus on revisiting these outputs, refining the targets set, and aligning the city plans towards attaining these 9-year targets.

2. *Working with existing and mandated local councils and special bodies as basic planning unit.* This involves tapping existing and mandated councils under the umbrella of the City Development Council (all of which have strong civil society representation) in coming up with sectoral components of both the land use and development plans. For instance, in regard to the social sector, the city worked with the children, women, youth, senior citizen and urban poor boards and councils in establishing the baseline data, assessing needs; crafting Programs, Projects and Activities (PPAs) that will respond to these needs in the context of the MDG and PGS targets; costing out these PPAs, and laying out a 9-year action plan for implementation, monitoring and evaluation.

3. *Stronger partnership with the academia.* Cognizant of the city's limited technical expertise in some specific areas of urban management, it tapped graduate students from the University of British Columbia School of Community and Regional Planning (UBC SCARP) in Vancouver, Canada – in partnership with their counterparts from the Ateneo de Naga University – to undertake action research on six areas vital to city development.

The research was conducted in the context of a studio course run by UBC SCARP in Naga from May 16-June 8, 2007. These areas include transportation and land use planning, investment promotion, urban agriculture, youth development, social housing and education. Their reports serve as another invaluable input to the planning process, aside from revitalizing town and gown partnerships which, in the past, has rather been weak in the city.

Outcomes and Insights

Does civic engagement under NGM work?

Our experience shows it does. For instance, Naga is nationally and international recognized for its innovations, whose common denominator is the premium being given to people participation in governance. These innovations include the initiatives I have described above, and more, which all redound to a more transparent local authority, quality yet cost-effective public services, a vibrant and inclusive urban community, and a participative society of empowered citizens.

More importantly, many of these outcomes are also measurable. That this unique people-centered public management approach works, for example, was recently affirmed in relation to the MDGs. Last year, UNDP selected Naga as one of the 10 leading-edge Philippine local communities in attaining these development goals. And a progress monitoring report commissioned by the Philippine national government showed it either already attained or is on track towards attaining all MDG indicators.

Insights

From Naga City's experience in pioneering various civic engagement mechanisms, we can draw the following insights:

1. *Confidence building is critical at the outset.* Especially in cases of changes in the political leadership, there is a need to clearly communicate the readiness and willingness of a new administration to engage its various publics in governance. This message should be matched with the appropriate initiatives, policy reforms and the corresponding resource allocations.

2. *The local society must secure a strong voice.* Our experience with the Kaantabay program is very instructive: it began with community organizing primarily intended to empower this marginalized sector, thereby giving it a seat in the table and a voice in governance. This is the first step in building up civic engagement and social accountability.

3. *A variety of civic engagement mechanisms exists, one often building up on others.* This is clearly demonstrated by the organization of urban poor associations, which led to their federation, which led to the reconstitution of the city housing and urban development board on one hand and the establishment of the NGO-PO and Peoples' Councils on the other. When the situation called for it, we also created mechanisms designed for individual citizens and households under the i-Governance program. These structures are by themselves mechanisms that will allow society to exact accountability from government.

4. *Local development planning can further institutionalize people participation.* The ongoing updating of local plans shows that Naga is coming full circle, with a twist. Traditionally, planning occurs at the initial phase of any process or activity. Here, it has emerged as the newest opportunity to integrate and tie in all these innovations together, when they already have individually achieved momentum and attained maturation.

5. *For optimum results, civic engagement must form part of the institutional development agenda.* This is perhaps what separates the city government of Naga from most other local authorities. Its institutional experience with people participation has evolved into its own governance framework that anchors all development initiatives of the city government.

Rebuilding Trust in Post-conflict Situation Through Civic Engagement: The Experience of Rwanda

Protais Musoni[103]

1. Introduction

Human society is sustained and advanced through the interactions of efforts of members of the society. One does not have to be very intelligent to realise that situations that promote and manifest collaborative efforts make people feel good and fulfilled, and therefore more productive. The corollary is also true; situations that promote and manifest conflicts tend to make people unhappy and less productive. Unproductive societies do not meet their collective needs and therefore enter into more conflicts. In Kinyarwanda language it is said that; *"Abasangira ubusa bitana ibisambo.* Literally translated, it says *"those who have nothing to share call each other gluttons"*.

In this paper I will briefly describe the situation after the conflict, drawing out the main challenges that the government of Rwanda undertook to deal with at different periods between 1994 and 2007 with specific leanings on programs that fostered civic engagement. This will be followed by a summary of lessons that I feel can be useful from the Rwanda case, and then come to conclusion.

2. Defining civic engagement and public trust

For the purposes of this presentation, over the various definitions of civic engagement, we would like to articulate one that is comprehensive, inclusive and, of course, one that speaks of the Rwanda we want. We understand Civic Engagement to mean *active involvement of citizens in resolving issues of public concern, shaping government policy, and ensuring that citizens' needs are central to program design and service delivery*. It means promoting the quality of life in a community, through both <u>political</u> and <u>non-political</u> processes.

The conceptual framework behind this definition started with a belief in deliberative democracy, which signifies an approach to democracy that puts citizens at the centre of the political process and that is more *'voice centred'* than *'vote centred.'* In this conception of democracy, citizens play a more robust role from the local to the global levels, in helping to set the public agenda and to decide about what will be the broad directions for public

---

[103]   Protais Musoni is a Minister of the Ministry of Local Administration, Good Governance, Community Development and Social Affairs of the Government of Rwanda.

policy. That way one can promote trust among citizens and between citizens and their Governments.

There is no one universal definition of trust. In one sense, trust is about *honesty* and *'telling the truth'*, but in the context of public services it can also be about wider considerations around service delivery. Scholars place a clear distinction between *confidence* and *trust*. If the former is referred to as a <u>*passive emotion*</u> accorded to the overall system or organization, the later is qualified as *more <u>dynamic beliefs and commitments</u>* accorded to people or systems (Sztompka, 1999). [104]

Here, trust has a direct relation with, but is not synonymous with, *'confidence'* and *'satisfaction'*, and is based on the *outcome* of the service and the *way it is delivered*. In fact, public service is a public trust. Citizens expect public servants to serve the public interest with fairness and to manage public resources properly on a daily basis. Fair and reliable public services inspire public trust and create a favourable environment for businesses, thus contributing to well-functioning markets and economic growth. Public service ethics are a prerequisite to, and underpin, public trust, and are a keystone of good governance.

Trust is the process by which government policies are carried out through the cooperation of citizens with public officials; trust building becomes the essence of governance. Governance issues are the major causes of conflicts both latent and open. Hence, to reconstruct a Nation, trust-building through civic engagement in governance[105] comes at the forefront.

3. Post-conflict situation in brief.

Rwanda passed through a long dark history of conflicts that culminated into the heinous and horrendous crime of genocide. The Tutsi genocide that occurred in Rwanda for 100 days in 1994 showed off the worst side of human beings; unprovoked killings in an attempt to exterminate people; it left behind animosities, chaos, a traumatized population, wrecked property and a failed state. Rwandans had lost trust and faith in humanity, in state machinery, the international community and even in religious organisations.

The genocide was stopped by the Rwandese Patriotic Front that had to fight the genocidal forces, as at the same time they tried to rescue survivors by carrying out missions behind enemy lines. On 19th July 1994, a broad-based government of national unity was installed that was composed of all political parties that participated in the ill-fated Arusha Peace Talks[106], with

---

[104]   Sztompka, P. Trust, a sociological theory. Cambridge: Cambridge University Press, 1999.

[105]   In the UN's paradigm, governance is defined as "the exercise of political, economic, and administrative authority to manage a nation's affairs."

[106]   Peace negotiations held in Arusha, Tanzania, between the then Government of Rwanda and the Rwanda Patriotic Front that were concluded on August 4, 1993, in a bid to stop war.

the exception of those political parties that had actively mobilised their members to carry out the Tutsi genocide. According to Linda Melvern [107]"*This was no triumphant victory. The country had been ransacked. There was no penny in the public coffers. There were no offices intact, no chairs, no desks, no telephones, nothing at all....Rwanda was divided, this time into victims, survivors, returnees and perpetrators.*"

Such a situation depicts the level of trust within Rwandan society in July 1994. All types of trust, including social, political, economic and even moral trust, in the society were at their lowest. Trust had to be rebuilt with whatever means available if the nation of Rwanda was to keep in existence at all. One must remember also that there were hundreds of thousands of refugees across all borders of Rwanda; in Congo, the then Zaire, in Tanzania, Burundi and Uganda, not to mention the political leaders and other elites of yesterday that had flown to Western Capitals. Among these were tens of thousands of Interahamwe militia members and former members of the Government of Rwanda army and police that collectively had participated and actively led the population in the Tutsi genocide. They were being armed to attack the new and still fragile administration. To quote Melvern again *"the camps were described as an unfettered corridor of arms shipment. Goma settled down into a state within a state, a new 'Hutu land' carved out of Zaire"*.

4. Post genocide Challenges;

In the aftermath of the war and genocide that deeply divided Rwandan society, the Government of National Unity (GNU) established in July 1994 was, therefore, faced with numerous challenges not only in rebuilding the public administrative system and the social and physical infrastructures severely destroyed during the war and genocide, but also to reconcile, empower and build confidence and trust in the local Rwandan population. This had to be done within a deeply traumatized society that had for decades been denied the opportunity to determine their own destiny, and had been ruled with *"divide and rule"* tactics.

The main challenges faced by the Government of National Unity can be summarised as follows:

1. The country was still under internal and external security threats from the defeated former army elements. There was a climate of fear and anxiety among the population, especially the survivors of genocide.
2. The country had to build national institutions of governance and administration from scratch, as over 97% of the top cadres of the state were not available to take up their previous posts.

---

[107]   Melvern, Linda (2000). A People Betrayed: The Role of the West in Rwanda's Genocide. London: Zeb Books.

3. Most of the population was either internally or externally displaced.
4. The social fabric of the society had been destroyed and feelings of mistrust were so high that members of different identity groups could not even travel together in the few public transport vehicles plying the Kigali streets.
5. The genocide had bruised the Rwandan society by creating hundreds of thousands of orphans, widows, and women and child-headed households. Cultural, social and religious values had been scorned, undermining the credibility of social symbols and institutions.
6. The social and public infrastructure had been destroyed; water was not running, the night in cities were dark as power infrastructure had been destroyed, houses of the survivors of genocide were now in rubbles, a large number of bridges were down, and the old-case refugees returning were occupying properties of those fleeing into neighbouring countries. Rwanda was in a total mess.
7. The damage to the economy was extensive; banks had been looted, crops rotted in the fields as there were no people to harvest them, Industries were not in operation and there were no service sectors to speak of. Worse, the Rwandan Government inherited an enormous debt that was contracted by the previous government, part of which had been used to prepare and carry out the mayhem.
8. The justice sector in particular was heavily affected and yet this was one area that had to deal with the consequences of genocide.
9. *Rwanda* had lost confidence and faith in international community in the light of the behaviour of some of its members during the genocide.

5. Recovery programs

The Government of National Unity, based on the above challenges, adopted an eight point program soon after its installation. It is the program that guided its policies throughout the interim period of 1994 to 2003 when the national constitution, popularly adopted through a referendum, guided the installation of the state democratically elected institutions. Interestingly, this program corresponded to the RPF Political Program, which it fought for, except that it was made more concrete and addressed issues of the day.

The program centred on stabilising the security situation, repatriating all Rwandan refugees that wanted to return, instituting the economic recovery program, working to bring about national unity, fighting corruption, developing a social assistance program for the many vulnerable in Rwandan society, establishing diplomatic relations in the region and internationally on the basis of mutual respect and equal benefit and finally, preparing the country for establishment of democratically accountable institutions. The interim program was supposed to end in 1998 but because of the many border incursions from Congo, it was extended and ended in 2003.

Looking back in time, one can see sets of two year periods with specific programs standing out. 1994-1995 were mainly years of situation stabilisation that included security stabilisation, national institutions installation and consolidation; 1996-1997 were mainly characterised with repatriation and resettlement and grassroots consultations on the Governance systems that would best help the country to recover from the effects of the long periods of misrule, war and genocide and also to create institutional frameworks that would promote good governance programs for national wellbeing.

During the consultation sessions the subject of the consultation was *"What are the causes of disunity among us?"* The question would be given to a target group comprised of two members from each of the five identity groups from each Cell. They would be *elected by members of each identity group at the cell level.* This could have been the first election in Rwanda after genocide! The identity groups as was apparent throughout Rwanda at that time, fresh after the massive repatriation excise from mainly Congo and Tanzania, were: the Tutsi survivors of genocide, the Tutsi old-case refugees recently repatriated, the Hutu that had just been repatriated, the Hutu that had stayed within the borders of Rwanda after the genocide and the Hutu elites (former government workers and business class).

These were brought together for a period of a week at the level of a Sector (there were at that time 1545 Sectors throughout Rwanda). Of the causes enumerated, the most frequently pronounced was of bad governance, followed by ignorance, poverty and the consequences of the genocide. The consultation process required the groups to give remedies they thought were appropriate to each cause. These initial grass-root consultations indicated that people wanted to have a say on issues that affected them. They recognized that blind obedience exposed them to manipulation and injustices. Analytically, the answer to the collective demand for effective participation was *democratic decentralization.*

The next two year period of 1998-1999 was characterised by deep consultations at the National level. It was carried out in the Presidential offices, commonly known as Urugwiro Village, every Saturday from early May 1998 to late March 1999. It was during these discussions which were very open and soul searching that most of the programs that have guided Rwanda in its political and social economic development up to date were suggested, debated and agreed upon. Because of the broad representation from the public, private and civil society and adequate coverage by the national radio and television, a broad consensus was reached on a number of programs of great national importance.

The major programs agreed upon were: The program on National Unity and Reconciliation, the National Democratic Decentralisation Program, the Gacaca program, the Vision 2020 framework and a program on National

Security. The thread across all these programs is that they were all people-centred. Every person speaking would recognise the primordial importance of involving citizens in all Government programs. In agreeing to use traditional practice of conflict resolution, the elite mould was broken.

It was a shared recognition that *within our culturally accumulated wisdom, we could find solutions that modern institutional practices could not provide.* Moreover, since these were traditional, the population was very comfortable with them, understanding them emotionally and thus fully participating with full knowledge of where they are coming from, where they are and where they are heading to. This was the start of a painful process of *re-establishing social trust and community spirit.* More and more programs drawing on the cultural practices have since been adopted. I will talk about them later. Let me first talk about the interim governance program that Rwanda developed with assistance of UNDP while the Urugwiro Village debate were still raging on.

In April 1998 a conference Governance was held in the town of Gisenyi. An Interim governance programme (1998-2000) was developed, which was extended through 2001. During this transition period, the Government of Rwanda highlighted the following governance areas to be revisited:

-   Improving public management and civil service reform;
-   Promoting decentralisation to ensure participatory decision making practices;
-   Strengthening the parliamentary institutions to ensure adequate capacity for legislative and oversight functions;
-   Improving economic and financial management practices;
-   Supporting broadly civic education programs and reinforcing civil society organisations;
-   Strengthening the judiciary to promote the rule of law and restore people's trust in the judicial system;
-   Promoting understanding of and protection of human rights;
-   Demobilisation, conflict prevention and peace building through Unity and Reconciliation Commission and other mechanisms;
-   Advancement of women and promotion of gender issues; and
-   HIV/AIDS prevention and control.

In March 2002, the Government of Rwanda developed a National Strategy Framework Paper and a corresponding Programme document for strengthening Good Governance for Poverty Reduction in Rwanda. These were based on the recommendations of a national conference held from 2nd to 5th November 2001, to assess the achievements of the Interim Governance program, to flesh out the remaining challenges and to propose strategic actions for strengthening good governance in Rwanda.

Five areas of priority focus agreed upon were as follows:
* Institutional strengthening and coordination;
* Unity and reconciliation, peace and security;
* Social welfare of the population;
* Civil society and Private sector; and
* Economic planning and management.

This allowed avoiding scattering efforts into a wide range of programs that were not addressing particular problems of the moment. Such focused vision was mainly led by the citizens preoccupations of the moment and aimed at regaining their ownership and trust.

6. Civic engagement programs

In prior decades, Rwanda had been characterized by divisive and exclusive political leadership, manifested through exclusive civil service and administration, nepotism and regional privileges to part of the Rwandan society. Ethnic polarization around purposely conceived social bias marked the community. For all these reasons and others stated above, there followed the upheaval that tore apart the Rwandan society, seriously shaking the existing rather unstable trust in governing mechanisms and the very questionable civic engagement.

In the aftermath of genocide, in order to reverse the gear, the Government of Rwanda undertook to rebuild a new society around a state governed by the rule of law, equality and equity, promoting national unity, banning all forms of ethnic, regional and other divisions and endeavoring a constant quest for solutions through dialogue and consensus[108]. It is around these core principles that a number of programs were initiated to restore trust among citizens and thus enhance civic engagement. Those programs include, but are not limited to, the following:

* **The generalised use of kinyarwanda**, the sole national language used in the country and even beyond, as an administrative language at all levels. This indeed reinforces unity and the sentiment of national ownership and pride.
* **Participation**: stirring people's participation to empower them toward confidence building; this involves administration through constant consultations and people involvement. An implementation tool was effective decentralization and democratic governance at all administrative layers.
* **Reconciliation programs**: a long process that involved the integration of social values promotion for enhanced understanding and ownership by the people:
    * o **Gacaca** or reconciliatory justice for genocide suspects, introduced five years after genocide (1999) and involving commu-

---

[108]   Constitution of Rwanda, 2003.

nity-level councils adjudicating cases and allowing the guilty to serve most of their sentence on community service. ·

o **Abunzi**: community arbitrators who handle civil cases to relieve courts from the congestion of unavoidable minor cases in a post-conflict situation. National attention is accorded to the vulnerable as we fight against impunity through restorative justice.

o **Ingando**: solidarity camps, seeking to demystify and break down barriers between people by freeing free expression, were at first used to help reintegrate refugees and former combatants returning to Rwanda, and later extended to include government officials and students candidates to higher education, aiming at better internalizing ideas of unity and reconciliation. Plans are underway to institutionalise leadership development centres (Itorero) at National, District, Sector, Cell and village levels.

o **Umuganda**: community works bringing citizens together to accomplish a task in common and giving them an opportunity to share views, plan public utility activities and socialize. Now institutionalized, this program is meant to supplement the national budget in infrastructure building.

o Newly established **Itorero**: leadership school aiming at strengthening ties among citizens around the broad theme of civic engagement.

- Non-segregative **service delivery** that is bound to results, through a merit-based, realistic management by objectives system. The new service delivery orientation is responsive to the quests of citizens and client-centred performance.
- **Civil society** that acts as a watchdog for public affairs management and even as a service provider under the principle of subsidiarity.
- **JADF** where all development actors in the Districts and Sectors plan with the leadership what should be done in those entities and closely monitor implementation.

7. Challenges

Reconstructing trust in a post-conflict situation takes time and definitely has to do with all sorts of hindrances, either internal or external. Major challenges encountered today include the long built and held ideologies of division and hatred, entertained by the so-called experts on the African Great Lakes Region, masters of "theories of origin" of peoples inhabiting the area, and other writers on Rwanda history who advocated differences and exacerbated divisions among Rwandans. While Rwanda is striving to uproot the evil on its territory, such ideologies are still flourishing in neighbouring countries and constantly fuelled to destabilize Rwanda.

Further, there is a dialogic reality of balancing the fight against impunity and the reconciliation process. Indeed, seeking justice for the deprived survivors of genocide through the classical juridical system was inconceivable as it involved a fastidious task of handling more than 825,000 cases in tribunals. A new system based on traditional values was devised to respond to that task and address swiftly the issues that otherwise would have taken more than two hundred years to be settled. On the other hand, survivors are to be rendered justice and compensation, culprits have to be punished to eradicate the culture of impunity that had long prevailed, yet the community must be reconciled and live together again in harmony. This is the huge task Gacaca courts are faced with.

Public administration has long been characterized by over-centralization, segregation, corrupt practices and rampant bureaucracy. New approaches are often met with resistance and reluctance to release "power" and to refrain from such ill practices. Public administrative attitude has been slow moving towards embracing new management concepts of effective decentralization and citizens' empowerment. Even today, it could not be surprising to meet some remnants of such behaviours, which raises in minds the spectre of the past era and contributes to check civic engagement and subsequent trust in a public-citizen shared responsibility governance model.

8. Lessons to be learnt

Building trust in a post-conflict situation involves a number of tasks to be performed, and behaviours and attitudes to be adopted, that will make citizens feel secure and confident toward public administration, and consequently accord their trust to the governing system. This in turn will make them civically engaged. In this process, among lessons we learnt in Rwanda are the following:

- Grass-roots consultations are necessary to identify the "missing link" by the people themselves. In Rwanda this allowed the recognition that blind obedience exposed people to manipulation and injustices and corrective measures were devised.
- Appropriate analysis of the situation. Decentralization in Rwanda was not initiated as a response to the new global wave of governance, but rather as an answer to the people's demand for effective participation through "democratic decentralization", after identifying the root cause of their tribulations.
- The major programs adopted to respond to the needs of the citizens were appropriately designed through a large consultation basis of national actors.
- For better appropriation of well understood initiatives, a large call was made on traditional long-held and accepted values based on

accumulated wisdom that had long proved to bring lasting solutions to community problems.

- External models of governance have inspired hybrid forms that were aligned to Rwanda's particular context and citizens have always been allowed a say before adoption of any initiative. Never has it been a question of importing a particular model to impose it to citizens, provoking unnecessary increased resistance.
- In seeking to engage Rwandans through accepted programs, an inclusive approach involves all layers of the population for empowerment (women, youth, disabled, widows, orphans, etc) Well-understood and shared programs have been initiated and instituted to bring reliable solutions to problems people were encountering.
- A strong National Vision and unwavering commitment on the part of leadership to involve people in the journey the vision sets.

9. Conclusion.

Owing to bad leadership and poor governance systems through its history, Rwanda experienced a series of tribulations, the last and by far the worst of them being the Tutsi genocide of 1994. It has been generally identified by the population that the mayhem occurred due to blind obedience that subjected citizens to manipulation. Bringing together a torn-apart society in the aftermath of genocide was a tremendous task to the new broad-based government that includes all sensitivities of the population. Citizens had lost trust in governing systems and civic engagement was at its lowest.

Through consultations and dialogue, programs to enhance citizen engagement, offer and demand driven, were launched and have proved their pertinence and are beneficial to a citizenry that is recovering gradually its trust in the Government. Challenges are still persistent, both internal and external, and today's government is striving to increase inclusive citizens empowerment, with citizens not only demanding their rights but also exerting their duties and responsibilities in an engaged way, thus building trust in government. It is not a fashionable governance system; it is a way of life!

Can Civil Society Engagement in Budgeting Processes Build Trust in Government?

Vivek Ramkumar and Warren Krafchik

1. Introduction

The Aide de Memoire for this meeting alerts us to the disturbing results of a survey presented to the World Economic Forum in 2005. The survey, conducted by Globescan, measured citizen trust in government in a diverse group of 17 of the world's richest and the poorest countries (World Economic Forum 2005). [109] When asked why they did not trust government, citizen respondents from across these countries provided the following reasons:

(i) government is not accountable to citizens (31 percent);

(ii) government is failing to deliver services (27 percent);

(iii) government is inefficient and corrupt (16 percent); and

(iv) government restricts public access to information (UNDESA 2007).

Each of the four deficiencies identified in the Globescan survey – accountability, responsiveness, efficiency, and transparency – play a critical role in undermining trust in government.

These results are congruent with the work of United Nations Development Program (UNDP), which includes each of these factors as necessary building blocks in good governance. According to the UNDP, governance is the exercise of economic, political, and administrative authority by a government. It is expressed through the mechanisms, processes, and institutions by which citizens articulate their interests, exercise their legal rights, meet their obligations, and mediate their differences (UNDP 1997). The United Nations Economic and Social Commission for Asia and the Pacific (UNESCAP) defines good governance to include:

- participation
- consensus-orientation
- accountability
- transparency
- responsiveness
- effectiveness and efficiency
- equity and inclusiveness
- legality

The question to be addressed in this paper is: What role can civic engagement play in rebuilding trust in government? This paper will focus

---

[109] Countries surveyed include Italy, Indonesia, France, Turkey, United Kingdom, Germany, Nigeria, India, United States, Spain, Canada, Argentina, Mexico, South Korea, Brazil, Russia, and China.

specifically on the opportunities and impact of civic engagement in public budgeting and auditing processes. Our evidence is drawn from the recent, dramatic growth of civil society organizations (CSOs) in over 60 countries with the capacity to understand, analyze and influence public budgeting.

Our conclusion will assert that emerging evidence shows that civil society engagement with public budgeting and auditing can help to substantially improve budgetary processes and outcomes in diverse developing countries. Greater engagement of CSOs in public budgeting is associated with a realignment of public priorities with public expenditures, improvements in the efficiency and effectiveness of public service provision, reduction of corruption and other leakages in the public expenditure chain, and improvements in the transparency of government budgeting and auditing systems. By engaging in public budgeting and auditing processes, CSOs can assist with efforts to rebuild public trust in government specifically by strengthening government accountability, responsiveness, efficiency, and transparency.

2. Impact Achieved by Civil Society Budget Advocacy

Over the past 12 years, CSOs in over 60 developing countries have been investing in capacity to monitor and influence public budgeting decision-making and outcomes. Civil society budget-focused organizations share three common strategies:
- They employ a combination of applied fiscal research and action;
- They specialize in producing timely, accessible and useful information to a wide range of stakeholders; and
- They focus on the impact of the budget on budget transparency and accountability, especially with regard to poor and low-income households.

In many other respects, civil society budget-focused efforts are diverse. Budget work has grown strongly in both low-income and middle-income countries. It has been successfully undertaken in both presidential and parliamentary systems of government; and it has proved adaptable to democracies and autocracies. The trend involves a wide range of types of organizations from think-tanks and NGOs to social movements and grassroots organizations. These organizations employ a diverse range of budget analysis methods to track the impact of the budget, including public expenditure and tax analysis, expenditure tracking, and impact measurement.

Although the interest and capacity of CSOs to engage in public budgeting is recent, emerging evidence points to the substantial potential impact of these organizations on budget transparency and accountability. Over the past two years, the International Budget Project has worked with the Institute for Development Studies (IDS) at the University of Sussex[110] to undertake in-depth case studies of six CSO budget-focused organizations in order to

---

[110] Detailed information on the research project is available at http://www.internationalbudget.org/casestudies.htm.

assess their impact on good governance practices and poverty reduction. The research project covered the following six civil society organizations:

Development Initiatives for Social and Human Action (DISHA) was founded in 1985 in Gujarat (India) to promote the rights of tribal communities (indigenous people) and laborers. The organization has focused on budget analysis and advocacy to represent the demands for land and labor entitlements for its constituents.

The Institute for Public Finance (IPF) is a non-governmental organization based in Croatia that undertakes public finance research and analysis to improve national policymaking and the effectiveness and efficiency of public budgeting. Founded in 1970, IPF's main purpose is the production and dissemination of high quality research on public finance issues conducted as part of a long-term effort to improve public education on public finance and the quality of public finance decision-making in Croatia.

Instituto Brasileiro de Análises Sociais e Econômicas (IBASE) is a Brazilian non-governmental organization that focuses on deepening democracy and increasing public participation in governance. IBASE set-up a budget advocacy unit in 1990 to focus on disseminating budget information in accessible formats to the public, and to conduct extensive trainings for the public in order to develop their capacity to analyze and influence government budgets.

The Uganda Debt Network (UDN) was established as a non-governmental organization in 1996 to campaign for debt relief from multilateral donor organizations. After Uganda was successful in achieving debt relief, UDN focused its activities on ensuring that the savings from the debt cancellations were utilized to support pro-poor expenditures in the country. UDN has trained community-based monitors to keep tabs on the effectiveness of government social service delivery.

The Institute for Democracy in South Africa (IDASA) is a non-governmental organization that focuses its activities on supporting the consolidation of democracy in South Africa by building effective civil society and governance institutions. IDASA started budget work in 1995 to provide timely and accessible public policy information on the impact of the budget on poor South Africans. IDASA has pioneered approaches to budget advocacy focusing on the impact of the budget on people with HIV/AIDS, children, and women.

Since its establishment in 1999, Fundar Centro de Análisis e Investigación (FUNDAR), has developed into a major research institution in Mexico that uses budget advocacy to highlight social justice issues in the country. FUNDAR works on transparency, human rights and governance, and citizen capacity building through partnerships and coalitions with other civil society groups in the country. The organization is particularly well-known in Mexico for its budget advocacy work on maternal mortality and HIV/AIDS.

The IBP-IDS research study examined the impact of the work of each of these organizations using a case study approach. Each case-study involved one academic and one practitioner spending two-weeks with each organization extensively interviewing the organization's staff and the users of the organizations work, as well as carefully reviewing the publications and other outputs of the organization. Interviews with users covered a wide range of stakeholders in the executive and legislature branches of government, the media, civil sector, and auditor-general.

The results of the research are exciting and very pertinent to the topic of this workshop. Across the six case-studies, civil society organizations show substantial capacity to promote the types of behaviour associated with good governance and thereby greater trust in government, including improvements in budget transparency, responsiveness, accountability, as well as increases in the effectiveness and efficiency of service provision. (Information on method and results of the case studies, as well as the individual case studies and synthesis papers is available at http://www.internationalbudget.org/casestudies.htm).

a) Improvements in budget transparency

Each of the CSOs under review developed highly sophisticated programs to enhance the transparency of public budgeting. The organizations developed accessible reports, briefs and summary documents (including guidebooks) that enable a much broader range of citizens and legislatures to understand budget decisions and the decision-making process. In many cases, organizations have also developed complementary training and technical assistance programs to build the capacity of citizens and legislatures to engage more effectively with the budget process. These efforts help to build the capacity of citizens to understand and commit themselves to difficult trade-offs inherent in budgeting and secure opportunities to make inputs into the budget process. To take a couple of examples:

IBASE in Brazil has developed training packages to promote awareness on budget policies and to strengthen the capacity of the public to monitor public budget. The training modules include innovative exercises that require participants to formulate the budget of a small town while responding to pressures from different constituencies and complying with federal regulations and guidelines. Another exercise requires participants to explore different strategies to obtain and interpret information on municipal budgets and to lobby local officials on specific issues (Shultz and de Renzio 2006).

Recently, IBASE examined "off budget" expenditures incurred by Brazil's National Economic and Social Development Bank (BNDES). The BNDES is a very large lending institution, with an annual budget larger than the World Bank's global lending portfolio. Concerned that many important decisions regarding public investment are being taken outside the budget process, IBASE has launched a dialogue between BNDES and Brazilian civil society. IBASE publishes a news bulletin to raise awareness about the role of BNDES in national development strategies and to provide information and analysis about important projects sponsored by BNDES (Shultz and de Renzio 2006).

The IPF in Croatia has published a "Citizens' Guide to the Budget" and a "Citizen's Guide to Taxation" that provide a general introduction to that country's budget and taxation processes. The guide provides an accessible historical analysis and government taxation and expenditure priorities, and clearly describes the Croatian budget process. The guide has been widely distributed and is widely used by the public and legislators. The following anecdote attests to its usefulness. The guide was published at the time that the national budget was being discussed in Parliament. On receipt of the guide, one of the Members of the Croatian Parliament stood up brandishing the document, and said to the Deputy Minister of Finance: "Now we don't have to simply listen to you anymore, we have a guide!" (Shapiro 2001). This and other IPF-published guides are regularly updated and made available on the organization's website (Van Zyl and Shultz 2006).

In India, the state government of Gujarat presents only a budget summary on its website, but not its full budget. After requests for detailed budget reports were turned down by the government, DISHA obtained these budget documents from members of the state legislature belonging to the opposition party. DISHA staff members undertake to analyze each of the budget reports and prepare accessible summaries for civil society and legislatures in time for the legislature hearings on the budget. Today, DISHA is the major source for budget information in Gujarat (Malajovich and Robinson 2006).

b) Increased government responsiveness

Each of the case study organizations has played an important role in increasing government expenditures on the needs of poor citizens – ensuring that the government is responsive to the priorities of citizens. While the total amount of funds involved in each case may be modest, the impact on citizen's lives is substantial. Examples of the successes achieved by FUNDAR in Mexico and IDASA in South Africa are presented below.

In 1999, the newly elected Mexican government committed itself to eradicating rural maternal mortality in the country. To evaluate the degree to which the government was living up to its commitment, FUNDAR joined a coalition of non-governmental organizations to examine reproductive health care in the country. FUNDAR analyzed the government's health budget and highlighted glaring problems in the maternal mortality prevention programs. Specifically, its research showed that the government was not allocating sufficient resources for these programs and the budget allocations for poorer states were disproportionately smaller than those for richer states. FUNDAR's findings were used by the coalition of non-governmental organizations to pressure the government to increase the budget for maternal mortality prevention programs. The coalition's efforts paid-off when the government approved a ten-fold increase in national allocations for maternal mortality prevention programs (Robinson and Vyasalu 2006).

In South Africa, the government provides a Child Support Grant to support the poorest families. Analysis conducted by IDASA's Children's Budget Unit showed that the program was being administered poorly in large part because of poor institutional capacity in local governments. As a result, the program was not fully accessible to its primary beneficiaries – rural and marginalized families. Further, IDASA's research highlighted the fact that program funding was not keeping up with increases in the cost of living (inflation). IDASA used these findings to launch an advocacy campaign to demand that program funding be increased in proportion with inflation rates, that the age limit of eligible children under the program be increased, and that additional resources be allocated to improve the institutional capacity of local government. In a major success for IDASA, the government increased funding for the Child Support Grant and raised the eligibility age from seven to 14 (Hofbauer 2006).

c) Increased government accountability

The case study organizations also achieved some success in ensuring that governments are held accountable to the public for their budget decision-making and implementation. As the examples from South Africa, India and South Africa show below, these impacts were achieved by successfully advocating for stronger public finance laws, ensuring that government budget commitments are actually met, and that appropriated funds are spent effectively and efficiently.

In South Africa, IDASA successfully advocated for changes in that country's new financial management legislation to make the law more transparent and accountable to parliament. IDASA insisted on the inclusion of stronger virement rules and of a provision requiring direct departmental responsibility for overspending. Virement rules determine the extent to which a government department can spend funds for purposes not congruent with budget plans without having to seek legislative approval (Hofbauer 2006).

In India, DISHA undertook activities that focused on ensuring that government departments spend their entire program budgets to address chronic under-spending by public agencies in India. The organization began by tracking funds allocated for programs targeted to support the socio-economic advancement of indigenous peoples. Analysis undertaken by DISHA revealed that the allocations to tribal communities in particular were frequently under-spent – sometimes by more than 20 percent of the total budget. DISHA undertook a public mobilization campaign to highlight these deficiencies and, as a result of its advocacy, the organization was successful in achieving a steep increase in actual spending levels in program budgets targeting tribal communities (Malajovich and Robinson 2006).

One strategy used by DISHA to ensure that program budgets are spent is to inform elected councilors in the rural administration of the specific allocations for local projects and to make follow-up enquiries once implementation begins. If implementation does not begin, DISHA writes to the relevant government minister, who then compels the local administration to release the funds. This strategy has proven to be a very effective way of placing pressure on the machinery of local government to ensure that financial resources for local infrastructure development are being utilized for their designated purpose (Malajovich and Robinson 2006).

In 2002, UDN and its partners in the Teso region of Eastern Uganda publicized the misuse of funds from the Schools Facilities Grant (SFG) – which support the construction of primary schools – in Katakwi district. The UDN report highlighted major shortcomings in the SFG guidelines that prevented effective oversight from being exercised over contractors who, in the absence of oversight, were constructing poor-quality schools. Sustained pressure brought to bear by UDN and its partners led to the revision of SFG guidelines to improve the quality of construction of school buildings, classrooms, and toilets. Among other changes, contractors are now required to submit performance guarantees declaring they will do quality work and ensure timely delivery of all projects. Further, contractors are required to submit bank guarantees that cover any advances that are released to them for project costs. In this way, if a contractor reneges on contract terms, the government is able to recover the amount advanced to the contractor directly from the contractor's bank (de Renzio et al. 2006).

d) Increased efficiency and effectiveness of public spending

The case study groups also achieved some success in combating leakages and in improving the efficiency and effectiveness of public expenditures. These successes have been achieved by the careful monitoring of government expenditures at the local level. We present examples of this work from Uganda and Mexico below.

In Uganda, UDN sought to tackle corruption and inefficient service delivery by training community-based monitors to check the quality of local service delivery, with a particular focus on local infrastructure projects. The community monitoring process culminates with an annual "district dialogue" during which the monitors present their findings to the district authorities. UDN community monitoring committees have achieved numerous successes. For example, monitors reported that patients in one community health center were treated poorly and forced to bribe hospital officials and buy their own medicine (which is supposed to be free). The resulting investigation by district officials led to a complete overhaul of the center, and subsequent reports by community monitors present a much improved picture (de Renzio et al. 2006).

In 2002, the Mexican legislature approved an increase of 600 million pesos for programs dedicated to women's health. Subsequently, the president of the budget committee of the legislature requested the Minister of Health to allocate 30 million pesos of these funds to eight non-governmental women's centers. The minister complied but the arbitrary and irregular allocation of funds created an uproar in the legislature. A network of six civil society institutions, including FUNDAR, came together to examine this issue. FUNDAR obtained hundreds of pages of accounting records from the Ministry of Health using the national freedom of information law and subsequently identified large-scale corruption in a contract awarded to a private agency, Provida, under an HIV/AIDS prevention program. FUNDAR's findings were corroborated by an official investigation conducted by the national supreme audit institution. Subsequently, pressure brought to bear by the FUNDAR-led campaign resulted in the initiation of government proceedings to recover misappropriated funds and the implementation of changes in the policies governing the management of discretionary funds, including the HIV/AIDS prevention program. The internal auditor imposed a huge fine of 13 million pesos on Provida, which was also asked to return the funds and was barred from receiving public funds for 15 years (Robinson and Vyasalu 2006).

In sum, these findings provide exciting, emerging evidence that by engaging in budgetary processes, CSOs can play a substantial role in improving governance and reducing poverty. More specifically, civil society budget work is associated with a number of outcomes – such as increasing the transparency, responsiveness, accountability and effective of government operations and service delivery – that may work to improve citizen trust in government.

3. Recent Trends in Civil Society Audit Activities

Most civil society budget-focused work to-date has concentrated on examining the passage of the budget through the legislature and the subsequent implementation of the budget by the executive. There has been much less civil society engagement with the auditing process and with supreme audit institutions (SAI), in particular. Yet, there would seem to be the space for a strategic partnership between civil society organizations and SAI's. CSOs often lack access to timely, accurate data, but can offer analytical capacity, citizens with direct experience of service delivery, and the ability to engage effectively in policy processes. In turn, SAI's can offer access to data, but often struggle with access to sufficient analytical capacity and are prevented from ensuring that their results reach the policy process and are taken seriously.

Reflecting these strategic opportunities, both SAIs and CSOs have increasingly been finding ways to engage with each other to exploit their relative strengths. Although this work is very recent, it promises several fertile opportunities for even broader civic engagement in budgetary processes, and concomitantly, broader opportunities for obviating the obstacles to trust in government.

An overview of civil society audit work

Work at the IBP has uncovered several innovative institutions that are using auditing methods and processes to engage in public budgeting. Despite the fact that most of these projects are very young, several are already indicating new opportunities to improve government transparency, accountability and responsiveness. We briefly describe five of these experiences below. [111]

In India, the Mazdoor Kisan Shakti Sangathan (MKSS) – a peasant and workers' union – uses public hearing forums to conduct social audits of local government expenditures in village communities. During these social audits, local communities check accounting and other records of public works programs executed in their areas in order to identify instances of unfulfilled works, fraudulent billing for project activities, and falsified labor rolls. MKSS' social audit methods are now being used all over India by citizen groups to monitor a recently introduced entitlement program -- the National Rural Employment Guarantee Scheme – under which rural households are eligible to receive minimum wage employment for 100 days in a year.

In South Africa, the Public Service Accountability Monitor (PSAM) – a research and advocacy organization – works closely with the legislature to track government agency responses to instances of financial misconduct and corruption identified in the Auditor General's reports. PSAM has highlighted the large number of audit disclaimers issued by a provincial audit agency – which was unable to access financial information during the conduct of its audit – and led a public campaign that subsequently resulted in the strengthening of financial management practices within provincial government agencies.

In the Philippines, a participatory audit was successfully conducted as a joint undertaking of the national Commission on Audit and a non-governmental organization called the Concerned Citizens of Abra for Good Government (CCAGG). CCAGG specializes in monitoring infrastructure projects within its province and uses the assistance of local monitors (volunteers drawn from the area) to verify that road construction projects are executed as per contract norms.

Also in the Philippines, Procurement Watch, Inc. (another non-governmental organization), specializes in building systems of transparency and accountability into government contracting and procurement practices. PWI's most recent initiative is to participate with the national Commission

---

[111] This section draws on Ramkumar 2007.

on Audit in a pilot test of a new tool to measure corruption and inefficiency in public procurement. The tool seeks to determine the true (fair-market) cost of a publicly procured good or service and then compares that cost to what was paid for the good or service. The size of the difference between the actual price paid and the fair-market value serves as a precise and objective measure of the extent of the problem.

In South Korea, the Concerned Citizens for Economic Justice (CCEJ) – the oldest non-governmental organization in the country working on economic rights issues – routinely uses the national citizen audit request system to request government audit investigations of public projects that are plagued with corruption and/or result in wasted resources. In one case, the organization's dogged pursuance of a case led to action against corrupt officials even after the agency had been cleared by the audit. In another case, changes were made in procurement policies in part as a result of the organization's advocacy campaign that demanded a limit on the issuance of no-bid contracts by the government.

In Argentina, La Asociación Civil por la Igualdad y la Justicia (ACIJ) – a human rights organization – successfully filed a law suit against the country's congressional commission responsible for reviewing public audits (this commission examines reports filed by the Supreme Audit Institution and initiates action based on audit recommendations) to obtain the minutes of meetings of congressional hearings. Subsequently, ACIJ used these records to highlight the lack of action taken by the commission to require corrective action in response to audit recommendations.

The increasing engagement of CSOs with SAIs is not only initiated by CSOs. In the following examples, it is the SAIs that have designed programs to engage with CSOs. The potential impact is however much the same – increasing opportunities for government transparency, accountability, responsiveness, efficiency and effectiveness[112].

In South Korea, the Board of Audit and Inspection (BAI) introduced the Citizens' Audit Request System under the Anti-Corruption Act of 2001 to allow citizens to request special audits from the BAI on public agencies suspected of corruption or legal transgressions. Applications are made under this scheme to a Citizens Audit Request Screening Committee, comprising citizens and audit officials who screen requests to identify frivolous complaints and decide which requests merit a full audit. Further, some local governments have decided to address complaints and grievances filed by citizens by appointing citizen auditors. These auditors, who are not public officials, are appointed to review petitions for a certain period and, if necessary, conduct audits and notify the petitioners of the results.

In 2002, the national Commission on Audit (COA) of the Philippines entered into a partnership with several NGOs, including CCAGG, to con-

---

[112]   This section draws on Ramkumar 2007.

duct participatory audits, in particular performance audits to determine whether government programs/projects had achieved anticipated results. Audit teams included members from COA and NGOs. In another instance, COA is cooperating with another NGO, Procurement Watch, Inc., by providing access to procurement documents of agencies that it is auditing to test a tool that measures corruption in procurement processes.

In India, inspired by the MKSS social audit process, the Andhra Pradesh state government is leading a social audit campaign together with a consortium of non-governmental organizations. All over the state, local communities receive information on the use of funds under the National Rural Employment Guarantee Scheme, and social audit forums are organized to discuss the veracity of expenditures incurred under this scheme. The state government acts on findings from social audits to improve the functioning of the scheme.

Taken together, the innovative civil society – SAI initiatives are still at a nascent stage and much needs to be done in order to deepen and document this work. However, the examples that we presented above do point towards the potential for civic engagement to have much the same impact in strengthening governance through the audit process as we observed in work on civic engagement on budget allocations and execution.

4. Conclusion

This workshop was presented with evidence of declining public trust in government, both in developed and developing countries. The argument advanced was that declining trust in government is the result of citizen perceptions of government as secretive, unaccountable, unresponsive, inefficient, and ineffective. While there is no silver bullet to addressing these issues or one prescription that will suit all contexts, it is essential to identify and document those practices that can contribute substantially to this rebuilding trust in government.

This paper has argued that civic engagement – and specifically CSO involvement in public budget analysis and advocacy – represents an important part of the solution to rebuilding citizen trust in government. We provided evidence from six initiatives around the world to show that CSO budget-focused work is able to contribute substantially to both improved governance and reduced poverty. In each case, the organizations concerned addressed these challenges by designing and implementing innovative methods to improve budget transparency, monitor the responsiveness of government to citizen priorities, reduce corruption and other leakages, and improve the efficiency and effectiveness of service delivery.

Moreover, experience shows that there is a natural partnership between civil society budget groups and other institutions attempting to enhance oversight of budget processes. The engagement of civil society in public budgeting can help to bolster the role of the media, legislatures and the SAI in the budget process by providing training, expanding available independent research capacity and improving data access. Thus civil society budget work can help to catalyze a systemic shift in domestic budgetary transparency and accountability.

While restoring public trust in government is a complex endeavor and well-beyond the ambition of this paper, strengthening opportunities for civic engagement in the use of public resources is a powerful and feasible necessary condition towards this end.

Bibliography

de Renzio Paolo, Vitus Azeem, and Vivek Ramkumar. "Budget Monitoring as an Advocacy Tool Uganda Debt Network Case Study." International Budget Project. 2006.

de Renzio Paolo and Warren Krafchik. "Lessons from the Field The Impact of Civil Society Budget Analysis and Advocacy in Six Countries." International Budget Project. 2006.

Hofbauer Helena. "Sustained Work and Dedicated Capacity: IDASA's Experience with Applied Budget Work in South Africa." International Budget Project. 2006.

Malajovich Laura, and Mark Robinson. "Budget Analysis and Social Activism: The Case of DISHA in Gujarat, India." International Budget Project. 2006.

Robinson Mark. "Budget Analysis and Policy Advocacy: The Role of Nongovernmental Public Action." Institute of Development Studies. 2005.

Robinson Mark, and Vinod Vyasalu. "Democratizing the Budget: Fundar's Budget Analysis and Advocacy Initiatives in Mexico." International Budget Project. 2006.

Ramkumar Vivek and Warren Krafchik. "The Role of Civil Society Organizations in Auditing and Public Finance Management." International Budget Project. 2005.

Ramkumar Vivek. "Expanding Collaboration Between Public Audit Institutions and Civil Society." International Budget Project. 2007.

Shapiro Isaac. "A Guide to Budget Work for NGOs." International Budget Project. 2001.

Shultz Jim, and Paolo de Renzio. "Budget Work and Democracy Building: The Case of IBASE in Brazil." International Budget Project. 2006.

United Nations Development Programme. "Governance for Sustainable Human Development." UNDP. Retrieved on May 24, 2007.
< http://mirror.undp.org/magnet/policy/chapter1.htm#b>

United Nations Department of Economic and Social Affairs. "Building Trust Through Civil Engagement." UNDESA Aide Memoir 2007.

United Nations Economic and Social Commission for Asia and the Pacific. "What is Good Governance?" UNESCAP. Retrieved on May 24, 2007.
<http://www.unescap.org/pdd/prs/ProjectActivities/Ongoing/gg/governance.asp>

Van Zyl Albert, and Jim Shultz. "Croatia and the Institute for Public Finance: Budget Work in a Transitional Democracy." International Budget Project. 2006.

World Economic Forum. "Trust in Governments, Corporations and Global Institutions Continues to Decline." Press Release. 2005. Retrieved on May 24, 2007.

http://www.weforum.org/en/media/Latest%20Press%20Releases/
    PRESSRELEASES87.

Oversight Offices and Civil Society Insights: The Case of India

Amitabh Mukhopadhyay

" **The concrete is concrete not because it is the particular of the general, but because it is the product of many determinations, the unity of the diverse.** "

Karl Marx, Grundrisse

Introduction: The Insurrection of Knowledges

Centrally planned economies, whether of a Stalinist variety or of a Keynesian persuasion, were in vogue until three decades ago. Techno-bureaucracies were the master-spirits of the age. Globalisation and information technology ushered in changes that enabled markets to assail the pre-eminence of nation-States. The nature of the public sphere started changing. Regulation of industries, private-public partnerships and decentralization to provide basic services are the order of the day. Even as re-engineering of governance in democracies to make room for greater intensity in deliberative processes is undertaken, cultural technologies of rule persist. There is a palpable disquiet about capability deprivation of human agency, whether manifest as abject poverty or as marginalized voices in everyday encounters with the State.

Compared to the excitement about government as an agency of development that was celebrated in the 1950s the world over, the trust of citizens in government has touched a new low. Some have argued that the rule of law has assumed different meanings, which is particularly relevant in the Asian context for the marginalized poor, women, tribal groups and the minorities. Others have appealed for an ethical globalisation where, for example, immigrants of all kinds enjoy human rights and corporations involve themselves in producing cheaper drugs to fight HIV aids. Feminist notions of what constitutes 'trust' have challenged the idea that trust can be built with reference to a static edifice of laws, rules and regulations[113]. There is interplay between the feelings of trust and distrust in the life-worlds of people which needs to be grasped and worked on.

Foucault's writings since 1965 showed us that the mere substitution of the sovereignty of the king by the sovereignty of the people does not by itself empower people because the acceptance of sovereignty as an idea in the minds of men and women continues to govern them. Conferring and re-organising rights into any type of sovereignty creates its own mechanisms

---

[113]   See Annette Baier's Tanner Memorial Lecture on 'Trust,' delivered at Princeton, 1991.

of domination. The notion of a right has to contend locally with the arms of hierarchical structures of legislative, juridical and administrative law the moment there is an assertion of the right in practice. Local assertions are countered by disciplines that legitimize hierarchical structures and the contests are easily doused, buried and perhaps papered over with greater finesse in democratic states than despotic ones.

Local memories and narratives of such contests lie as bric-a-brac in the social terrain until they are constituted by civil society into knowledges which contend or forge a relationship with disciplines. Tabling these subjugated knowledges as truth by civil society at various forums -- evident in acts of martyrdom, in liberalism, pluralist engagement and more recently, in postmodern critical vigour -- have gathered momentum. These critiques have helped democracies to gain a wider vision than the straitjacket of legislative/juridical/administrative law would otherwise have allowed.

While Montesquieu marveled at the separation of powers in American democracy, de Tocqueville pointed out that in modern democracies, the freedom of association is the real safeguard, not only against the authority of the state but also against the tyranny of the majority. More recently, as the willingness of some States to put more and more information in the public domain has grown, the contributions by civil society to this process of an 'insurrection' of knowledges have increased. A global movement of civil society is clearly in evidence.

Of course, this engagement or contestation could not have been a linear development. Precisely because it *is* a contest, various means have been deployed on both sides. On the one hand, there is co-option of civil society institutions and deployment of ideas and knowledges based on local experience, by the State, to continue its domination by inscribing them with its own institutions that trap popular justice. There are innumerable examples of local NGO initiatives being converted into national programs where critical concepts are debased into vacuous jargon. On the other hand, civil society is not coextensive with society; the former consists of individuals that enjoy higher life chances. Having been invited to high table by bureaucracies to deliberate policies and programmes, many of them easily lose the initial contact they had with the life-world of people. As a result, some of them don pretensions to *representing* the interests of people, in parallel with elected representatives, and others are reduced to serving as agencies for agendas of the State.

The 'insurrection' of knowledges has happened unevenly. For instance, environmental concerns constitute an area where this has occurred with considerable intensity in recent times. In which domain is the voice of challenges to established knowledge less audible? In this paper I argue that Supreme Audit Institutions (SAIs) have not been the subject of civil society debate till very recently[114]. SAIs have escaped an audit by civil society per-

---

[114]   The debate in the UK regarding the Audit Commission for local authorities leading up to the Act in 1998 was an important development.

haps because SAIs themselves have been regarded as a check on the excesses of sovereignty.

Do SAIs perform any sovereign functions or do they merely express an opinion? In some countries, like in France, they clearly issue legal judgments. In others, like the commonwealth countries, they may not pronounce judgments, but they do provide legitimacy for judgments by other sovereign organs within a framework of procedures for such judgments to be arrived at. In other words, even in commonwealth countries government audit is not just any opinion, but a privileged opinion, an opinion that carries the halo of power. It is the opinion of a person 'ordained' by the constitution and the laws.

In the wake of large development programs undertaken by governments in the welfare era, SAIs extended their concerns from regularity to performance audit. Issues about the effectiveness and objectivity of auditors have been raised by several commentators in this context of the progress from the confines of a narrow focus of a concern for compliance of laws (regularity audit) to wider avenues like performance/value for money/policy audits. As a Divisional Court in the UK observed, "Expenditure is only unlawful if it lacks authority or represents an abuse of discretion. Poor value for money is not, in itself, unlawful and the auditor has no specific power to force authorities to implement his value for money recommendations. His only sanction is to issue a public interest report to draw attention to unsatisfactory progress"[115].

Does this widening of concerns render them less capable of 'objectivity', of making judgments on their own? It is usually believed that it does. In my opinion, however, it is not this widening gyre that makes a difference. The very idea that 'objectivity' can be arrived at by isolated individual auditors or insulated institutions, whether in regularity or in performance/value for money (VFM)/policy audits, is questionable. In fact, in the flattened out post modern world, it makes no sense to cling to the archaic notion of a clinical 'objectivity'. Both kinds of audit can be better undertaken as they should be, if instead of deploying the expertise of individual auditors to arrive at objectivity and controlling that by hierarchical arrangements for issuing more and more abstract audit guidelines, SAIs were to ask their auditors to engage with activities of civil society and, in the context of audit of local bodies, experience objectivity in collective representations at local assemblies.

With the rising tide of decentralization, the ambivalent footing of SAIs in relation to audit of local bodies/authorities requires scrutiny. On the one hand, SAIs have kept themselves apart from the audit of local bodies/authorities that actually deliver social services. On the other, they continue to comment on the delivery of social services by acting as auditors on behalf

---

[115]   Hazell versus Hammersmith and Fulham LBC (1990) 2 WLR 17.44.

of 'donors' (national/provincial governments or international donor agencies) by means of reports on 'performance audits' or 'VFM audits' or 'audit of policy'. By constituting their 'public' as an abstract monolith at a national level, SAIs may have gained the respect and regard of other organs of the State but fail to meet the expectations of citizens who in fact exist in everyday life as several 'publics' and often constitute persistent minorities. I put forth the view that the SAIs should be poised to assume sentinel functions for common citizens in tandem with civil society instead of exclusively catering to the representatives of the people in legislatures.

Another worrisome trend in the practices of SAIs must be noted. While the origins of the audit discipline lay in anxieties of people about fraud and corruption, most SAIs, over time, distanced themselves from these as core concerns. INTOSAI's Auditing Standards do mention checking against fraud as part of 'due care' to be excercised during regularity audit but this is mere lip service. Other than in France, *few cases of fraud or corruption have been reported by SAIs*. It is customary for SAIs to shrug these off as the responsibility of the executive and best left for investigative and legal action by them. A separate forensic discipline of fraud detection has sprung up and offices are being established under the executive wing. Corruption, requiring investigation to reconcile what is on paper with what is not on paper and involving third parties, is left to vigilance commissions under the executive. The increasing emphasis of SAIs on the distinction between responsibilities of internal (executive) audit and external audit (statutory) and their over-emphasis on the need to strengthen internal audit by the executive is symptomatic of their insular formalistic concerns and frustrations about their own weak ineffectuality in handling mismanagement and corruption in the public sector through reporting to legislatures.

In the wake of the computerization of accounts worldwide and electronic data processing (EDP) techniques of audit, an interesting development is that fraud and corruption are being revisited by SAIs. The World Bank's exhortations[116] might revive interest of SAIs in these matters. The UN Convention on Corruption signed in September 2005 and ratified by an overwhelming majority of countries in 2006 might also help to bring these concerns back as expectations of people from their SAIs. As of September 2005, however, only a pilot practice note of INTOSAI on SAIs' involvement in detecting fraud and corruption was in the offing.

I dwell on the emergent methodology of social audit in India in the context of local bodies and compare this with individual-based audit or process documentation and monitoring. I argue that the inter-relations between SAIs and civil society can be forged on the basis of social audit if SAIs are

[116] Kenneth M Dye and Rick Stapenhurst, 'Pillars of Integrity: The Importance of SAIs in Curbing Corruption,' The Economic and Development Institute of the World Bank, 1998.

willing to move from an insular mode of functioning to an interventionist orientation for accountability to specific publics which are the focus of national concerns.

What appears to be marginal in the affairs of the State may well turn out to be central. The macroeconomic basis of the Millennium Development Goals with their predominantly finance-driven approach to end poverty, HIV/aids and delivery of social services begs the question of the accountability of the machinery that is expected to deliver. There is a perceived notion of accountability which reduces it to compliance with hierarchical structures of law and administration. The subterranean domain of social accountability, which is far more meaningful and relevant especially in the context of local bodies, can be constructed, in my view, by a realigned dialogue of SAIs with civil society.

Section II : Decentralisation and Social Audit

Insurrections of knowledge are part of the social history of every locality, province and country. What excites me about the emergence of social audit practices in India is the manner in which, by means of social audit, citizens are able to relate their life-worlds to systems of accountability and how this process generates an ethical tone in the public sphere. To facilitate an appreciation of this effervescence which drowns all clichéd differences in the audit discipline between subjective-objective, external-internal, regularity-performance in a collective undertaking, I contrast this with government audit and process documentation and monitoring.

The legacy of colonial systems that codified government audit in India is essential to an understanding of its current practices. The practices of British auditors were introduced by the East India Company for the presidencies of Bombay, Bengal and Madras, prior to the British Crown taking over the territories and creating the Office of an Auditor General in 1857 to audit supplies from UK and their application. With posts & telegraph, then railways and defence departments added to the responsibilities of the British Government of India, the ambit of Auditor General in India increased. He reported to the Governor General. Since 1881, when local bodies and authorities on the British pattern were created, the presidencies and later provinces enacted laws for the audit of local funds falling within the provinces. The Examiner/Director, Local Funds Audit reported to the Finance Secretary of the provincial governments.

The Constitution of India adopted in 1950 created the institution of an independent Comptroller and Auditor General of India as an officer not of the House, but submitting reports to it. However, in other respects, it only formalized the earlier existing arrangements. He continued to decide on accounting matters, maintaining accounts at the Centre and the States, as

well as auditing them[117]. He continued to leave the audit of the local bodies/
authorities to the Examiner/Director, LFA. Even in 1992/93, when by means
of Constitutional Amendments, 'local self-government with a development
orientation' was ordained, the audit of these bodies remained circumscribed
by archaic Local Fund Audit Acts. The Union Finance Commissions that
periodically decide on the sharing of proceeds of taxes and on obligatory
grants by the Centre to the States have commented repeatedly on the state
of complete disarray in the accounts of local bodies.

Since 2002, the Comptroller and Auditor General (CAG) of India has
made efforts and obtained the consent of State Governments to provide
technical and administrative guidance to offices of Examiners, Local Fund
Audit. These are not mandatory functions and performance reviews of
implementation of social services and programmes financed by the Centre
and the States but implemented by local bodies, are submitted by him to
Parliament/State Legislatures just as they used to be reported prior to the
Constitutional Amendments in 1992/93. CAG does not submit any reports
to the local bodies (except in 3 out of 28 provinces where provincial acts
mandate him to do so). Even where he does submit reports to local bodies,
as in West Bengal, Bihar and Karnataka, the standards of audit practices
leave much to be desired. The orientation of CAG in India to serving what
may be termed only donor interests (Centre & State Governments) vis-a-vis
local bodies and authorities underlines the disjunction in the audit of social
service delivery.

There is certainly an immediate need to revamp the local fund audit
acts. These are archaic in that : (i) they are still cast in the mold of accountability of local bodies to senior officials of the State Government and State
legislatures; their focus is more on classificatory issues and disallowances
along with imposing surcharges as a mode of control of State Governments
over local bodies rather than a concern for service delivery by the local bodies
in and for themselves and (ii) they continue to prescribe the impossible task
of audit of cent per cent of the vouchers with the result that faced with this
impossibility, local fund auditors simply certify the final accounts without
auditing any voucher at all! Nevertheless, apart from revamping the audit
acts, audit as a discipline of practices will need to be critically refashioned as
well by forging ways for the auditor to hear the complaints of residents in
each locality. An alternative paradigm to organically link the national and
local concerns is also necessary.

We need to step back at this juncture to consider monitoring processes
before reverting to audit again. There are various ways in which projects are

---

[117]   The separation of accounting and auditing functions are regarded as part
of internationally accepted standards. While the accounting functions have been
handed over in 1976 by the CAG in India to the Finance Ministry at the Centre, the
CAG continues to maintain them for the State Governments.

monitored by management within the executive wing. These rely on statistical frames of surveys and reports/complaints from a wide range of sources which are scrutinized. Even in the best of circumstances, such monitoring constantly gropes for more and more information while progressively doing less and less, in terms of decisions taken by administration, with the information at hand. This happens for at least two reasons. One, individuals that make up bodies are often swayed by career considerations, professional networks as well as rivalries and loyalties that are removed from a service orientation. Second, because increasingly, contemporary service delivery is by public bodies which secure actual provision of services by an agency or under contract from private providers, and this not only introduces corruption in the interstices but also compromises online correction due to a   negotiated and contracted efficiency that gets legally frozen in time.

A more recent usage is Process Documentation and Reporting (PDR). This refers to a different independently conducted exercise by civil society institutions. PDR records *site-specific information* about the interface between actors/institutions involved in a project or programme[118]. While economists provide this service for the private sector, only some beginnings have been made for this service in the public realm. Of course, participatory processes and techniques for data collection have become ever more sophisticated. Yet, the inevitability of political factors in the conversion of data into information has been acknowledged by social theorists.

As against social theorists who make a sharp distinction between knowledge and opinion, appearance and reality, others reject 'objectivity' in an appeal to solidarity. They look for as much inter-subjective agreement as possible. "As a partisan of solidarity, the researcher's account of cooperative human enquiry has only an ethical base, not an epistemological or metaphysical one"[119]. Consensus as a criterion which legitimates knowledge can be viewed in different ways. It may or may not be a consensus of free individuals through dialogue. It may well turn out that the system of governance manipulates a consensus to rule the roost.

In the professional world of audit and corporate scandals such as the ones related to Enron or Worldcom, it was even argued on the basis of the legal obligation of corporate executives to maximize shareholder value and the fact that organizations comprise multiple individuals and agendas, that corporations do not have ethics; they have instead, only public relations!

We can see that the problems of 'objectivity' are confounding in a schema of deploying individual researchers in process documentation and moni-

---

[118]   See an excellent review of literature on PDR by Pari Baumann, Information and Power : Implications for Process Monitoring , Working Paper No. 120, Overseas Development Institute, London, Sept., 1999.
[119]   Rorty, R (1996) 'Solidarity or Objectivity' in Cahoone, L (ed) From Modernism to Post Modernism: An Anthology, Oxford : Blackwell Publishers.

toring and can only be worse when SAIs deploy individual auditors or a team
of them with constraints of time and the straitjacket of audit missions.

The good governance agenda, which emerged with the publication of the
World Bank's report *'Governance and Development'* in 1992 has two objectives – one is to encourage greater transparency, accountability and administrative efficiency and the other concern is with democracy, human rights and
participation. The precise mechanisms to link the latter set with the former
are not very clear. Accountability is being pursued without any priority being
assigned to its major components that are simply listed: accounting/auditing,
decentralization, micro-accountability of public agencies to direct consumers
of locally provided services and government and NGOs. There is no attempt
to answer the questions 'accountability to whom? through what mechanisms
? and to what degree ?'[120]

An alternative mode of a collective process of social audit, deserves
greater attention. The contrast between social audit practices and the existing practices of process documentation and monitoring (PDR) are : (i) that
social audit is collective and PDR is normally carried out by a non-project
individual researcher; (ii) social audit *verifies* the records of project implementation to not just cast doubt on parts of the records but investigates the
social story which explains the false part of records whereas PDR follows a
parallel ; (iii) social audit is undertaken for a local public whereas PDR aims
at enlightening a wider public at a remove.

The practices of Mazdoor Kisan Shakti Sangathan (MKSS), a union
of labourers and peasants in Rajasthan, India in developing the methodology of social audit since 1990 have been documented and acclaimed as
remarkable. A demand for minimum wages to be paid to workers at famine
relief works near Dev Dungri village in Bhim tehsil of Udaipur district in
Rajasthan led to an interesting development. The demand was refused on the
grounds that 'they did not work'. The workers protested, but were told that
the measurement books for the works filled in by junior engineers of PWD
showed they had not worked. Their hard labour had been penned off! The
stupefied workers naturally demanded to see the records. Administrators,
who quoted the Official Secrets Act of 1923, told them that they could not
see the records.

The need to access records was hammered home and rural workers
organized themselves as a union of workers and peasants – Mazdoor Kisan
Shakti Sangathan (MKSS) – to struggle for ways and means of wresting their
right to know from government. The first public hearing was held by MKSS
at Kot Kirana, Rajasthan in December, 1994. Known as a *jan sunwai*, this
became an incredibly powerful step in revivifying the centrality of citizenship
in a democracy.

[120]   Moore, M. (1995) 'The Emergence of the Good Government Agenda: Some
Milestones', IDS Bulletin (26) 2.

People from about 18 surrounding villages gathered. Small public works of 1993-94 were probed, muster rolls were read aloud and were found to be fake. Fingers pointed at a retired school teacher, the gram sevak and the junior engineer who certified the muster rolls. People fearlessly spoke against the deputy speaker of the vidhan sabha (provincial legislature) who had camped for a week in the village to intimidate people. Thereafter, when the bills related to construction of a patwar ghar, stated in the accounts to have been completed but visibly roofless, were read out, people burst into laughter. Soon, however, laughter gave way to anger and people went all the way to lodge an FIR. A month later, the retired teacher's son lost the panchayat election.

The struggle illustrated that the right to information was not just a component of people's right to freedom of speech and expression but was also a part of their fundamental right to life and liberty. It was needed to obtain the basic living wage, entitlements under the ration quota at the fair price shops, the medicines the poor ought to receive in public health centres and for contending with coercive abuse by the police.

By January 1995, when the fourth Jan Sunvai was held, it was clear that this mode of struggle was widely feared by the gramsevaks (official secretary of the gram panchayats). An order had been obtained by MKSS from the collector (district magistrate) in Ajmer that all records should be given by panchayats and preparations for the Jan Sunvai at Jawaja were on. Gram sevaks of the district staged a dharna at the collector's office agitating that records should be shown only to government auditors. Gram sevaks then organised for a state-wide protest. Though records were denied to MKSS, the Jan Sunvai was held on January 7, 1995. People from seven panchayats gathered to give oral evidence. Within two days of the hearing the sarpanches and gram sevaks started paying back the pilfered money. Many workers received full payment of wages. It is from this point onwards that MKSS focused on the people's right to information on a statewide basis. The fact that the people's right is crowded out by institutional privileges of the organs of the state – courts, legislatures, government audit and the media – was brought home.

Leading up to a jan sunwai, typically, the MKSS first obtained the records related to the public works carried out by the panchayat. Once the documents were accessed, the Sangathan took the records to each village where the works were supposed to have been executed and checked them out by asking the village residents and the workers who had been employed on the site to authenticate the records. On the day of the public hearing in front of the general assembly of the village residents, the details were read out and testimonies sought. A panel of 'men of letters' from different walks of life, like lawyers, writers, journalists, academics and government officials, were invited to the public hearings to act as a jury. In the presence of officials from the district administration, an effort was made to arrive at appropriate corrective measures for the irregularities identified. Communicative action characterized the movement for social audit and the right to information. By means of puppetry, street plays and folk songs, on every occasion, the attention of large audiences was gathered and brought to a friendly temper rather than an inquisitorial mood.

Jan sunwais have touched a social chord. The malpractices usually uncovered at sites for anti-poverty employment generation works are over-billing in purchase of materials, fake muster rolls, under-payment of wages and, in some very interesting cases, ghost works (construction works that are there on record but do not exist on the ground). Workers denied payment after repeated visits to the sarpanch over years have been often paid overnight at the mere announcement of a jan sunwai. Cases where, after an embezzlement being proved at a public hearing, the sarpanch has promised and has in fact paid back the amount into the panchayat account are not rare. Action has sometimes been initiated by government against officials without whose complicity the embezzlement could not have occurred or remained unnoticed.

Triggered by these experiences gained from social audit in Rajasthan and experiences of civil society groups engaged in human rights and displacement issues, a concerted national campaign for the right to information and for an employment guarantee act was launched in 1996 in India[121]. The campaigns succeeded in wresting both a Right to Information Act (RTI) and a National Rural Employment Guarantee Act (NREGA) from the Government of India in 2005.

Spontaneous activist efforts that seek to influence state outcomes through outside pressure have been contrasted by social scientists in a theoretical frame[122] with a model of deliberative democracy for which the Kerala campaign for decentralized planning in India is cited as an example. Professors Fung and Wright, for instance, draw the contrast in terms of (i) the larger reform scope of deliberative democracy experiments, (ii) their being characterised more by an external deliberation process (ie. with people in participative activities) as against the reliance on internal deliberations by activist groups, the results of which are then taken to people and (iii) the focus on transforming mechanisms of power rather than trying to gain power vis-à-vis the state. Since each of these criteria for the contrast lend themselves to a wide range of interpretations, it is difficult to accept this as a conceptual contrast between activist efforts and campaigns like the one in Kerala. The Kerala campaign for decentralized planning which was based on

---

[121]   Neelabh Misra, 'People's Right to Information Movement: Lessons from Rajasthan,' Discussion Paper Series-4, Human Resource Development Centre, United Nations Development Programme, New Delhi, 2003.
[122]   Archon Fung and Eric Olin Wright, Deepening Democracy: Innovations in Empowered Participatory Governance, Politics and Society, Vol. 29 No. 1, March 2001, pages 5-41.

the exercise of State power earned the dubious distinction of being dubbed a case of decentralization of corruption. Not even its greatest proponents, like Thomas Isaac, contest that corruption was in fact in evidence though they do question its extent. The Report of CAG of India on the campaign is, however, quite damning. The complete rollback of the experiment in Kerala since 2005 calls into question the scope of reflexivity in State-sponsored initiatives which are invariably propagandist.

In contrast, we have the counter-example for the theoretical framework of Fung and Wright in the story of MKSS in Rajasthan which has throughout dwelt on developing concrete practices of social audit built around the workers trying to investigate the whys and wherefore of the denial of the benefits of anti-poverty programmes by collusive corruption of the local elite and officials. The self-learning modes of MKSS and reflexive modes led on, through struggles to undertake social audit, creation of a national campaign for people's right to information and finally to enactments on right to information in seven states and finally by Parliament.

In 2006, MKSS undertook an audacious leap from engaging in exercises of post-implementation audit to one for monitoring the implementation of the Rural Employment Guarantee Scheme in Rajasthan. The twin objectives of NREGA are to provide wage employment/create assets and establish the *right* to employment. As participants in the first district-wide monitoring exercise, at Dungarpur, Rajasthan in April 2006, where persons from NGOs, unions of workers, individual activists and officials undertook investigations along 30 different routes in groups of 30 persons, what struck all of us over the few days was the quality of the verbal transactions that occurred when the groups interacted at sites with workers and their supervisors. These were adult–to-adult transactions on concrete matters like a wage payment to a worker, measurement of a pit, distance from the habitation/village, lead and lift of earthwork, schedule of rates, measurement books, job cards, etc. – in complete contrast with the nature of child-to-adult (think about it!) transactions of patronage when anybody goes to people with the imagined mission of raising their 'awareness' about programmes.

The specific methodology adopted, of transacting/interacting on the *details* of matching what's on the ground with original records of applications, job cards, works estimate, muster rolls, measurements and assets being created, is clearly most appropriate. It is in contrast to transactions in abstract terms, like responses to multiple choices in an administered monitoring questionnaire or to the nature of transactions at meetings of beneficiaries with experts where abstract opinions are expressed. The method of social audit as a monitoring device added value in two ways : (i) the very process of monitoring catalyzed the administration and (ii) the method of reporting collectively, which condensed a large number of narratives to produce a conjoined local representation allows for refinements/corrections to be made by government *in situ*.

Participation in such collective local gatherings leads to an objectivity in a defined local context that comes home as a collective representation. Some truths are attested and other novel representations are forged. For example, at Dungarpur, Rajasthan, the lack of deliberations to decide on the nature of works that can be more fruitfully undertaken (eg. watershed based land development of the workers' land holdings) and hastily sanctioned earth excavation works for deepening existing village ponds or fortifying a huge existing anicut and non-payment of wages for more than 15 days were discussed. The major unintended mechanism of benefits to manual workers in terms of the reduced compulsion to seasonally migrate to places outside the village where exploitation by contractors was far more intense, were noted. The reasons for poor record keeping of measurement of works – to allow more powerful non-workers to grab wage payments -- come across as new truths apprehended in the effervescence of local assemblies. The blank application forms, not filled in but signed or thumb-impressed by workers lying at the local body's office, a few with a mention of 15 days' requested and just three or four with 30 days written, tell the tale of an instruction somewhere along the line that the demand can be entered after the supply is made! Blank application forms signify an abject surrender of workers to the powers that be. With no payment for work done and an acceptance of whatever mandays might be allowed by the village elected headman and the local official, the gathering wondered if the *rights* to information and employment were anywhere in evidence even though in aggregate terms, a large amount of funds were being spent.

It is arguable that such facts can be captured by statistical reporting as variances in data. However, such variances do not lend themselves to immediate explanations nor are they immune from doctoring of information. If anybody looks at the data in the portals of national and state governments in India related to NREGA, the aggregate figures of demand and supply of wage work will be found to be identical. This is simply due to the fact that instead of being compiled from figures in the application for work submitted by the workers (which is politically discouraged by implementers on the ground), they are derived from the estimates of mandays in work orders. By contrast with social audit, monitoring by the State machinery creates a situation where failure is seldom admitted.

MKSS inspired the State Government of Andhra Pradesh to take the movement further in September, 2006. A campaign for social audit at local assemblies was undertaken by the State Government in partnership with a consortium of NGOs in Anantapur. Investigating teams consisting of persons from NGOs, MKSS and government gathered and attended local assemblies across the district. I was privileged by an invitation from the State Government, to participate in the campaign.

A feature of NREGA in Andhra Pradesh was that wage payments under NREGA in Andhra Pradesh had been arranged to be made by the post offices in savings accounts for workers. What came through to all of us during the *padyatras* and village assemblies was that by and large, wage payments ranging from Rs 80 per day to Rs 200 had been received (compared to the prevalent agricultural wage rate of Rs 47 for men and Rs 36 for women which remained stagnant over a decade), the wage rate paid to men and women was the same, works had by and large been sanctioned on workers' own lands (the opposite of what happened at Dungarpur) signifying the same thing again, i.e., sanction by administrative fiat rather than any basis in local-level planning. It also brought home the involvement of postal officials at some places in fraudulent withdrawals of money from savings accounts of workers. The last signifies the political fact, of how even when administration tries to get around frauds in cash transactions by means of payments credited to accounts of workers, the local mafias and local officials collude to get at the money. The timeliness of the social audit monitoring exercise, however, raised hopes that next year round, the problems will have been addressed to a large extent due to the transparency and publicity to the process which therefore cannot be laid aside as merely sectional or individual *opinion*[123].

It is this nascent social movement for social audit that calls for the participation of SAIs with civil society institutions to establish good governance. Here I propose that the distinctiveness of social audit from other kinds of process documentation and monitoring methods should be fleshed out to develop the notion of 'objectivity as collective representation'. Realigning relations between SAIs and civil society along this channel would be productive.

The first step towards this endeavour is for SAIs to break out of the division of internal and external audit regimes in the sphere of audit of delivery of social services. It must be remembered that as against the concerns of departmental auditors for classification of transactions under relevant schemes and programmes, citizens are interested in the veracity of the details in BPL surveys, vouchers and muster rolls. The actual construction of permanent assets along proper specifications also matters to them.

The auditors of local bodies including audit clerks, should be required to attend local assemblies called by civil society institutions at the gram sabhas (village assemblies mandated to authenticate accounts of the village panchayats) held in each year to familiarize themselves with the working of the local bodies bottom up. The bogey of 'conflict of interest' is raised whenever any participation of an auditor in the activities of auditees is suggested. A problem of ethics is sought to be bureaucratically solved by making insulary the cornerstone of the independence of audit. Evidence shows

---

[123] Documentation Team, New Concept, Hyderabad, 24 January 2007, Social Audit-Tool for Empowerment, jointly organised by NGOs and CSOs of Ananthapur and Department of Rural Development (GoAP), supported by Mazdoor Kissan Shakti Sangathan (MKSS) and Action Aid India.

that this has never succeeded; the wining-dining and gift-giving to auditors is rampant the world over. The effective safeguard against unethical/arbitrary practices is to enhance the transparency in the auditor's proceedings. Another change required in India is to give the powers and responsibility to auditors of local bodies *in person* as is the practice in UK. That is the only way auditors would be liable for any miscarriage in person too, and their job would not be protected institutionally.

Auditors for local bodies should be trained by asking them to actually write the accounts of the village/municipal level local bodies and then set to work and first help civil society organizations and the poor in particular villages to monitor programs/projects. It is only after such rigorous training, rather than chalk and talk sessions, that they should be allowed to certify accounts. Such certification should be undertaken only after they have heard the residents in at least 5 percent of the local assemblies (called by gram sabhas or by any civil society institution) and have reconciled what's on paper with what is not.

Section III: Decentralisation and Supreme Audit Institutions

Ironically, while the role of SAIs has been expanding in many spheres as a response to emergent national concerns, their purview does not extend directly to the audit of local bodies and authorities in the commonwealth countries, India included. There are separate Acts governing the audit of local authorities in UK and India. We have earlier looked at the genesis of SAI in India and the continuance of separate provincial audit acts for local bodies. It is instructive to go over the genesis of audit of local authorities in UK to highlight the general problem posed by ambivalence of SAIs – remaining external to audit of local authorities and yet exerting bureaucratizing controls on actual audit processes – which is clearly an unacceptable situation.

Independent scrutiny of accounts of local public bodies existed since the 14th Century in England but *the audit system developed due to the cost and complexity of the poor laws since 1601*. Initially, poor law accounts were presented to the justices of the peace for their approval but by the 19th Century, the practice of engaging specialist auditors was established. In 1834 the Poor Law Commissioners were provided with the power to appoint paid officers with such qualifications as they thought necessary for auditing the accounts. The Poor Law Amendment Act of 1844 further authorised the chairman and vice-chairman of the boards of guardians in each district to elect an auditor of the district. The elected auditor was provided full powers to examine, audit, allow or disallow the accounts and to charge those responsible for any deficiency or loss as a result of neglect or misconduct. The same Act gave ratepayers a right to see the accounts and to attend the audit to raise any objections.

With the diversification of local public services, district auditors assumed new areas of responsibility. From the beginning of the 20th Century, these included local boards of health, schools, sanitary authorities, highways, county councils, uban/rural district and county councils and the London boroughs. The Local Government Act, 1972 put the laws and procedures for audit of all local authorities in England and Wales together. The District Auditors, inducted into the civil service in 1968, were appointed by the Secretary of State. The Layfield Commission commented on the compromised independence of the district auditors, and urged that they be brought under the Comptroller & Auditor General. Due to the inappropriateness of the national legislature intruding into the business of local authorities, this was not accepted. However, Layfield Commission's concerns were addressed in an ingenious manner by the changed procedure for appointment of auditors under the Audit Commission Act, 1982.

Several features of the Audit Commission Act, 1982 are noteworthy[124]. First, the Commission is self-financed by means of audit fees paid by local authorities and is not a Crown body. Second, its jurisdiction was extended by the National Health Service and Community Care Act, 1990 to include health authorities and other NHS bodies in its purview of arranging for audit. Third, while the Commission appoints auditors and employs them, the Act maintains the tradition of conferring statutory powers and duties *on the auditor in person*, who remains accountable only to the Courts for the way in which he discharges his professional responsibilities, independent of the Commission which only lays down a Code of Audit Practice with which auditors must voluntarily comply. Fourth, there is the clear provision in the Audit Commission Act, 1982 that *the auditor must hear the ratepayers before certifying accounts.*

Of course, controls of the SAI operate in practice. The reappointment of the auditor depends on the judgement of the Commission of how well the auditor has performed with reference to the Code and information circulated by the Commission has to be taken into account by the auditors. They have to also apply the Commission's recommendations to promote good management practice. Besides, Section 27 studies of the Commission provide the basis for reports by the SAI to Parliament on any relevant matters arising from them.

Though the Commission in UK, like the Comptroller & Auditor General is independent, and can appoint independent auditors, the members of the Commission themselves are appointed by the Secretary of State who is also empowered to give directions as to the discharge of its functions, with which the Commission is bound to comply. To the onerous duties of

---

[124]   Mike Radford, Auditing for Change: Local Government and the Audit Commission, The Modern Law Review, Vol.54, No. 6, Law and Accountancy. (Nov, 1991) pp 912-932.

the Commission and auditors for regularity audit have been added on the obligation to promote value for money. This involves the auditors in how the authorities operate and to take interest in the day-to-day activities of the authorities and creates a clash of interest between the role of auditors acting both as adjudicators and quasi-prosecutors. This gave rise to the phenomenon of 'creative accounting' whereby loopholes were found by local authorities to defer current expenditure to later years. In order to control this, the Commission preferred not to rely on strict application of rules of local authorities but to issue its own interpretations of the laws of local governments, for instance, about competition law as applied to tendering by local authorities (the controversy about values of tenders of contractors vs. costs of local authorities' own supply of services) which were often idiosyncratic (eg. differed significantly with CIPFA interpretations). This has led to the problem of authorities being 'intimidated' into accepting the Commission's interpretation for fear of risking allegations of illegality. From a conventional 'objectivity' point of view, it also prejudices the independence of auditors.

A significant contrast is provided by the judicial status of audit in France. Decentralisation was carried out in France by law in 1982. In preparation for this increase in competences of the local communities, in each area a regional room of accounts was created whose members are magistrates for life. A Regional Chamber of Audit has jurisdiction over all territorial communities in its region. Members of the Regional Audit Chambers are magistrates who hold their position for life. Their duty is to verify accounts of public accountants of these territorial communities and their public institutions, review management of these communities as well as the management of their public institutions, which, depend or receive directly or indirectly financial assistance from them, help in verifying budgets of communities and their public institutions, through advice, formal notice or proposals, under certain circumstances, and according to procedure set by the law. The Decree of 23rd August 1995, has updated the organisation and functioning of the regional audit offices and has introduced the *system of hearing local voices before open court for imposing a fine on public accountants.*

Competences of these new jurisdictions of the State are essentially defined in the same law and in the Code of the Financial Jurisdictions: to judge the accounts of the public accountants of the local authorities and their publicly-owned establishments; to examine the management of these communities like that of all the organizations which, directly or indirectly, depend on them or receive from them financial grants; to contribute to the control of the budgetary acts of the local authorities and their publicly-owned establishments, by opinions, proposals or settings in residence, in circumstances and according to a procedure defined essentially by the law itself.

The Regional Chambers of Audit in France have reportedly done a marvelous job of cracking down on corruption in the working of local authorities. It must be noted that this happened in a context where elections are publicly financed and austere limits have been imposed on this spending. The earlier connection between spending by local authorities and election-eering funds has been removed by law.

This is of immense relevance to the situation in countries like India where anti-poverty programmes have been dubbed 'political slush funds' by noted economists. As a result of the sluggish and ineffectual response of the Public Accounts Committees at the provincial and national levels to the reports of the Comptroller and Auditor General of India, people have moved courts of law by means of public interest petitions to agitate the right to food and employment. The courts have responded by appointing commissioners to oversee implementation of anti-poverty programmes. However, the orders of the commissioners too have been mired in the 'inquiries' by the very state agencies that are involved in the mismanagement. The hierarchical structures of rule are easily circumvented in the labyrinthian world of government pro-cedures by bureaucrats crafty for comfort and other vested interests in the spoils of development funds. Building trust in government requires the SAI in India to hold hands with the civic engagement already under way in the practices of social audit where facts are collectively shared and deliberated transparently in public assemblies.

Section IV: Conclusion -- Agency and Accountability

The macroeconomic approach of the MDGs cannot be a success unless the risks of misappropriation of resources to be mobilised are lowered signifi-cantly. At the moment, the international community is lagging way behind the target of raising 0.7 per cent of GDP of developed donor nations for the MDGs. The funds are not forthcoming, among other reasons, because the agency of the marginalized, which alone can provide an assurance about the delivery mechanism, has not been given sufficient attention to create the confidence of donors.

'Agency' is usually construed to mean organizing the poor to lend them a voice. For instance, it is customary to characterize the poor in India as suffering due to their being in the 'unorganised' sector. By implication, it is argued, that their agency can only be created by organizing them into trade unions, after the image of the working class that went on to create the wel-fare state in England. This is neither based on facts nor very imaginative in today's context. Albeit in wrong hands, the poor actually happen to be orga-nized, whether by contractors of labour or *dubbawallahs, kabariwallahs,* etc. in cities. Such organization for survival renders them prey to exploitation. Programmes of government which are expected to enable the poor to break out of the shackles of such organization are frustrated by these 'organizers' in collusion with officials implementing the programmes. They do so by dint of knowledge/power, by being crafty in wielding the fine print and law-ways that circumscribe what 'law' means in society.

To counter the craft of misinformation and cowing down of people by 'superior' knowledge and closed-door practices, the agency of the poor has to be created, not by efforts at unionisation, but by supporting their efforts at investigating their local experiences. The agency of the poor is created in local assembly when they are assisted to piece together the information required for them to make sense of their actual experiences, gain confidence to act and contest the received knowledge about what needs to be done, how best it can be done and what *should* be done in the circumstances. It is this enhancement or enrichment of the public sphere in terms of knowledge/ power that is creative of agency, not as a sectional voice but as a common concern. In local assembly, a moral sphere of impersonal and communicable truths or objectivity is generated and a trust is built among citizens that cooperation on a dignified and equal footing, though vexed, is indeed possible. Participation by SAIs and civil society are required at this point to dispel the notion of accountability as a submission to 'superiors'.

By participating in social audit used as monitoring exercises, studying the programmes and investigating details on the ground along with people, attending local assemblies to gather collective representations of experiences, the district auditors and civil society would be able to discern the substantive parts and assail the narrowly technical/administrative binds in guidelines/ rules of programs. They would be able to grasp concepts of accountability as social concerns in the moral world of people in flesh and blood rather than merely as administrative or legal matters buried in papers/files. The differences between internal and external or regularity and value for money audit would naturally dissolve simply into one integral audit.

Elected representatives of the people are familiar with the truths generated and agitated by local assemblies in their constituencies. They give credence to such accounts which are somehow belied in executive reporting on the subject when they sit for meetings of the committees in Parliament. By forging mediation *at* local assemblies, SAIs can provide a richer account of actual implementation which resonate far more with the representatives' knowledge of the field.

The reporting by SAIs to legislatures should not be supplanted by social audit but can be enriched by it. At present, audit comments presented to Union and State legislatures are based on audit checks married to a systemic and statistical analysis peppered with a questionnaire-based assessment of 'impact' of programs for the poor, all of which presume that the wisdom of those who formulated the programmes exhaust the universe of all concerns. These comments urge further investigation of matters by the program executives who in turn come up against elusive truths, limited at any rate to 'what's on paper', scattered at various removes from them. By reporting on performance of programs based on participation in processes to gather not only paper records but also collective oral representations in local assemblies, SAI of India (and other SAIs) would be able to serve far better as an instrument for accountability.

SAIs jealously guard their independence in a schema of separation of powers. This comes in the way of their relating to civil society engagement with public affairs. Rather than construe independence of audit as connoting an institutional preserve, SAIs must recognize independence as a matter of speaking truth to power, like the judiciary in India which has so creditably opened up its windows to the winds of public interest litigation. It is time that a highly formal kind of democracy where citizens vote in an electoral process for the purpose of selecting competing elites bows out to a robustly egalitarian democracy that has political legitimacy and the social strength to pursue accountability.

Civic Engagement in Queensland Australia: Participation in Road System Management A Case Study of Main Roads Experience, Queensland

Neil Doyle

Introduction

Citizen expectations to be involved in the decisions made by government are increasing world-wide. Citizen participation democratises decision-making with specific, tangible objectives and enhances knowledge, capacity, skills and expertise social goals, including public education and enhancement and incorporation of citizen values (Todman, 2004).

In response, the Queensland Government's policy commitment acknowledges the right of Queenslanders to have a say and get involved in government planning and decision making. This commitment extends to priorities and outcomes that all departments, such as Main Roads, Queensland, must demonstrably contribute to.

Roads are essential to support improvements in the standard of living of citizens. For government departments responsible for planning and managing roads as part of an integrated transport system, citizen participation presents considerable challenges as decision makers balance national, state and local road needs, often within a constrained fiscal environment and also the benefits to future generations against short-term costs. By their very nature, roads can sever or unite communities and have both positive and negative impacts on people's quality of life. It is fundamental, therefore, that the decision-making process of government departments such as Main Roads, Queensland, accounts for the needs and expectations of citizens in an open, collaborative and meaningful way.

This paper examines how Main Roads is working to achieve the goals of civic participation in road system management — management of the physical road asset within broader land use, transport, land, social and environmental systems. As a road system manager, Main Roads has invested significant time and resources establishing and maintaining connections with citizens, communities, businesses and other levels of government through community engagement.

The paper outlines concrete steps taken to: 1) include government-citizen engagement across all phases of business and 2) encourage a values base and institutional framework that addresses leadership, managerial capacity and civil capacity to engage elements of the model of engaged government proposed by Guthrie (2003).

The paper presents Main Roads' integrated approach of public participation, governance and government-to-government relations as key strategies in assisting public participation in road decision making. This process acknowledges that public involvement must be an early and continuing part of decision making to understand and respond effectively to community and citizen values and to avoid, minimise and mitigate impacts.

The paper outlines community engagement as a process practiced by Main Roads to provide opportunities for the public to understand the constraints and trade-offs associated with road system management and to 'buy-in' to the problems and 'own' the solutions.

The paper outlines experiences in meeting the challenges of public participation whilst simultaneously managing Queensland's largest community-owned asset with an estimated replacement value of AUD$30 billion – the state-controlled road network. With the sheer volume of road infrastructure development planned for Queensland, on any given day Main Roads' staff will be working with hundreds of communities across the state. This presents new issues such as increasing public frustration with traffic/delays, public scrutiny of road budgets/estimates, perception of regular changes to project scope/briefs, and increased lobbying from industry, economic groups and others with vested interests. This, in turn, exerts even more pressure on Main Roads to build trust and confidence with key external stakeholders to engender support and 'buy-in' to ensure delivery of core business.

Within this environment, learning from experience and building capability to engage communities is ongoing. The paper looks at the department's learnings and evaluation of community engagement.

Finally, looking to the future, the paper provides an overview of the Roads Alliance, a world-class, innovative government-government collaborative relationship model as a contribution to reinventing government. The paper also outlines the department's innovative research and development agenda to ensure ongoing improvements to community-government relations.

The Global Perspective

Khan (2006) provides a comprehensive overview of global and local forces impacting on citizens' power in government-citizen relationships, empowering some and disempowering others. Khan discusses the engaged governance model as a construct for mainstreaming citizens at all levels of governance (legislative and executive) to ensure inclusiveness in decision making.

At the 2005 International Conference on Engaging Communities led by the United Nations and Queensland Government, a number of common issues were raised with respect to government-citizen relationships and engaged governance, relevant to both developed and developing countries.

These issues included:
- the universal challenges of trust, participation, legitimacy, accountability and efficacy in government;
- the relational nature of governance and business in the public, private and community sectors;
- the fundamental need for 'community connections' to achieve sustainable economic, social, cultural and environmental development; and
- the lack of 'engagement' and 'equity' in the era of 'New Public Management' efficiency and effectiveness dialogue.

Figure 1: Australia's Mainland State and Territories

The Brisbane Declaration for Community Engagement was an important outcome of the Conference, as it formalised an ongoing commitment to community engagement and participatory decision making by representatives from over 40 countries, international institutions, government, academia, business and civil society (see Attachment One). The intent of the Declaration is captured in Main Roads' community engagement practice, as presented in this paper.

Australia in Perspective

Australia comprises six states and two territories, as well as external dependencies such as the Australian Antarctic Territory, Cocos Islands, Norfolk Island and the Coral Seas Island Territory. Australia is the world's largest island and smallest continent (see Figure 1). Australia covers around 7.6 million km and represents just 5 per cent of the world's land area (149.45 million km2), but is the sixth largest country after Russia, Canada, China, the United States of America and Brazil. It is also the only one of the top six that is completely surrounded by water. The nation's land mass is almost as great as that of the United States of America, about 50 per cent greater than Europe, and 32 times greater than the United Kingdom.

With an annual average rainfall of 465 mm, Australia is about one third drier than all other continents except Antarctica. Around 70 per cent of the nation is unable to support agriculture in any form and much of it can be used only for the grazing of a limited number of sheep or cattle. About one third of this area is classified as desert. The remaining area is split roughly in half, with a little more than 15 per cent falling in a temperate region between the arid zone and the coastal belt. This has played a significant part in the nation's settlement pattern and development of a transport system to meet population and industry needs.

Figure 2: Australia's Human Settlement Pattern, 2001 (Newton, 2001)

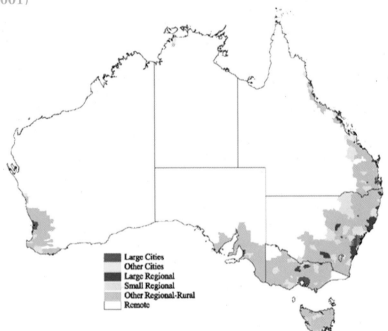

On 28 March, 2007 Australia's population was estimated at 20.79 million. Australia's growth rate of 1.3 per cent at September 2006 was about the same as the overall world growth rate (Australian Bureau of Statistics, 2006a).

The nation has one of the lowest population densities in the world at 2 persons per km. The nation's pattern of human settlement is characterised by particularly high rates of urbanisation and low-density cities. Around 85 per cent of the population live within 50 km of the coast in mainly in two crescents: the south-eastern coastal corridor between north of Brisbane and west of Melbourne, and the south-west of Western Australia centred on Perth (Newton, P, 2001) (see Figure 2). While the large capital cities dominate in population terms, many Australians live in smaller towns and remote areas. Many of these areas are where the nation's lucrative, high export-earning mining and agricultural industries are located.

Irrespective of where people live and industry is located, all Australians expect to have access to other places, people, goods and services. This presents considerable challenges for road infrastructure providers like Main Roads in providing fair and equitable access and safety.

Government in Australia

There are three levels of government in Australia — Commonwealth, State/Territory and Local[125].

The Commonwealth Government is responsible for laws in relation to a range of specific subjects listed in the Constitution. Major areas include taxation, defence, external affairs, trade and immigration. Over the years, the power of the Commonwealth has also broadened, through its increasing capacity to raise revenue through taxation (including customs and excise duties, and income tax on individuals and businesses), as well as growing trade and commerce across state and national boundaries. More recently, the Commonwealth Government has taken an active role in transportation planning.

State Governments are responsible for state laws that regulate important areas such as education, health, roads and criminal law. Their parliaments can pass laws on a wider range of subjects than the Commonwealth Parliament, on any subject of relevance to the particular state. The Commonwealth Parliament is empowered by the Constitution to make laws for the government of any Australian territory.

A large measure of self-government has been conferred on three territories, namely the Australian Capital Territory (location of the federal capital city, Canberra), Australia's largest mainland territory, the Northern

---

[125]   For more information on government in Australia, go to the Australian Government website at *http://www.apsc.gov.au/about/exppsreform3.htm*.

Territory and Norfolk Island. The remaining territories, which include the Australian Antarctic Territory, are offshore and sparsely populated.

There are in excess of 673 local governments across Australia, all with varying rate bases, revenue streams, skills and capabilities. The constitutional responsibility for local government lies with the state and territory governments, and therefore their roles and rresponsibilities vary. Examples of responsibilities include infrastructure and property services, recreation facilities, health services, community services, building services, and planning and development[126].

Civic engagement responsibilities

Responsibility for civic engagement sits with individual governments at all levels (the Queensland Government position is discussed below). While each state and territory has developed its own vision, policies and strategies and use different ways to describe the relationship between government and citizens, there is a common ground in that all seek, to varying degrees, to incorporate citizens' views.

At a local government level in Australia, civic engagement is undertaken by individual councils. The Australian Local Government Association is the overarching body that guides local councils and its state/territory counterparts, with individual state/territory local government associations having a strong commitment to connecting communities and strengthening democracy[127].

Working together

With three levels of government in Australia, ensuring that all representatives work together has always been challenging. One mechanism for providing this opportunity is the Council of Australian Governments (COAG), a body comprising of the Australian Prime Minister and all state/territory Premiers and national president of the Australian Local Government Association, established as a forum to initiate, develop and implement national policy reforms requiring cooperative action between the three levels of national, state/territory and local government.

The Commonwealth and state/territory governments also cooperate in many areas where states and territories are formally responsible, such as in education, transport, health, and law enforcement.

Later in this paper, Main Roads' experience in inter-governmental rela-

---

[126]   For more information about local government in Australia go to the Australian Local Government Association website at *http://www.alga.asn.au/about/*.
[127]   For examples of peak local government bodies go to the Australian Local Government Association website at *http://www.alga.asn.au/about/*, the Local Government Association of Queensland at *http://www.lgaq.asn.au/portal/dt* and Victorian Local Government Association at *http://www.vlga.org.au/*.

tionships and collaborative decision making with local government will be highlighted to demonstrate meaningful ways to achieve better outcomes for communities and government.

Queensland in perspective

Queensland is located in the north-eastern section of Australia (see Figure 1). The state has a sub-tropical climate in the south-east of the state, semi-arid and arid conditions in the western interior, and a tropical climate in the north. Queensland is the second largest of Australia's six states and two territories, covering some 1.7 million km2. The state is four times the size of Japan and seven times that of the United Kingdom.

Population growth

At June 2006, Queensland's population reached just over 4 million, an annual growth rate of 1.9 per cent. Queensland's population density is 2.34 persons per km2 (Australian Bureau of Statistics, 2006b).

In June 2006, Queensland recorded its fifth consecutive year as Australia's fastest growing state (Department of Local Government, Planning, Sport and Recreation, 2007). While 19.7 per cent of Australia's population lives in Queensland, by June 2006 the state gained 28.7 per cent of Australia's population growth. Natural increase is the largest component of population growth, followed by interstate migration and overseas migration. The top ten birthplaces for settlers arriving in Queensland are New Zealand, United Kingdom, South Africa, Philippines, India, China, Sudan, Fiji, United States and Malaysia.

Around two-thirds of Queenslanders are concentrated in the south-east corner, which totals one per cent of the state's land area.

The population is governed by the Queensland Government and 125 local government authorities. In the north-west the state's largest city in area is Mt. Isa, covering some 43,000 km2 but with a population of around 23,000. In contrast, there are 18 local government councils in south-east Queensland serving a population of 2.7 million covering an area of approximately 22,500 km2. Queensland has the nation's most diverse industry sector, with industry supporting thriving cities, towns and communities across the state, making Queensland the most decentralised state in Australia in terms of industry and population.

While Queensland's population growth continues to be strong, future growth will depend on the drivers of migration, specifically, employment opportunities, lifestyle/family reasons and house price differentials.

Meeting the demands of growth across Queensland

The Queensland Government has embarked on a significant infrastructure development program to meet the infrastructure needs of and demands by an increasing population and strong economic growth. Queensland-wide the state government is spending AUD$11 billion in 2006/07.

Over the next 20 years, the Queensland Government is also investing significantly in the south-east corner through the South East Queensland Infrastructure Plan and Program (SEQIPP)[128]. The SEQIPP outlines an investment of AUD$27.7 billion to major transport infrastructure, of which AUD17 billion is allocated to roads[129].

Figure 3: State-controlled road network, Queensland

---

[128]   The South East Queensland Infrastructure Plan and Program is located at *http://www.coordinatorgeneral.qld.gov.au/pmo/index.shtm.*
[129]   The $ values for SEQIPP are expressed in 2006 values. A new SEQIPP is due for release mid-2007 and will be available on the above website.

The VITAL role of roads in Australia

Australia has one of the most extensive road networks per capita in the world. Australian roads comprise a national network, state roads and local roads. Roads have a vital role in contributing to national, state, regional and local economies, linking people, goods and services across vast geographic distances in Australia. Roads also play a critical part in maintaining the social fabric of communities, as people may need to travel long distances to access basic services, see friends and family and meet work commitments.

While local governments are responsible for about 80 per cent of the nation's road network, but these carry mainly low traffic volumes. State and territory governments manage the majority of roads of national and state significance.

Given that roads are managed across jurisdictions, how decisions are made about roads management is critical to maintaining the road system as part of an integrated transport system which ensures the social, economic and environmental well-being of citizens.

Queensland roads

Queensland has around 178,000 km of roads. At 19.8 person/km, Queensland has a more dispersed road network than the Australian average of 23.6 persons/km.

Main Roads, is responsible for almost 34,000 km of the state-controlled road network, the biggest in Australia (see Figure 3). This comprises 20 per cent of the state's total road network, but carries 80 per cent of the traffic. The remainder of the road network is managed by the state's 125 local governments.

State-controlled roads are a high-speed network connecting major centres across Queensland and interstate. This includes the Auslink National Network[130]. Volumes of traffic on the state-controlled road network range from less than 50 vehicles per day to more than 140,000 per day.

The state-controlled road network is a valuable community asset owned by the Queensland Government, with a replacement value of approximately AUD$30 billion. Main Roads has responsibility for planning, designing and delivering this road network across 14 districts.

Maintaining network condition and enhancing network capacity to fulfill the state's emerging social and economic needs, while sustainably managing the natural environment, is an enormous undertaking, particularly as the road network ages. The challenge for both the state and local governments

---

[130] The Auslink National Network links major population and economic centres and facilitates the movement of people and freight internationally, nationally and between regions. The network also connects to major ports and airports.

is to meet community expectations of the road network by achieving the best possible network performance from available resources.

This requires us to:
- effectively plan and prioritise works on a network-basis, rather than the management by individuals in an uncoordinated manner to produce inconsistent outcomes;
- achieve the most efficient and effective use from available resources across the state, including funding, plant and equipment and technical expertise, capability and capacity; and
- build high-quality road-management capability throughout the state, which is particularly critical in those regions where communities' size and resource-base may not be proportional to their network management responsibilities.

Most governments managing state-wide programs or providing services on a state-wide basis will recognise they face similar issues. Clearly, there is a need to establish ways that levels of government, communities, citizens and wider stakeholders can work together to consistently address concerns, expectations, issues and opportunities so that the road network best fulfils all stakeholders' needs.

THE QUEENSLAND GOVERNMENT'S COMMITMENT TO ENGAGED GOVERNMENT AND ENGAGED COMMUNITIES

The Queensland Government has adopted a Queensland Public Service Charter as a statement of commitment to the people of Queensland (Queensland Government, 2003). Within this Charter is a commitment to working across boundaries as a professional public service " …We will cooperate across structural boundaries to develop innovative multi-agency programs to address complex issues. Our actions and behaviours will foster public trust and confidence in the integrity of the public service".

Recognising the importance of public participation in decision making, the Queensland Government has adopted the Organisation for Economic Cooperation and Development (OECD) public participation continuum to involve communities and citizens on a range of policy, program and service issues (OECD, 2001):

- INFORMATION
- CONSULTATION
- ACTIVE PARTICIPATION

The Queensland Government has seven key priorities as a guide to policy development, planning and reporting. These are endorsed by Cabinet, and all departments must contribute to these through their core business, or by working collaboratively across departments on integrated service delivery[131]:

- Improving health care and strengthening services to the community;
- Realising the Smart State through education, skills and innovation;
- Protecting our children and enhancing community safety;
- Managing urban growth and building Queensland's regions;
- Protecting the environment for a sustainable future;
- Growing a diverse economy and creating jobs;and
- Delivering responsive government.

Under the priority "Delivering responsive government," engaging the community on the government's directions and processes is a key strategy to understand and respond to community needs.

In 2001, the Queensland Government provided an institutional basis for community engagement through:

- a **vision** – "Involved Communities – Engaged Government" is about communities and government working together to achieve better policy making, solutions for a sustainable future, enhanced trust in government and active citizenship;
- a **concept** of engagement that refers to the "arrangements for citizens and communities to participate in the processes used to make good policy and to deliver on programs and services"; and
- a set of **six principles** incorporating inclusiveness, reaching out, mutual respect, integrity, affirming diversity and adding value (Guthrie, 2003:6).

A legislatively-based Charter of Social and Fiscal Responsibility (Queensland Government, 2004a) demonstrates the government's commitment to communities through whole-of-government outcomes. As with other countries, the Queensland Government recognises the need to deliver better social, economic and environmental outcomes for people in the long-term.

The Queensland Government is also committed to a "seamless" coordinated government approach to achieve better outcomes. This approach recognises that improvements to citizens' quality of life require the combined efforts of all departments. The government (2003b, 2004b) released Realising the Vision: Governance for the Smart State, a framework to guide this approach, along with Seamless Government: Improving Outcomes for

---

131   For more information about the Queensland Government priorities go to *http://www.thepremier.qld.gov.au/priorities/*

Queenslanders, Now and in the Future. The approach requires state government departments to work together as a single entity and with federal and local governments to achieve the best possible outcome.

The Queensland Government has reaffirmed this commitment to whole-of-government outcomes for communities, and identified community engagement as a key priority for all departments. As previously mentioned, the government released a vision, concept and principles moulded on OECD work, along with a community engagement improvement strategy.

The Government emphasis is on:

- having a vision for governance that is participatory, consensus-oriented, accountable, transparent, responsive, effective and efficient, equitable and inclusive, following the rule of law (Queensland Government, 2003);
- implementing community engagement across departments; and
- building public sector capacity to engage communities and citizens.

MAIN ROADS' COMMITMENT TO COMMUNITY ENGAGEMENT

Main Roads is the Queensland Government agency responsible for managing Queensland's road system as part of an integrated transport system. The department is part of the transport portfolio which includes Queensland Transport, Queensland Rail, state-owned ports corporations, and Queensland Motorways Limited, the latter responsible for tollways and their associated motorways.

The Queensland Government's priorities and outcomes guide road system planning and delivery to take account of external inputs. The Transport Infrastructure Act 1994 and the Integrated Planning Act 1997 both mandate consultation as the critical element in planning activities (Guthrie, 2003). As well, the Transport Coordination Plan (TCP) is a transport portfolio-level direction document guiding all modes of transport in Queensland.

Prior to the Queensland Government initiating institutional arrangements, Main Roads had developed its own vision, concept and principles for civic participation through the process of community engagement. This was due to the department having a number of highly sensitive road projects which encountered growing community concerns about impacts on their well-being.

For Main Roads, community engagement involves arrangements for citizens and communities to participate in the processes used to make good policy and to deliver on programs and services. Community engagement is defined as the many ways that government, communities and individuals connect and interact in developing and implementing policies, programs, services and projects. In this paper, community is defined as all relevant stakeholders including government, industry and individuals.

Main Roads recognises the many types of communities to be considered in decision making, including:

- communities of place such as a region, suburb, town, catchment area;
- communities of interest such as government, special interest groups, regulatory bodies, industry and education; and
- communities that form around an issue such as environmental protection and community amenity.

These communities comprise the department's stakeholders — those individuals, groups and organisations who are likely to be affected by, and/ or have an interest in, the department's decisions and actions.

Since the 1980s, Main Roads has taken a forward-looking approach to engaging communities. Our learnings are that the civic participation road is sometimes 'bumpy' as hard decisions are made, not only for local communities but also for regional, state and national reasons. To address this, a number of interventions have been put in place over time, including policy, systems, processes and staff training and mentoring. These continue to be recognised by other state departments and levels of government as a critical level of individual and organisational capacity to work innovatively with diverse communities and collaboratively with other departments on complex, multi-faceted problems (Guthrie, 2003).

Based on past experiences, Main Roads is moving towards a collaborative approach that focuses on outcomes, process and relationship building, accountability and community development.

Districts, a Key to Successful Relationships

In a state as vast as Queensland, a decentralised department presence in local communities is essential for staying connected to community issues, being responsive to local needs and building trusting and meaningful relationships. Central to the success of the department's relationship with Queenslanders are 14 district offices and their staff who live and work in their local communities. In regional and remotes areas, this local presence has underpinned community and citizen satisfaction with engagement processes and outcomes reached.

In more built-up areas of the state, especially the south-east corner where high levels of infrastructure development are taking place and communities can become blurred, the department has increased the level and type of information to communities and citizens as part of the engagement process.

Having a strategic long-term view

As outlined previously in the paper, the department faces significant challenges and tensions in managing Queensland's largest physical asset within broader land use, transport, social, cultural, economic and environmental systems. Challenges include balancing community expectations in a high growth population environment while maintaining an ageing road asset, building new infrastructure, supporting Queensland's strong economic growth, supporting traditional industries while responding to the transport needs of new and emerging communities, protecting indigenous cultural heritage, and protecting the natural environment for now and future generations.

Figure 4: Integrated Planning Framework

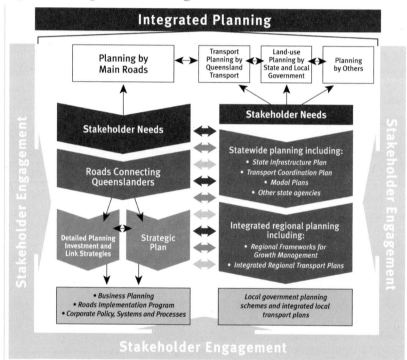

In response, in 2002 a long-term, stakeholder-focused strategic policy framework was developed for the Queensland road system and the organisation to respond to the challenges ahead, stakeholder needs and expectations and the impacts of integrated planning and service delivery. Main Roads released Roads Connecting Queenslanders (RCQ)[132] to demonstrate the

---

[132]   A copy of Roads Connecting Queenslanders is located in Corporate Publications section of Main Roads' website at *www.mainroads.qld.gov.au.*

department's response to external drivers and inputs and contributions to the Queensland Government's priorities. Both the RCQ and TCP are supported and informed by Integrated Regional Transport Plans which provide a blueprint for how the transport system will be developed regionally, through an integrated method.

RCQ is the first of its kind in Australia and guides all strategic and business planning in Main Roads. It incorporates four outcomes to connect social, economic and environmental policy within an infrastructure context, and contribute to broader whole-of-government outcomes and priorities:

- safer roads
- efficient and effective transport
- fair access and amenity
- environmental management

RCQ emphasises the need for integrated planning to achieve balanced decisions that will result in better outcomes, and where relevant outlines a shift from a single agency output to multi-agency outcome planning. RCQ is the road perspective within the broader integrated planning framework, as shown in Figure 4. Importantly, the policy framework prescribes that engaging stakeholders is an essential part of business from strategic planning to policy development, road system and corridor planning, business planning and program development, delivery of works, and monitoring and review.

The outcome areas in RCQ are incorporated into the department's annual strategic plan (see Figure 5) and in the department's business planning process and Roads Implementation Program (the department's rolling program of works). The Strategic Plan provides strategies to guide investment and operations over a five-year period to deliver the goals of the long-term planning horizon of the RCQ and TCP.

Figure 5: Main Roads' Strategic Plan 2007-2012

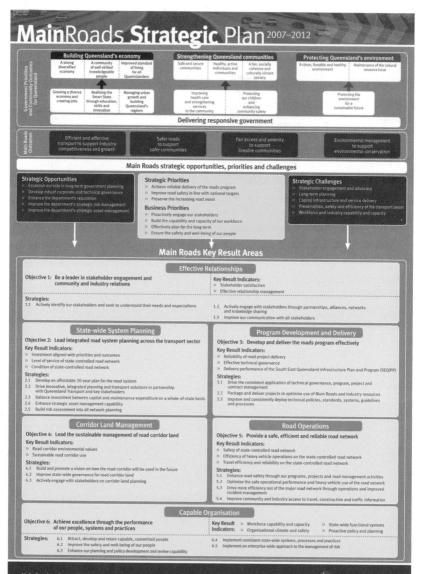

Community engagement in Main Roads

Following the release of RCQ, a targeted state-wide evaluation was undertaken, involving senior management, middle management and staff with experience in community engagement. Stakeholder feedback from past community consultation was also reviewed, including the learnings from case studies of specific projects. This led to the development of a community engagement policy, standards and guidelines, resource guide, planner and toolkit[133]. These apply equally to staff undertaking community engagement as well as contractors and consultants acting on behalf of  the department. A new community engagement training program was launched to continue to build capability in this area, using a mix of theory, case studies, facilitation and relationship skills.

---

[133]   A copy of the resources is available on the Doing Business with Us section of the Main Roads' website at *www.mainroads.qld.gov.au*

Figure 6: Community engagement planning in Main Roads

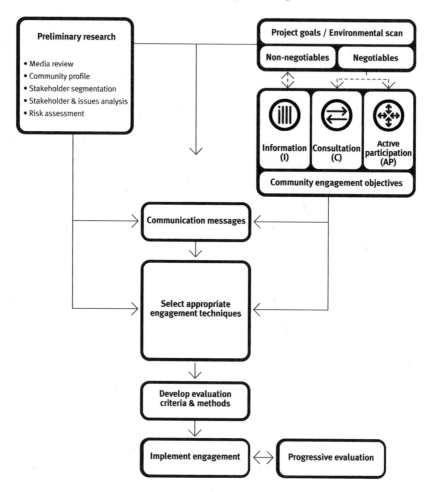

The department's approach is to have a fit-for-purpose community engagement planning that considers when, how and the extent of engagement and on what issues, by looking at the negotiables and non-negotiables (see Figure 6):

- Negotiables are choices and options and outcomes that can be changed to reflect community input – for example, possible route options for future corridors, possible locations of interchanges, some visual and noise mitigation measures, and integration of state and local government transport issues.
- Non-negotiables are usually those things that reflect conscious policy decisions of government already set and which cannot be changed or negotiated by the department – for example, decisions that have already been made such as a pre-determined transport corridor linking community a to community b, technical standards to which the department has to adhere (especially for safety, cultural heritage and environmental issues), time and resources available, the available skill levels to implement, and the opportunities available for community input.

This approach assists in alleviating controversy resulting from poorly managed community engagement processes that result in a difficult climate for future road infrastructure projects. It is also important for meeting the increasing expectations of well-educated and politically-savvy communities demanding increased influence in decisions relating to infrastructure development.

Matching the level of community engagement to the issue

The type of interactions or engagement possible depends on a number of factors, including:
- the issue
- the decision to be made
- available resources
- the communities and citizens affected or involved
- any sensitivities (political, community)
- available time

The extent of information, consultation or active participation undertaken depends on what is negotiable and the levels of sensitivity. When the negotiable aspects of a project increase, so do the possibilities for consultation and active participation (see Figure 7). The higher the sensitivity and impact, the more the department considers active participation, particularly if there are many negotiable aspects in a project.

Support for community engagement

Main Roads is unique in Australia in having 15 mandatory standards with supporting guidelines to ensure the principles of good governance are incorporated in engagement practice The department's policy statement gives a clear message about what the public can expect from Main Roads (see Box 1).

Figure 7: Negotiables and Impacts

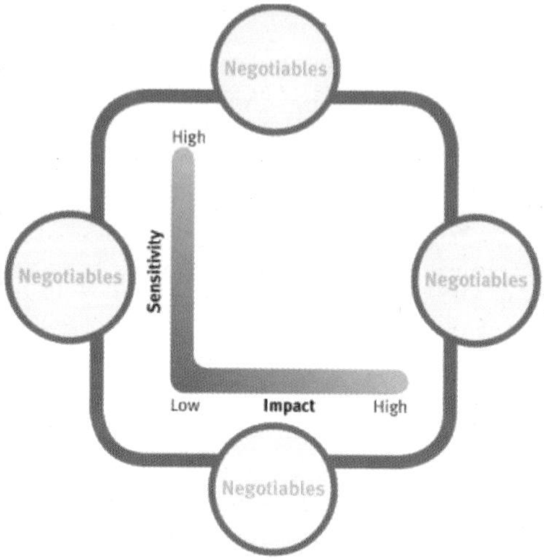

Box 1: Community Engagement Policy Statement

The Department of Main Roads is committed to effective and appropriate community engagement, recognising that is essential to improve decisions and listen and respond to community needs. Main Roads will be valued for the way it works with communities, industry and across government, to deliver outcomes.

Main Roads' commitment builds on legislative requirements, its strong public consultation experience and on-the-ground relationships, includes authority for local managers to make decisions about when and how to use Information, Consultation and Active Participation - the three levels of community engagement – to connect and stay connected with communities. Community engagement will vary in intensity and complexity as appropriate for the issue or task being addressed in each phase of business under the Road System Manager. Responsibility for any final decision is with the department and Minister.

The standards cover three broad areas which are incorporated into evaluation of community engagement objectives and outcomes (see Box 2).

* community values;
* a commitment to better organisational practice; and
* a commitment to continued learning through evaluation and improvement.

Box 2: Main Roads Community Engagement Standards
Community values

Standard One – An appropriate engagement process will be undertaken for each phase of business to identify and respond to community needs and values.
Standard Two – Engagement with a range of stakeholders is to occur early in decision making to identify their range of interests and issues.
Standard Three – The decision-making process must be open, accountable and transparent.
Standard Four – Stakeholders must be given sufficient time to participate in the engagement process in accordance with social justice principles regarding individual rights, equity, participation and access.
Standard Five – Engagement processes will give communities and individuals the opportunity to participate by helping facilitate people's ability to contribute to the process.
Standard Six – Information on the engagement activity will be easily and freely available and understandable so that people can be fully informed.
Standard Seven – Feedback will be sought on the engagement process, outcomes and decisions, to acknowledge participation and encourage continuing involvement.
Standard Eight – All stages of the engagement process, including the final decision, must show respect for the needs, views and concerns of stakeholders.
A commitment to better organisational practice
Standard Nine – Stakeholder databases will be continually reviewed and updated.
Standard Ten – Stakeholder privacy and confidentiality must be respected before, during and after engagement has taken place.
Standard Eleven – A written engagement plan must be developed for all engagement activities and be approved at the appropriate level before the activity commences.
Standard Twelve – Staff with decision-making responsibilities will be identified at the outset of the engagement activity and be available to participate in those activities to add credibility to, and understanding of, the process and to build and sustain relationships.
Standard Thirteen – The roles and responsibilities of stakeholders must be clearly defined, discussed and agreed to at the outset of engagement.

A COMMITMENT TO CONTINUED LEARNING THROUGH EVALUATION AND IMPROVEMENT

Standard Fourteen – Community engagement activities will be evaluated with input from stakeholders.
Standard Fifteen – Adequate training is to be provided for departmental staff involved in community engagement.

While the department embraces the OECD community engagement continuum of information, consultation and active participation, the planning, delivering and operation of roads means that community engagement is not a linear process, but is a 'cradle to grave' process. This means that connecting and staying connected with communities and citizens starts at the visioning stage some 15–20 years into the future when there are more negotiables in decision making, to on-the-ground delivery of road projects in communities when there are less negotiables. The intent of the policy is that community engagement is not an end in itself, but a way of doing business to get the best possible outcome for Queenslanders by revalidating, over time, community issues and responses.

The Road System Manager framework

Choosing priority projects in an environment where community expectations often exceed available dollars, presents an ongoing challenge. With a 'cradle to grave' approach to business, Main Roads has developed a consistent state-wide understanding of how the department conducts its business with communities over time within a Road System Manager framework (RSM) (see Figure 8). The RSM demonstrates the process used to make program choices.

Within the RSM, community engagement is a cyclical, linked process that takes place at the outset of departmental decisions and continues over time to ensure that the stewardship of the road system is integrated with the overall transport, land-use, social and environment systems and that ongoing and changing stakeholders' needs are responded to.

Phase 1 - outcomes and direction – this involves the choices and direction the department takes in terms of outcomes. It is informed by the external drivers, including legislation, whole-of-government priorities and outcomes, transport outcomes, stakeholder needs, land use and integrated transport planning and funding.

Phase 2 - road-system planning and stewardship (15+ years) - takes the policy directions, strategic choices and priorities from Phase 1 to guide plans of action for improving the state-wide road network. Visionary targets and implementation strategies are set for a 15-20 year period, for scenarios of funding and a total system view of the road network, including wider transport and land-use issues. Previous engagement in Phase 1 links to engaging stakeholders in the second phase to help understand the road needs into the future to guide our investments and planning.

Phase 3 - corridor planning and stewardship (<15 years) - involves forward plans and road investment strategies at the corridor level consistent with the state-wide view in the previous phase. Community engagement is undertaken to ensure corridor planning resolves alignment and future land requirements for routes and assesses wider impacts on stakeholders.

Phase 4 - program development (7 years) - involves prioritising a list of investment candidates across and within the categories that make up maintenance, operations and enhancement of the network. Long-term planning undertaken in earlier phases is integrated at this stage, along with relevant external and internal considerations. As the work program takes into account a total needs analysis, engagement is essential to identify priorities necessary for inclusion in the Roads Implementation Program, a plan for road-related infrastructure as required under the Transport Infrastructure Act 1994.

Phase 5 - program delivery - involves the efficient and effective delivery of the Roads Implementation Program to ensure that infrastructure projects and operations meet the standards identified in earlier phases. Engagement is undertaken to confirm and relay decisions in previous phases, and to understand and respond to impacts of roads on communities, including design, construction and maintenance.

In *Phase 6* - program finalisation - involves a review of project and activity performance against targets in the Roads Implementation Program and other departmental policies and directions. This phase is informed by stakeholder evaluation to ensure concerns have been identified and addressed.

Phase 7 - review – measures the actual outcomes against desired outcomes identified in Phase 1. This phase is informed by market research targeted at stakeholders to gauge their needs on an ongoing basis. Performance is also informed by stakeholder evaluation of community engagement processes and outcomes.

Embedding community engagement and building capability

Main Roads has invested significantly in project management to achieve results through managing opportunities and risks and making the best use of resources. This is to ensure that the outputs from each project will deliver outcomes that are consistent with government policy and departmental strategic objectives. Community engagement is embedded in project management methodology, recognising that it will ensure projects are delivered on time and in scope and contribute to stakeholder confidence in the decisions made by the department.

Building capability continues to be a priority for Main Roads. As mentioned, the department's public consultation training program was revised with inputs from staff around the state, taking into consideration stakeholder feedback about the way the department does its business. The new program includes the government's direction in community engagement as well as in RCQ to help build skills and capability. It is delivered as an introduction to community engagement, a refresher course for past participants, or just-in-time training for new staff with real-time projects used as case studies in the phases of the RSM. These assist staff working in the field in developing a community engagement strategy tailored to their specific needs. To date, over 400 staff have completed the course.

Importantly, the department understands that working with communities requires complex processes that do not readily translate into discrete competencies that fit easily into a standard training format (Guthrie, 2003). It is recognised that people need to be systems thinkers and strategic managers; they need to be able to understand and respond to community dynamics. As such, community engagement training is enhanced by on-the-ground experience on real time projects. Meta level skills that may be needed in engagement include understanding community dynamics, how communities learn, how to match managerial style to engagement strategy, how to assess when there has been 'enough' engagement and how to integrate conceptually distinct community and technical inputs.

Figure 9 demonstrates how Main Roads has framed community engagement practice.

Building and sustaining strategic stakeholder relationships

With multiple strategic stakeholders, many with vested interests in the department's service and who can potentially impact or influence business operations, the department is taking a more proactive approach to strategic stakeholder relations and management. The approach involves Key Account Managers. The senior management group will have responsibility for building and maintaining relationships with stakeholders relevant to individual manager's area of business delivery. It is expected that this approach will ensure that Main Roads is more responsive to strategic stakeholder needs/views, that stakeholder views are understood and reflected in the planning and delivery of the road system and the department's reputation and performance are enhanced.

Figure 8: Road System Manager Framework

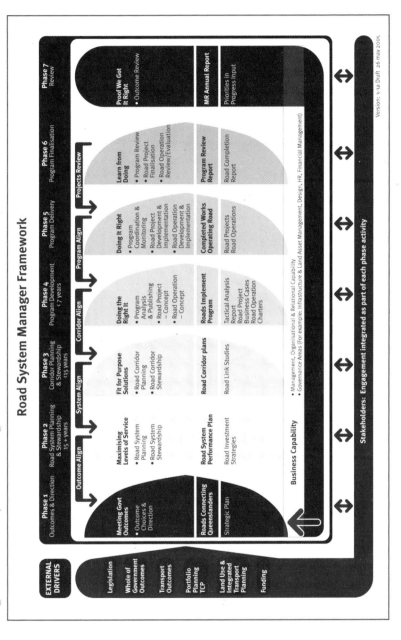

Figure 9: Community Engagement Practice in Main Roads

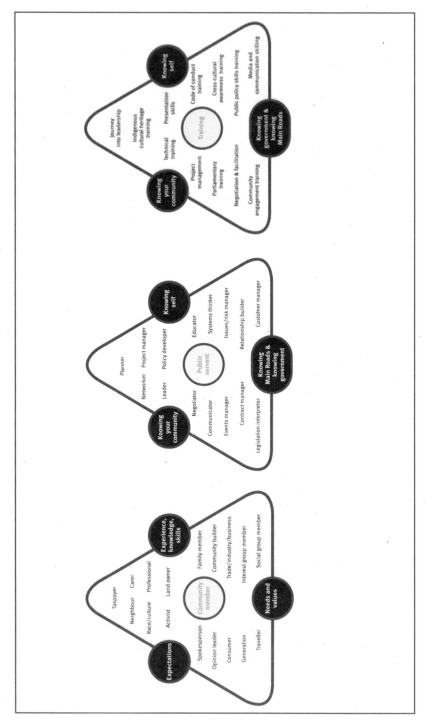

EVALUATING CITIZEN PARTICIPATION IN MAIN ROADS' DECISIONS

As an infrastructure builder and manager, Main Roads faces considerable support as well as some opposition for its work. Even with the best systems and processes in place, there are times when communities and citizens express dissatisfaction with their participation in department decision making and the solutions reached. With the best of intent, 'win-wins' are not always possible. As Irvin and Stansbury (2004) contend, dissent is not rare. They provide strategies that lead to meaningful outcomes, arguing that these are locale dependent. Strategies include careful selection of representative groups of stakeholders, transparent decision making, clear authority in decision making, competent and unbiased facilitators, regular meetings, and adequate financial support to the group process (Irvin and Stansbury, 2004:61).

The Key Account Manager approach to strategic stakeholder management is an important step to mitigate the impacts of the department's business and address stakeholder concerns, by building and maintaining long-term stakeholder relationships.

Evaluation is also an integral element of community engagement practice to learn and share experiences and improve stakeholder satisfaction with the department and its activities. Evaluation is undertaken at two levels:

- State-wide annual market research – undertaken by an independent social research organisation to glean stakeholder perceptions of the department and satisfaction with their involvement in community engagement activities.
- Project-based evaluation:
  - Formative evaluation. This is about what we do better and is used for incremental, continuous improvement as part of total quality management and to achieve better organisational practice from what was learned.
  - Summative evaluation. This is about how successful the engagement process was and is used for accountability and performance evaluation, evaluation against the department's 15 standards, and evaluation against community engagement objectives.

In the evaluation process differentiation is made between satisfaction with the process of community engagement versus the outcomes achieved. Table 1 gives an example of some methods and approaches used.

Table 1: Methods and approaches used

	Criteria (What is needed to be known)	Measure (Quantitative or qualitative)	Method
Information	Level of awareness of project	% of stakeholders who are aware of the project	Random telephone survey
	Whether stakeholders found the information kit adequate	Level of satisfaction with type and amount of information provided	Response form included in information kit and random telephone survey
Consultation	How satisfied were stakeholders with the opportunities to provide comment	Level of satisfaction with mix of consultation methods	Response form from information kit and random telephone survey
	Extent to which stakeholders were consulted	Number of stakeholders who provided feedback	Record number of stakeholders participating or responding to methods
Active Participation	Extent to which local government representatives felt network outcomes were collaborative	Perceived level of collaboration in decision making	Local government forum feedback forms and verbal feedback from councilors, mayors
	Extent to which participation lead to effective outcomes	Level of satisfaction with how outcomes were derived	Focus group meeting

The Roads Alliance: An Example of an INTERGOVERNMENTAL Partnership for Road System Management

The Roads Alliance is a joint initiative between Main Roads and the Local Government Association of Queensland (LGAQ). It is an example of two government 'communities' (state and local) working collaboratively in a coordinated approach to manage Queensland's roads. The Alliance is about more than working together to build and maintain roads. It is a new way of thinking about governance, including but not limited to roads, and represents a commitment by Main Roads and 124 local governments in Queensland to get better value out of all available roads' dollars through improved planning, better purchasing and resource sharing, and investment in and improvement of our capability.

The Roads Alliance is recognised nationally and internationally as a genuine shift in emphasis from a functional approach, based on ownership, to an outcomes approach. The Roads Alliance is about skilled people, using advanced technology and information to make better decisions to contribute to better community outcomes.

For the broader community, this results in improved consistency in road standards across Queensland. Through this partnership, Main Roads and local government jointly address issues of increased demands on roads' budgets and greater expectations from motorists, while continuing to provide a safe and reliable road network for the community.

How the Roads Alliance functions

Queensland's road managers know that collective action is needed to achieve systemic, state-wide improvement in planning, resource-use and capability if they are to deliver the outcomes required by their stakeholders. A consistent state-wide improvement is not possible if parties act individu-

ally, regardless of their individual excellence, but instead requires effective collaboration by all parties. Accordingly, the Roads Alliance builds on the existing relationships between local and state governments.

Significant features of the Alliance include that it:

- builds on the strengths of an existing relationship between Main Roads and local government;
- has voluntary membership (124 out of 125 Queensland local governments are members);
- is based on 17 "political" groups of council representatives, Regional Road Groups (RRGs), deciding road priorities and funding priorities at a regional level, with each group supported by a Technical Committee which makes recommendations;
- shifts emphasis from a "road ownership" approach to a network-function approach to achieve best network outcomes through improved planning, better purchasing and resource sharing and investing to improve delivery capacity, all of which serve to make the best use of available dollars;
- provides a vehicle for setting 20-year road investment strategies that span state and local election cycles;
- takes a joint management approach to network planning of road works to ensure sustainable employment in rural and remote areas;
- enables agreed visions when planning to meet communities diverse expectations across a regional road network servicing both high growth and low growth environments (population, economic);
- takes a flexible approach, recognising that 'no one size fits all';
- is guided by a state-wide framework for investment decision making and road management strategies; and
- goes well beyond normal collaborative approaches – control of priorities for state government expenditure is transferred to Regional Road Groups (currently around AUD$200 million) where Main Roads is only one voice/vote and with 8-10 mayors.

Roads Alliance critical issues and success factors

Since its inception, the Alliance has successfully addressed some critical issues, generating learnings that will help with future collaborations of this type (see Table 2).

Table 2: Roads Alliance Issues and Success Factors

Critical issues	Success factors (Learnings)
The need to establish and embed a strong Alliance culture and working relationship to enable participants to continue to collaborate and work in parallel on a range of issues and challenges	High-level up-front commitment from partners' leaders to agree a governance structure, a clear Alliance vision outlined in a *Memorandum of Agreement* and a set of guiding principles to which members can subscribe (*Diverse partners will more readily commit to a tangible arrangement where the obligations and benefits are clearly articulated*) Linking the Alliance to the business strategies of the Main Roads and LGAQ stakeholders' business strategies (*Joint ventures will be better supported when they align and link to the strategies of participating partners*) Developing joint Alliance strategies as one entity across Main Roads and the LGAQ. (*Joint planning ensures that new knowledge is effectively shared across Main Roads, local government and others*) Fostering a professional relationship that clearly defines and sets future parameters. (*Clear professional relationships create trust and long-term commitment*)
The Alliance comprises 125 different partners, each with differing circumstances, individual strengths and weaknesses and facing a mix of challenges and opportunities. Establishment arrangements will need to effectively accommodate their diverse situations, while achieving consistent outcomes.	Willingness to design roll-out that accommodates diverse situations in achieving a common objective, rather than trying to force diverse stakeholders to "fit" into a single implementation timetable and approach. *Enabling a range of flexible approaches to achieve an outcome is more effective than preoccupation with a single, often-mandated approach to an outcome)* Understanding and responding to time factors in the relationship. (*An awareness of partners' time constraints enhances elements of the relationship, for example, communication and information sharing.*) This "relational approach" requires commitment to invest time and resources in establishing and embedding arrangements over a period of time. (*Managing partners as individuals requires an investment of time and resources but is more likely to achieve a strong and understanding relationship.*)

Critical issues	Success factors (Learnings)
Significant difference in individual partner's capacities and capabilities.	Establishing a framework of desired capabilities and working closely with and investing with each partner on an individual basis to achieve that capability outcome. *(Assistance, guidance and advice needs to target individual, rather than "generic", needs.)*
Because roads are owned by different governments, there is inconsistent knowledge of the condition and performance of all roads throughout the state – an obstacle to robust prioritisation of network-wide investment.	Agreed common road network asset management approach, systems, standards and capabilities, with associated systems development and training. *(Sponsors of change need to identify and make available practical tools to achieve that change if they want that change to be consistently achieved, particularly where individual partners may not have the resources to develop those tools on their own)*
Consistently achieving the best possible regional road infrastructure from Main Roads and the Local Governments' available funds.	Better joint-funding applications, joint purchasing and resource-sharing. Transparent group decision making and prioritisation of works throughout a region. Commitment of Main Roads and local government to a minimum level of funding to the Local Roads of Regional Significance (LRRS) network. *(Collective planning, open and integrated decision making and aggregation of resources significantly improve network investment outcomes)*
Partners coming from different positions may not consistently understand, see value in or commit to particular initiatives.	Piloting initiatives with appropriate support has helped to test implementation approaches, generating reference sites and credible champions among the stakeholders themselves. *(Examples of successful implementation can generate support and ownership of an initiative and provide a credible source of knowledge upon which other partners can draw. It is also advisable to test concepts through piloting them before wider implementation)*
Planning and asset management on a region-wide basis often encounters issues beyond the scope of individual participants to manage.	A willingness to tackle issues and challenges together – collaboratively. *(Two tiers of government can work very successfully as partners to build capacity and improve their collective and individual performance.)*

Roads Alliance outcomes and achievements

Notable outcomes to date include:

- that the Roads Alliance has gained national recognition as leading the way through extensive collaboration, capability building and engagement to develop an innovative model for smarter delivery and management of Queensland's road network;
- establishment of a robust mechanism that enables communities to build better cases for road funding;
- a safer, more effective and consistent road network for all road users across Queensland;
- a coordinated asset-management approach and uniform arrangements for collecting, analysing and reporting data on the state's road assets, supporting better investment decisions;
- increased efficiency in delivery through resource sharing and group purchasing, producing better value in planning, design, construction and maintenance;
- funding certainty and longer-term commitment through a rolling four-year works program;
- capacity building in Main Roads' districts and local government through knowledge sharing and experience;
- strengthening of the local government role in regional decision making and economic development;
- identification and reduction of capability and capacity duplications and gaps; and
- improved skill-base and capability contributing to the sustainability of rural and regional communities.

Application of the Roads Alliance model

Although focused specifically on roads, the Alliance approach may suit other planning and service delivery situations. Opportunities exist in the areas of transport planning, water, sewage and waste infrastructure planning, financial and contract management, technical support and advice, environmental management, disaster management and so on. The model also has potential for replication across many areas of public policy.

Other INTERGOVERNMENTAL, Cross-agency Initiatives

There are many other examples of cross-agency, intergovernmental initiatives of community engagement and capacity building in which Main Roads has a role. These include:

- Community engagement index - trial of a whole-of-government community engagement activities in south-east Queensland. The trial involves identifying opportunities for joined-up, collaborative

community engagement. Current and future community engagement is input to a database to give an index that all departments can
access to plan and coordinate engagement. The aim is to minimise
uncoordinated agency consultation in communities and, in turn,
reduce over consultation and consultation fatigue'[134] experienced in
some communities.

- Integrated Regional Transport Plans (IRTPs) — the department is
actively involved in the development of IRTPs which are plans to
help meet emerging transport needs for a given region. An example
is the Capricornia IRTP which was developed by Main Roads and
Queensland Transport in partnership with Livingstone, Mount
Morgan and Rockhampton City Councils to address population
growth, employment and industry in the Capricornia region[135].

- Community Renewal Program — Community Renewal is a
Queensland Government initiative, delivered in partnership between
the state and local governments, business, residents and the community sector to deliver projects that improve people's lives in selected
Queensland communities[136]. The program includes community
centres and youth arts projects, to traineeships and family support
services, bringing communities and governments together to find
new solutions to local needs. Main Roads works with its portfolio
partner Queensland Transport on access and mobility issues in these
socio-economically and locationally disadvantaged communities.

- Engaging Indigenous Queenslanders — Indigenous Queenslanders
are some of the state's most socio-economically disadvantaged people.
Working with Indigenous Queenslanders is a high priority for the
department. The approach taken is to go beyond the identification
of Indigenous communities' priorities, to resolving their issues while
simultaneously building community capacity and skills. Indigenous
reconciliation and capacity building play a significant part in the way
Main Roads manages the road system. Main Roads has an obligation
to manage the impact of roadworks, work closely with Indigenous
people and, in doing so, help alleviate disadvantaged communities
and protect the cultural heritage of Australia's oldest culture. The
department does this within the context of whole-of-government
priorities, programs and policies. This includes nationally with
COAG and the Australian Transport Council, along with other state

---

[134] Consultation fatigue is where people feel over consulted. This can place an
unfair burden on citizens and communities and diminish the likelihood of good
participation.
[135] For more information about the Capricornia IRTP go to *http://www.transport.
qld.gov.au/qt/tpSite.nsf/index/capirtp.*
[136] For more information about the Community Renewal Program go to *http://
www.housing.qld.gov.au/initiatives/cr/index.htm.*

departments and local government. The department has developed nationally-recognised Cultural Heritage Guidelines and Procedures that demonstrate commitment to embracing and building sustainable relationships with Indigenous Queenslanders. In addition to this, the department has actively embraced capability development for Indigenous people so they can gain employment and improve their quality of life:

- The department established a Remote Communities Services Unit to provide training and mentoring to Indigenous people across Cape York Peninsula and the Torres Strait[137]. On offer is an accredited training program that helps local Indigenous councils increase their capacity to undertake infrastructure maintenance in their community.

- The department established an annual Education to Employment Scheme in 1999 to provide practical work experience, financial and employment assistance to at-risk young Indigenous Queenslanders, generating self-sufficiency and greater self-confidence. The scheme has grown to include 17 departments across government. In 2007, 97 students were awarded grants bringing the total to 258 students currently involved in the scheme. Main Roads currently sponsors 40 students.

RESEARCH AND DEVELOPMENT

Interagency partnerships and collaboration with other levels of government are not without their problems. More needs to be done, especially in such a large and regionally diverse state, with multiple systems, processes and views of dealing with regional issues. There is a growing interest in governance mechanisms for regional areas stemming from perceptions that the current system could be improved, and from recognition that a variety of different approaches to regional governance are being trialed in Queensland. For example, there are efforts to involve communities in planning approaches, to devolve some governance to regional or local bodies, or to consult and collaborate at a range of levels with communities in the provision of services. These initiatives occur across different departments and groups, and across a spectrum of government services and roles, so that the matrix of different activities is complex.

---

[137]   The Remote Communities Services Unit has offices and training facilities in both Cairns and Thursday Island. The training aims to increase the skill level of council employees. Main Roads encourages participation in this program by offering culturally and technically appropriate competency based training. By participating in this training program councils will increase their capacity to undertake infrastructure maintenance in their own community.

At the same time the Roads Alliance was established, the department began work with a group of other state government agencies and the LGAQ on the Engaged Government Project[138]. The project involves two stages:

- A scoping study investigating barriers and enablers to joined-up decision making. The findings showed strong similarities to elsewhere, nationally and internationally, including:
    - Barriers at the regional level relate to fragmentation of purpose amongst departments, lack of integration in structures and systems and poor capability for working in new ways. Specific examples of barriers include 'silo-based' objectives and budgets and associated judgments about what is not 'core' business, bureaucratic accountabilities, and risk aversiveness (Guthrie, 2002).
    - Enablers, the opposite of the barriers, relate to the adoption of a common purpose, aligning structures/systems with regional needs and priorities. Developing capability for innovation within the public service leadership and culture and amongst the sectors in the regional system is also important. Specific themes include the need for Ministerial support for collaborative agendas in Queensland's regions, a strengthening of the articulation between government priorities and outcomes, departmental programs and budgets, and a budgetary system that supports shared regional objectives and planning processes (Guthrie, 2002).
- A three-year (2004/05-2006/07) Australian Research Council (ARC) linkage study "Engaged Government: A Study of Government-Community Engagement for Regional Outcomes", exploring sociological, public policy and economic dimensions of collaboration. The United Nations is the peer reviewer for the project which focuses on addressing the barriers and enablers, outlining recommendations necessary for an engaged government focused on regional outcomes. The project team has worked closely with the Central Queensland

---

[138]   For more information about the Engaged Government Project go to *www. griffith.edu.au/projecteg.*

Regional Managers' Coordination Network as a regional decision-making mechanism[139].

The research findings are relevant to governments world-wide and include a number of paradoxes that give conceptual form to the barriers and enablers to engaged government. Some paradoxes are related and may be viewed as conceptually linked:

- The paradox of competing expectations and demands: the role of public service managers is to meet the competing and often contradictory expectations and demands created by:
  - o hierarchical systems of organisation and governance within their departments
  - o a public service culture that is economically rational, departmentally (core business) focused, risk-averse and politically sensitive
  - o expectations of community, industry and politicians that departments from all tiers of government will work collaboratively with each other and engage with community, industry and politicians to meet identified needs and expectations
  - o a rhetoric of whole-of-government policy statements that lack legislative authority.
- The paradox of whole-of-state regional planning and service provision: public service managers should plan and provide services from a whole-of-state perspective while also ensuring that competing regional needs and expectations are met.
- The paradox of regional and local planning and services provision: public service managers must plan and provide services regionally while also ensuring that competing sub-regional and local issues are addressed.
- The paradox of silo/place and issue: public service managers must provide services at regional, sub-regional and local scales while also ensuring they meet competing demands of a departmentally organised, silo-based, centralist system of government.

---

[139]   Regional Managers' Coordination Networks (RMCNs) were set up by the Queensland Government with a mandate to play a stronger role in delivering on government priorities. The RMCN is a key coordinating committee which brings together state government managers from a range of portfolio areas to assist agencies in achieving economic, social and environmental benefits for Queensland regions by coordinating priority cross-agency initiatives. The RMCN aligns services with government priorities and community needs by supporting collaboration across government agencies and with local government, businesses and communities. The RMCNs are part of a three-tiered approach to improving outcomes in regional areas. The networks have a strong involvement in Ministerial Regional Community Forums as well as links to the new Regional Queensland Council, a Ministerial advisory committee made up of 10 members of parliament from regional areas across Queensland.

- The paradox of ideological/instrumental motivation: The engaged government approach is underpinned by an ideology of the public sector working collaboratively to provide improved service to citizens. However, the decisions and actions of public service managers can at times be driven primarily by the core business interests of a department.
- The paradox of participative/associative democracy - representative democracy: the ideals of participatory and associative democracy can sit uncomfortably within governance systems based on the ideals of representative democracy (Oliver, 2005).

The researchers found examples of rejecting the paradox or recognition and legitimisation of only one side of the statement, working to solve or use that portion of the paradox at the expense of the other. Within this environment, it is the role of elected government and its agents to balance and manage the tension caused by the competing demands of its citizenry.

Outputs from the research which will be discussed in the workshop at this forum include:

- an ideal collaboration model: a tool to help stakeholders with a common issue to think about and discuss the process of working together;
- Issue, Context and Stakeholder (ICASA) System: a tool to assess whether or not stakeholders should collaborate to address a common issue and, if so, how they may best work together;
- Collaboration, Monitoring and Evaluation Framework (CMEF): a tool to help those involved in an existing or planned collaborative activity to review and evaluate the effectiveness of their efforts;
- three PhD dissertations: based on sociological, economic and public policy dimensions of engaged government and governance; and
- four discussion papers on aspects of the research: focusing on regional budgeting, institutional structures for engaged governance, agency culture and engaged governance, and human resource management policy and engaged government.

Conclusion

The department's vision "Main Roads — Connecting Queensland" outlines our promise to Queenslanders. With a record road budget in excess of AUD$11 billion over the next five years, balancing the needs and expectations of an engaged citizenry with the volume of works planned and taking place must be carefully managed.

The public continually expects more from us and a say in what Main Roads does as an organisation. There will be times when agreement between all involved will not be possible, as the department grapples with meeting local, state and national priorities for roads.

Community engagement is therefore an ongoing priority and normal part of business for Main Roads as a road system manager, to ensure that diverse viewpoints and concerns are part of decision making. This commitment is embraced at the executive management level, recognising that leadership is essential to successful policy implementation.

The department has a long history of community engagement and connections with local communities. With the large road construction task ahead, this will remain a strong focus. In future, there will be more emphasis on opportunities for citizens and communities to be involved much earlier in decision making. This recognises that communities and citizens are a rich repository of knowledge and can actively contribute to state, regional and local transport futures. Early involvement will also thwart negative effects and give a real sense of ownership to issues and solutions.

The department will also continue to work across government structures, recognising that the delivery of improved economic, social, cultural and environmental outcomes require integrated and innovative responses. The findings from the Engaged Government Project will assist in this regard and will be disseminated widely for discussion across government, academia and in the public domain.

References

Australian Bureau of Statistics (2006a) Australian Demographic Statistics, September 2006
http://www.abs.gov.au/ausstats/abs@.nsf/0e5fa1cc95cd093c4a2568110007852b/6 949409dc8b8fb92ca256bc60001b3d1!OpenDocument <Accessed 9 March 2007>

Australian Bureau of Statistics (2006b) Australian Demographic Statistics, Catalogue 3101.0.

Department of Local Government, Planning, Recreation and Sport (2007) Queensland population update including regional population trends, Number 8, March 2007.

Guthrie, Dr. D.M. (2002) Engaged Government Summary Report, Government Community Engagement for Regional Outcomes, Paper prepared for Main Roads, Queensland Transport, the Department of Natural Resources and Mines and the Department of the Premier and Cabinet.

Guthrie, Dr. D.M. (2003) Building Public Sector Capacity for Community Engagement, Paper to Innovations in Governance and Public Administration for Poverty Reduction, United Nations Ad Hoc Expert Group Meeting, 13-14 February 2003.

Irvin, R.A. and Stansbury, J. (2004) Citizen Participation in Decision Making: Is it Worth the Effort? Public Administration Review, January/February 2004, Vol. 64, No. 1, pp. 55-66.

Khan, A. (2006) "Engaged Governance": A Pathway to Citizen Engagement for Social Justice, UNDESA.

Newton, P (2001) Human Settlement Theme Report
http://www.environment.gov.au/soe/2001/publications/theme-reports/settle-ments/settlements01.html <Accessed 26 March 2007>

OECD (2001) Engaging Citizens in Policy-making: Information, Consultation and Active Participation, PUMA Policy Brief No. 10, July 2001.

Oliver, Dr. P. (2005) Problems, Paradoxes, and the Way Forward, Paper arising from Research Team Meeting 11, October 2005.

Queensland Government (2003a) Queensland Public Service Charter
http://www.opsme.qld.gov.au/pubs/pub.htm <Accessed 3 January 2006>

Queensland Government (2003b) Realising the Vision: Governance for the Smart State, Office of Public Service Merit and Equity
http://www.opsme.qld.gov.au/pubs/realisingthevision.htm <Accessed 3 January 2006>

Queensland Government (2004a) Charter of Social and Fiscal Responsibility 2004
http://www.treasury.qld.gov.au/office/knowledge/docs/charter/index.shtml <Accessed 5 January 2006>

Queensland Government (2004b) Seamless Government: Improving Outcomes for Queenslanders, Now and in the Future
http://www.opsme.qld.gov.au/seamless/seamless_final.pdf <Accessed 4 January 2006>

Todman, L.C. (2004) Citizen Participation in the United States
http://www.consultmillennia.com/publications.html <Accessed 10 April 2007>

Role of Government Coordination in Civic Engagement: Experience of Queensland, Australia

Peter Oliver*

Introduction

Citizen trust in government is built on many factors. Among them is the ability of government to work effectively and efficiently to deliver the services and programs they desire. In representative democracies, citizens elect representatives to government to make decisions on their behalf. These governments may occur at several spatial scales – local, regional, state and national - with all spheres of government supported by a civil service to act as their agent and do their bidding. Government agencies able to work together seamlessly in their dealings with citizens are more likely to be trusted by citizens than those that cannot or will not work collaboratively when engaging with citizens, or delivering services.

This paper focuses on the idea of government agencies 'joining up' or engaging with each other to interact with citizens and deliver services. It describes three tools developed as part of a three-year research project on engaged or joined-up government. These are designed to assist civil servants in recognising when working together will most likely deliver better outcomes, and how to go about undertaking and evaluating such collaborations. The case study research, empirical evidence and literature on which the discussion presented below is based, show that successful engaged government depends on several factors. These include:

- the development and maintenance of social processes that incorporate how participants work together;
- their response to unchosen change;
- how and where decisions are made and informed by the best available knowledge and changes that occur as a result of this process, especially in terms of changing power dynamics; and
- the way resources are distributed within collaborative relationships over various spatial and temporal scales.

This paper is structured in three parts.

The first part discusses several concepts that are germane to the focus of the Engaged Government Project – namely the discourse of New Public

* Peter Oliver is a Senior Lecturer (Education and Training) at the International WaterCenter, p.oliver@watercenter.

Management, trust and the notion of agencies 'joining up' or collaborating to engage with citizens or deliver services.

The second part introduces the reader to the location and government institutional structures and governance arrangements of Queensland, Australia, the setting for the five case studies that comprised the Engaged Government Project. It also gives an overview of the project.

The third part summarises the outputs from the project, emphasising three of these:

- an Ideal Collaboration Model which provides a normative description of an inter-agency collaboration, differentiating between a non-collaborative and a collaborative 'space' and indicating agencies need to make a conscious decision about when to enter the 'collaborative space';

- an Issue, Context and Stakeholder Analysis System to support decisions about whether to collaborate, with whom, on what issue and the level of process discipline and care that may be required; and

- a Collaboration Monitoring and Evaluation Framework to guide the iterative and adaptive process of collaboration and provide methods to allow participants to reflect upon and evaluate their progress in an evidence-based, participatory manner.

These tools highlight that successful government inter-agency collaboration is as much about how participants understand their relationships with each other and how they are prepared to develop, invest in and take risks in these relationships, as it is about focusing on the effective and efficient achievement of goals and accountability – the concepts underpinning New Public Management.

New Public Management (NPM)

Over the last thirty years several important changes have occurred in public administration, especially in the way politicians, civil servants and citizens have related with each other. The concept of New Public Management (NPM) involves an increasing emphasis on efficiency, effectiveness, performance management and accountability, including the use of private sector solutions such as marketing and managerialism as remedies to public sector problems (Hood, 1991). The paradigm shift to NPM that occurred throughout governments of the developed world in the 1980s saw the public re-framed as consumers rather than citizens were allowed to complain about government services, but without the ability to play a part in determining them (Corrigan and Joyce, 1997; and Dixon, Kouzmin and Korac-Kakabadse, 1998).

However, many challenges facing governments today, for example, climate change, environmental, social and economic sustainability and addressing chronic poverty and health issues, are ones of emergent complexity. They have many dimensions. It is often difficult to establish causality between the parts that comprise them, and to predict what will happen next and therefore develop and implement policy to address them, using the concept of NPM with agencies and spheres of government working as unitary actors. These agency actors also must consider how to engage each other and the trust necessary to do so. Solving these complex problems may also involve agencies re-construing the public as citizens with rights and roles to play in working with agencies to address problems, rather than as passive consumers who lack the interest and expertise to be trusted with such important matters. It may also be as much a matter of whether citizens trust government and the agencies that serve them, if they are to work together to address problems requiring their input.

Trust

Trust is an important element of social capital. It is a term used by social scientists to refer to social networks, and the "norms of reciprocity, and mutual assistance and trustworthiness" that exist within them (Putnam and Feldstein, 2003. p.2). Scott and Marshall (2005, pp. 671-672) rely on the work of Giddens (1990) to distinguish between two types of trust. The first is where a person relies on, or has confidence in the ability of another, as personalised trust. The second is where a person is prepared to rely on a system to serve their interests – institutionalised trust. The trust people may have in government as a system can depend on how well government serves their interests, as well as how well they know or trust individuals within the system of government. A report carried out by GlobeScan, commissioned for the World Economic Forum, highlights declining levels of trust in government, particularly of national governments and the United Nations over the last two years (World Economic Forum, 2005).

A decline in generalised or institutionalised trust in many countries, particularly trust in government and associated political processes, has been reported by several authors (Cox, 2002; Putnam, 2000; Wuthnow, 2002). The more recent GlobeScan survey work of 17 countries, 14 of which were developed countries, indicated a decline in trust in government that was attributable to four main factors. In order of importance these were:

- lack of accountability (31%)
- failure to deliver services (27%)
- perceived as being inefficient or corrupt (16%)
- restricting public access to information (15%)

Of the citizens surveyed, 11% were uncertain as to their reasons for mistrusting their government (World Economic Forum, 2005).[140]

---

[140]   Approximately 1000 citizens were surveyed in each country.

Engaged Government

While other factors may come into play, a lack of ability on the part of agencies and spheres of government to work together when necessary to interact with citizens and to deliver services and programs may lead to lines of accountability becoming unclear, failure to deliver services, and inefficiency – three of the important factors contributing to a lack of trust in governments identified above. Good engaged government may overcome these factors and help to build trust.

Engaged government is about coordination and collaboration and is central to the task of building trust in government. Coordination refers to "the orderly integration of activities, while collaboration or joined up working refers to the behaviour that achieves this coordination" (Guthrie, 2002, p.10). Government agency attempts to build trust through civic engagement that does not pay adequate attention to engagement within government, may encounter difficulties. This is an important focus of the Engaged Government Project. The following section describes the location and government institutional structures and governance arrangements of Queensland, Australia, the setting for the project's five case studies.

About Queensland and Australia

The Commonwealth of Australia is a democracy and constitutional monarchy. It was formed in 1901 when six British colonies joined together to form a new nation — a federal system of government with powers divided between the central government and the individual states and territories. State and territory governments form local governments to take responsibility for local services. These local governments, also known as local councils, have powers defined by the state or territory that established them (Australian Government, 2005). The Engaged Government Project has focused on state and local governments in regional areas of Central Queensland (see Map 1).

Queensland, the second largest state in Australia has a surface area of 173,704 km2 and is home to 4.05 million people (Office of Economic and Statistical Research (OESR), 2007). The 2001 Census revealed that around 52% of the Queensland population lived in major cities, with the remainder living in regional and remote areas (Australian Bureau of Statistics (ABS), 2004). Large areas, long distances and dispersed populations contribute to many of the challenges faced by government staff in interacting with and providing services and programs for Queensland citizens.

Map 1: Districts that Comprise the State's Regions

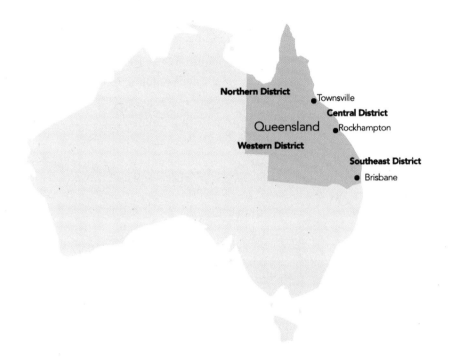

Engaged Government Project

The overall aim of the Engaged Government Project was to understand more about when, how and why government agencies should collaborate with each other and other spheres of government to work with community and industry to deliver services and programs. In essence, this research project was a collaboration about collaboration. The three-year study was set in Queensland, Australia, and was supported by three Queensland Government agencies, the Departments of Main Roads, Natural Resources and Water and Queensland Transport, as well as the Local Government Association of Queensland representing local government interests.

The government partners provided cash and in-kind support for the project. The Australian Research Council, the primary source of advice to the Australian Government on investment in the national research effort, also provided funding. Three universities were involved – Griffith University, The University of Queensland and Central Queensland University. The AUD$500,000 project involved a team of university investigators drawn from the disciplines of economic, public policy and sociology, along with three PhD researchers. The research team was ably supported by a group of Queensland Government regional managers from the Central Queensland Regional Managers' Coordination Network (CQRMCN), one of fifteen such coordination networks throughout Queensland (see Map 1).

Specifically, the Engaged Government Project sought to:

- **assess** the value of multi-sectoral collaboration to long-term positive regional and broader government outcomes;
- **determine** the enabling and accountability frameworks and mechanisms needed to encourage and manage multi-sectoral collaborative relationships;
- **decide** who or what makes best value collaborative partners and how much to invest in collaborative work vis-à-vis costs, benefits and outcomes; and
- **identify**, at an institutional level, what structural arrangements (regional coordinating mechanisms), managerial strategies (outcomes-based management) and participant capacities (negotiating, brokering) build the capacity for collaboration and, potentially, policy coherence. (Guthrie, 2003, p.1)

An action research approach (Kemmis and McTaggart, 1988) was used to address these objectives. Five case studies were chosen. These included: 1) local-state government collaborations to plan and provide transport infrastructure in three regional settings; 2) a whole-of-region Central Queensland planning initiative; 3) and a devolved grant scheme involving a regional natural resource management (NRM) non-government organisation in the provision of grants to farmers to carry out on-ground works on their properties.

While the 600 km distance between the Central Queensland case study setting and the research team base in Brisbane, the capital in the south-east of the state, made interaction with participants a challenge, every attempt was made to be as participatory as possible throughout the research process. The PhD researchers spent many weeks in the case study areas and the whole research team met with the CQRMCN for six full-day meetings over the project. The research team also held three full-day, annual learning seminars in Rockhampton, a major Central Queensland city of some 80,000 residents, over the life of the project. These were attended by 160 people in total, many of whom were public servants from various levels of government interested in how they could work better together to meet the needs of citizens in regional settings.

The project produced a range of academic outputs such as conference and journal papers and research reports, as well as three PhD theses which are in their final stages of completion.[141] A meta-study paper focusing on the nature of and barriers and enablers to collaboration between the agency and university partners involved in the project is finished (Leach, 2007). The meta-study uses the collaboration and monitoring evaluation framework developed in the project to evaluate the collaboration that occurred in the conduct of research project itself.

Of particular interest to government managers and staff, the project produced a folio of seven products designed to help improve the effectiveness of collaborations amongst agencies and spheres of government. The first three products are 'engagement tools' for inquiring into and finding solutions for improving cross-agency collaboration.

They are:

1. *An Ideal Collaboration Model (ICM)* – a tool to help stakeholders with a common issue to think about and discuss the process of working together;
2. *Issue, Context and Stakeholder Analysis (ICASA) System* – a tool to assess whether or not stakeholders should collaborate to address a common issue and, if so, how they may best work together;
3. *Collaboration Monitoring and Evaluation Framework (CMEF)* – a tool to help those involved in an existing or planned collaborative activity to review and evaluate the effectiveness of their efforts.

The products are discussed below.

The remaining four products are discussion papers focusing on central considerations for collaboration:

4. *Whose outcomes? A Proposal for Regional Budgeting* – information to assist stakeholders funding and resourcing collaborative activities to address a shared issue;
5. *Institutional Structures that Encourage Engaged Governance* – information to assist stakeholders find structural solutions for meeting cross-agency governance needs;
6. *Agency Culture and Engaged Government* – information to assist stakeholders recognise and work with the barriers and bridges that different organisational cultures present for engaged government; and
7. *Human Resource Management Policy and Engaged Government* - information on the Human Resource Management implications of Engaged Government. (Oliver, 2007, p.1)

The final section of this paper presents information on the first three tools mentioned above – the Ideal Collaboration Model, the Issue, Context

---

[141]   The project is due for completion in July 2007.

and Stakeholder Analysis System and the Collaboration Monitoring and Evaluation Framework. The relationship between the three products is shown in Figure 1.

Figure 1: Relationship between Engaged Governemnt Project Products 1, 2 and 3

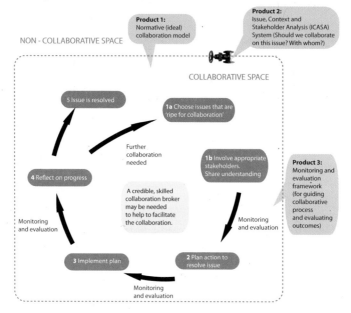

Ideal Collaboration Model

Figure 1 outlines the ideal or normative model for collaboration developed as part of the Product Folio. The project further developed this model from the work of Whelan and Oliver (2005). This Ideal Collaboration Model embodies products two and three (outlined above) and has the following key features.

First, it emphasises the notion of collaborative and non-collaborative 'space'. Project fieldwork showed the culture underpinning these two ways of working, or 'spaces' to be very different. The culture of the non-collaborative space was observed to be that typically found in government agencies – one of risk aversion and caution in decision making; valuing certainty and security; power imbalances in relationships; and hierarchical institutional structures. In contrast, the culture of the collaborative space is the antithesis of this, with field observations indicating participants who try to bring the culture of the non-collaborative space into the collaborative space have very limited success in working together.

Issue, Context and Stakeholder Analysis System

Second, the Ideal Collaboration Model shows a valve or a means by which issues and participants may move from the non-collaborative to the collaborative space. It emphasises that this should be a conscious decision on the part of all who may be involved, and should consider the need to embrace the different cultural values underpinning effective collaboration.

This valve is the Issue, Context and Stakeholder Analysis (ICASA) System - product two of the Product Folio. Again, based on the empirical work of the project researchers, the ICASA System emphasises some issues and situations which will not be amenable to a collaborative solution, while others will be. In essence, it gives agency managers and staff the basis of a business case proposition to their supervisor from which to argue why their agency should or should not collaborate, or should in fact take some other form of action. The steps involved in the ICASA System are shown in Figure 2.

Figure 2: Summary of steps involved in the ICASA System

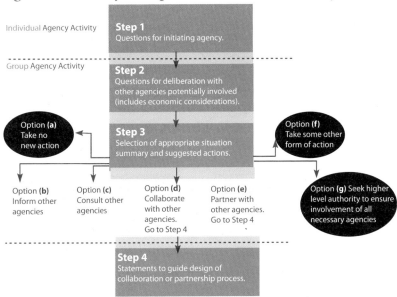

If the ICASA System indicates an issue may be amenable to a collaborative solution, it provides a checklist to guide the degree of process discipline that may be required to facilitate the issue to a successful conclusion, given the complexity of the issue itself; the number, nature and interests of the stakeholders involved; and the context within which the issue occurs.

Collaboration Monitoring and Evaluation Framework

Third, the Ideal Collaboration Model indicates the process of collaboration is iterative and adaptive and may require the services of a credible and skilled facilitator, depending on the complexity of the issue and context. It also shows the process to be driven by a Collaboration Monitoring and Evaluation Framework which guides the process and helps to monitor achievement of outcomes. Further developed from the work of Whelan and Oliver (2005), this is the third tool in the Product Folio.

The four-dimensional framework has two levels, one for collaborations and partnerships the ICASA System has indicated are relatively routine and a second, more detailed level for collaborations and partnerships the ICASA System has indicated are more complex and will require more careful facilitation and participant reflection. The four dimensions of the framework are shown in Figure 3.

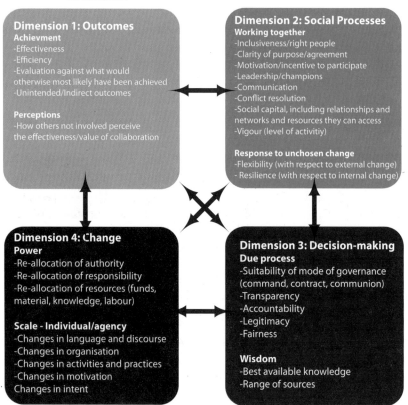

Figure 3: Expanded Monitoring and Evaluation Framework or Level 2

Dimension 1: Outcomes
Achievment
-Effectiveness
-Efficiency
-Evaluation against what would otherwise most likely have been achieved
-Unintended/Indirect outcomes

Perceptions
-How others not involved perceive the effectiveness/value of collaboration

Dimension 2: Social Processes
Working together
-Inclusiveness/right people
-Clarity of purpose/agreement
-Motivation/incentive to participate
-Leadership/champions
-Communication
-Conflict resolution
-Social capital, including relationships and networks and resources they can access
-Vigour (level of activitiy)

Response to unchosen change
-Flexibility (with respect to external change)
- Resilience (with respect to internal change)

Dimension 4: Change
Power
-Re-allocation of authority
-Re-allocation of responsibility
-Re-allocation of resources (funds, material, knowledge, labour)

Scale - Individual/agency
-Changes in language and discourse
-Changes in organisation
-Changes in activities and practices
-Changes in motivation
Changes in intent

Dimension 3: Decision-making
Due process
-Suitability of mode of governance (command, contract, communion)
-Transparency
-Accountability
-Legitimacy
-Fairness

Wisdom
-Best available knowledge
-Range of sources

Analysis of project case studies revealed those inter-agency engagements that considered the social processes listed in Dimension 2 of Figure Three, and the changes in power and scale indicated in Dimension 4, were more likely to achieve the outcomes of Dimension 1, as well as meeting accountability and other New Public Management-style requirements listed under Dimension 3 of the framework. The four dimensions may be viewed as inter-related with a collaboration or partnership being unlikely to achieve the outcomes it seeks, unless participants and those facilitating the process consider the other dimensions throughout the life of the process. The inter-related nature of these dimensions is highlighted in other literature on collaboration and partnership building (e.g. Dukes, Firehock, and Leahy, 2001; Linden, 2002; Oliver, 2004; Wondolleck and Yaffee, 2000).

The ICASA System and the Monitoring and Evaluation Framework each contain series of checklists and qualitative scales that allow participants systematically to gather evidence and reflect on their situation, so they may work in a participatory manner to continuously improve the way they work together to achieve the best outcomes possible.

Conclusion

As discussed in this paper, throughout most of the world, trust in governments and the agencies that serve them is declining. As stated earlier, government inefficiency and ineffectiveness rank highly as two key reasons for this mistrust (Globescan, 2005). Many of the problems challenging government in the 21st century are complex and fall across several agencies and spheres of government. It is unlikely that governments will successfully address these challenges through a more determined application of single-agency, silo-based applications of the ideas of New Public Management.

While the engaged government tools discussed here may need adaptation for use in specific situations, they are a sound first step towards developing 21st century 'technologies of government' to address these problems. They provide practical ways for agency managers and staff to decide if, when, where and how they will engage with each other, and how they will reflect on and continuously improve their practice in this area. The author and the remainder of the Engaged Government Project Research Team are keen to continue this work, by working with others in Australia to develop a community of practice in this area and to network this community of practice with others world-wide with similar interests. As Myles Horton and Paolo Freire, two of the great social change theorists and practitioners of the 20th century, remarked to each other when discussing how people may best work together to improve a shared concern or situation, "We make this road by walking" (Bell, Gaventa and Peters, 1990).

References

Australian Bureau of Statistics, 2004, Australian Bureau of Statistics – 1362.3 Regional Statistics 2004, accessed on 3 May 2007 from *http://www.abs.gov. au/AUSSTATS/abs@.nsf/productsbyCatalogue/9448A06F12B2AAA2CA2569 2E0007CA9E?OpenDocument*

Australian Government, 2005, Government in Australia, accessed on 2 May 2007 from *www.australia.gov.au/govt-in-aust*

Bell, B., Gaventa, J. and Peters, J. (Eds) 1990, We Make the Road by Walking: Conversations on Education and Social Change, Myles Horton and Paulo Freire, Temple University Press, Philadelphia.

Corrigan, P. and Joyce, P. 1997, "Reconstructing public management. A new responsibility for the public and a case study of local government", International Journal of Public Sector Management, Vol. 10, No. 6, pp. 417-432.

Cox, E. 2002, "Making the Lucky Country", in R. Putnam (Ed) Democracies in Flux: The Evolution of Social Capital in Contemporary Society, Oxford University Press, Oxford.

Dixon, J., Kouzmin, A. and Korac-Kakabadse, N. 1998, "Managerialism – something old, something borrowed, little new", International Journal of Public Sector Management, Vol. 11, No. 2/3, pp. 164-187.

Dukes, E.F., Firehock, K. and Leahy, M. 2001, Collaboration: A Guide for Environmental Advocates, University of Virginia, Virginia.

Giddens, A. 1990, The Consequences of Modernity, Stanford University Press, Stanford.

Guthrie, D. 2002, The Engaged Government Project: Government – Community Collaboration for Regional Outcomes – a Scoping Paper, prepared for Department of Natural Resources and Mines, Department of Main Roads, Queensland Transport and Department of the Premier and Cabinet, Brisbane, Queensland.

Guthrie, D. 2003, Australian Research Council Linkage Grant Application: Engaged Government: A study of government-community engagement for regional outcomes, Department of Politics and Public Policy ,Griffith University, Brisbane, Australia.

Hood, C. 1991, "A public management for all seasons?" Public Administration, Vol. 69, Spring, pp. 3-19.

Kemmis, S. and McTaggart, R. 1988, The Action Research Planner, Deakin University Press, Deakin University, Victoria, Australia.

Leach, G. 2007, 'A study about a study' - enablers and inhibitors to collaborative research about collaboration, Engaged Government Project, Queensland Department of Natural Resources and Water, Indooroopilly, Australia.

Linden, R.M. 2002, Working Across Boundaries: Making Collaboration Work in Government and Non-profit Organisations, Jossey-Bass, San Francisco.

Office of Economic and Statistical Research (OESR) 2007, Environment: statistics to do with the natural and built environment, accessed on 2 May 2007 from *www.oesr.qld.gov.au/queenslandbytheme/environment.*

Oliver, P. 2007, Engaged Government – In Search of Collaboration; Information Sheet One, Engaged Government Project, Department of Politics and Public Policy, Griffith University, Brisbane, Australia.

Oliver, P. 2004, Developing effective partnerships in natural resource management, Unpublished PhD Thesis, Griffith University, Brisbane, Australia.

Putnam, R. and Feldstein, L. 2003, Better Together: Restoring the American Community, Simon and Schuster Paperbacks, Sydney.

Scott, J. and Marshall, G. 2005, Oxford Dictionary of Sociology, Oxford University Press, Oxford.

Whelan, J. and Oliver, P. 2005, The place, limits and practice of collaboration: lessons from case studies of community participation in natural resource management, Cooperative Research Centre for Coastal Zone, Estuary and Waterway Management, Indooroopilly, Australia.

World Economic Forum, 2005, Trust in Governments, Corporations and Global Institutions Continues to Decline, a press release from the World Economic Forum accessed on 02 May 2007 at *www.weforum.org/en/media/Latest%20 Press%20Releases/PRESSRELEASE87.*

Wondolleck, J.M. and Yaffee, S.L. 2000, Making Collaboration Work: Lessons from Innovation in Natural Resource Management, Island Press, Washington DC.

Wuthnow, R. 2002, "Bridging the Privileged and the Marginalised?" in R. Putnam (Ed) Democracies in Flux: The Evolution of Social Capital in Contemporary Society, Oxford University Press, Oxford.

Local Government: A Pro-active Partner in Civic Engagement[142]

Greg Hoffman, Alan Morton and Desley Renton

Introduction

Since 1896 the Local Government Association of Queensland (LGAQ) has been representing and providing leadership to its member councils. This is done with the explicate intention of 'strengthening the ability and performance of Queensland Local Government to better serve the community'.

This Mission Statement sums up the LGAQ's purpose - to ensure Queensland Local Government operates within a 'good governance' framework in order to maximise the effectiveness and efficiency of the delivery of services, programs and initiatives undertaken by the state's 157 local government councils.

Irrespective of what aspect of work is undertaken by the Local Government - road construction, water desalination, rubbish removal, environmental protection, lifelong learning projects with senior citizens or delivering immunization programs to babies, ultimately, it's principal focus is local democracy and caring for people and their wellbeing.

Local Government undertakes these functions with the aim of making the State's towns and cities vibrant places to live, work and play. Maintaining and enhancing a quality lifestyle is the Local Government's core business. While the LGAQ's objective of service to community has remained the same since its creation 110 years ago, the way it goes about its business to achieve these outcomes has altered dramatically. Local Government, like other spheres of government, has to reshape itself in order to respond to change and to help shape a sustainable future.

The Local Government's mantra of the Roads, Rates and Rubbish, has expanded beyond its fore father's wildest imaginations. While still core functions, the 3 Rs (rates, roads and rubbish) as a symbol of Australian Local Government's 'purpose' is more representative of the past rather than the present or indeed the future. Today, Local Government has over 80 core functions and 400 career areas.

Local Government in Queensland employs nearly 37,000 people and spends $A5.5billion annually (2005/06). Across all Australian States and

Territories these figures are respectively, 165,100 employees and annual expenditure of $A18.265 billion.

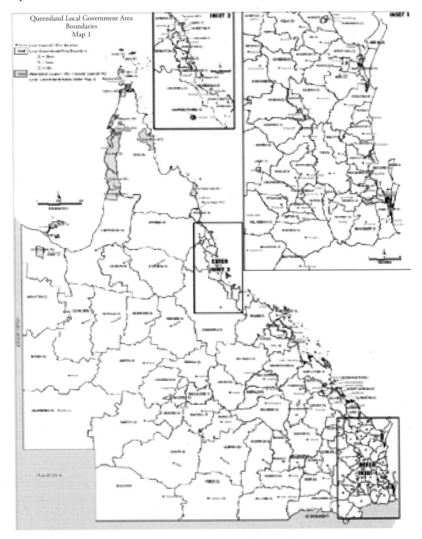

While the proportional de-emphasis on 'services to property' has affected some local governments more than others, there is unanimous agreement that this sphere of government is characterised above all else by diversity[143].

The call for a multidisciplinary approach has come from two main areas. It has come from citizens seeking transparent accountable government at all

---

[143]   Reshaping Australian Local Government: finance, governance and reform: UNSW Press. 2003.

levels which responds to local needs and aspirations. Local Government is more community-based than Australia's State or Federal Governments and is often the obvious choice for such activity. In addition to Local Government voluntarily incorporating a range of new functions and responsibilities, State Governments in Australia have 'devolved' considerable responsibility to Local Government from what has previously been regarded as State jurisdiction. The challenge is to ensure that these changes occur within a strategic policy framework based on mutual interest and responsibility and that they can be sustained and meet triple bottom line capability[144].

Councils are increasingly engaged in planning with the longer-term in mind. Councils are anticipating change - change in the way people live and work, change in the way they travel, change in demographic profiles and changes in cultural profile. Councils also want to influence the way things change and are increasingly examining the drivers of change. Councils are looking at what kind of future their communities are seeking – not just around the corner but in 30, 40 and 50 years time.

This role has required Local Government to look at its own future and role. This paper will explore how the LGAQ has reinvented itself in order to remain relevant and responsive in modern society and how it has applied civic engagement as the method by which to build trust in Local Government throughout the change process.

The paper will explore Local Government's civic engagement responsibilities and examine some of the partnerships LGAQ has brokered and developed, particularly with the State Government. This approach strongly reflects LGAQ's belief that all stakeholders are responsible for delivering on the complex issues facing communities and their future – and that one group or level of government cannot achieve success without the support and involvement of the people, and that there must be a commitment to working within collaborative decision making frameworks to 'make it count'.

Practicing what we preach

It is important to the Association that it models the change it wants to see. The following figure demonstrates LGAQ's commitment to engagement with its stakeholders as part of its annual policy and program development progress. Depending on the issue or decision to be made, LGAQ engages internal staff, member councils and other 'communities of interest' at an appropriate level on the engagement continuum to inform its strategic and operational planning.

Community members are regularly consulted for their opinion on a range of Local Government services and functions. Regional organisations of councils and professional bodies are involved in the broader strategic policy setting. Special purpose Reference Groups participate in the development

---

[144]   Triple bottom line refers to the economic, environment and social.

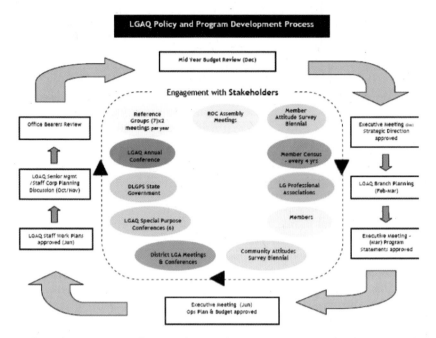

and implementation of LGAQ's agenda. Once a year at the Association's Annual Conference, members are empowered through an opportunity to vote on policy and advocacy agendas. This process keeps the LGAQ accountable and its decision making processes transparent.

Protocol Establishing the Roles and Responsibilities of the State Government and Local Government in the system of Local Government

The Protocol Establishing the Roles and Responsibilities of the State Government and Local Government in the system of Local Government represents a cooperative arrangement between the State Government and Local Government in Queensland (represented by the LGAQ)[145]. Unlike other Australian states, the LGAQ is the sole peak body representing Councils in Queensland. It is this unique position that brings universality of voice and opinion. LGAQ is not dictated by party and geographical politics that have divided Local Government elsewhere and can therefore speak with a clear and authoritative voice.

Currently in its third iteration (1997, 2003, 2006), the Protocol provides a framework for negotiation between the two spheres of government in order to 'enhance the wellbeing of communities'. It does this initially by acknowledging very clearly that the two spheres of government have a shared

---

[145]   Protocol Establishing the Roles and Responsibilities of the State Government and Local Government in the system of Local Government 2006.

jurisdiction and that each will effectively serve the people of Queensland if they operate in a spirit of mutual respect with an emphasis on partnership and cooperation. The Protocol also recognises the individual roles and strengths of each partner. Local Government plays a critical role in community governance as a democratic, accountable and efficient forum for local decision making. It also acknowledges the State Government's responsibility for establishing and providing coordination of state wide issues of strategic significance.

From a purely legal perspective, the Local Government is a creature of the State Government. However, the relationship shared and actively promoted is one of partnership. Each shares the same constituents, shares the same land area as Local Government in Queensland covers the entire State, and shares many roles and responsibilities through legislative and financial interaction. The Protocol demonstrates a maturing of this relationship beyond the traditional construct and reflects mutual respect and recognition.

It documents a formal set of principles that frame the engagement and interagency collaboration between the two spheres of government. It identifies shared understandings and expectations aimed at providing better outcomes through integrated and collaborative action.

So how does this work in reality? The implementation component of the Protocol documents the process that both spheres of Government adopt to promote a successful outcome. The State Government's Department of Local Government, Planning, Sport and Recreation (DLGPS&R) has the mandate of embedding the Protocol across all government agencies.

Notwithstanding the good intentions and best practice principles of partnership and collaboration embodied in the Protocol, its success is measured by the commitment of the parties to its implementation.

Regrettably, the relationship between the Queensland Government and Local Government in the State was severely damaged on 17 April 2007 when the State unilaterally abandoned the jointly conducted voluntary reform program entitled Size, Shape and Sustainability (SSS). This program, developed over two years in collaboration with the State and undertaken by Local Government with extensive community engagement, has been replaced by a State appointed seven member Commission which will undertake a state-wide review of council boundaries over three months leading to the forced amalgamation of councils from March 2008.

The SSS program was instigated in 2005 by Local Government in Queensland in recognition of the need to review its structures as well as its organizational and operational arrangements. With the focus on long term sustainability, the SSS program was voluntarily investigating change options involving amalgamations and boundary changes as well as collaborative resource sharing arrangements including establishing joint enterprises and service agreements. With 157 councils spread across the vast and diverse area of Queensland, this approach was designed to identify changes appropriate to not only densely settled metropolitan and coastal areas but also remote, sparsely populated rural and outback areas.

By its action the State not only repudiated the principles contained in the Protocol but also adopted a reform model and timetable which effectively denies the community any real opportunity to be engaged in a process of fundamental change of local government areas. The wishes and aspirations of local communities will not be heard in a process that will determine the structures of their local government bodies to operate for the next century.

This action is in complete contradiction to the objectives of the 7th Global Forum as it explores the reinventing of government by building trust through civic engagement. It also demonstrates the fragility of commitments to engagement and collaboration when jurisdictions are able to exercise their political power to achieve their ends.

The Community Satisfaction Benchmarking Survey

In 1997, LGAQ commissioned a project to develop a survey instrument and process to allow Queensland Local Government to monitor and track performance against the value system implicit to their customers.

Since 1997, the survey instrument developed at that time, has been used biennially by LGAQ to provide an overall benchmark by Council category (developed metropolitan, fringe metropolitan, provincial and rural) on the aggregate performance of Councils against a number of themes and topics. In addition, the surveys provide a time series on trends in aggregate performance of the Local Government sector in Queensland.

The survey methodology looks at both the importance of a function or service to the community and the perception of how well a Council is performing each specific function or service.

The premise of this approach is that there is not much merit in achieving excellence for an activity that has little value to the community. Nor is mediocre performance desirable in those functions which are judged as crucial by the community.

In developing the survey methodology, the market researchers employed by LGAQ held consultations with a cross-section of community representatives across Queensland. These consultations were aimed at gaining an insight on the range of services, activities and functions which were seen by the community as the essence of local governance.

This resulted in five broad themes being identified. Within each theme, a number of topics, services or activities were identified against which to measure both importance and performance. The themes and number of topics are:
- Basic Services and Infrastructure (12 topics)
- Community Lifestyle Services (12 topics)
- Managing the Shire/City (7 topics)

- Customer Service/Communication (6 topics)
- Qualities of Council (5 topics)

The following figure shows the trend in performance by theme over the five surveys undertaken to date. The 2005 scores showed a generally sound level of performance, and an improvement from the lower scores recorded in 2003 across all themes.

Figure 1: Performance Trend

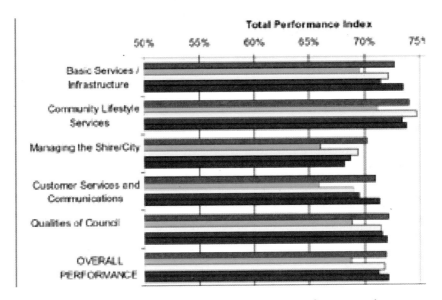

The surveys are used to highlight specific topics or functions where performance is below average. These become targets for performance improvement and are used by LGAQ to develop strategies and initiatives for capacity building.

The following figure shows the 15 performance improvement targets highlighted by the 2005 survey. The topic "Quality of the Elected Council" recorded the largest gap between importance and performance in the 2005 survey. This has been a focus of a number of LGAQ initiatives in recent years.

Figure 2: Performance Targets

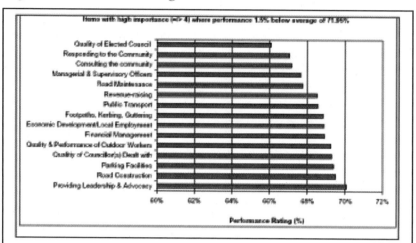

The Community Engagement project, discussed later in this paper, was a response to a community perspective, identified through surveys, that Local Government's engagement practices and techniques including community consultation required improvement. The following figure reveals that the gap between importance and performance narrowed significantly in 2005 following implementation of this initiative in 2003.

Figure 3: Performance Gap - Consulting the Community

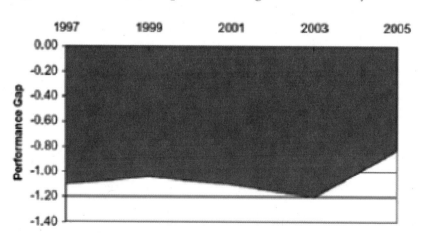

The survey methodology has also been used by a significant number of larger Councils in the State to track their own performance relative to the category benchmarks developed from the whole-of-state survey. The results then feed into individual Council Corporate and Operational Plans where initiatives are required to enhance performance.

The survey also provides the opportunity to include questions on emerging themes and topics. For example, in 2005 a number of questions focused on customer access to the internet and willingness to use this for information, business transactions and payment of accounts. This information has been used to further develop the e-business approach of Councils in the State.

The survey has also allowed LGAQ to track the performance of Local Government as a service provider relative to other Federal or State Government owned service providers. The question was first asked in a 1995 community attitude survey but has also been included in the Benchmark Surveys since 1999. As the following figure shows, the percentage of respondents regarding Councils as being just as good or better than these other service providers has steadily increased from 71% in 1995 to 86% in 2005.

Figure 4: Council Performance as a Service Provider

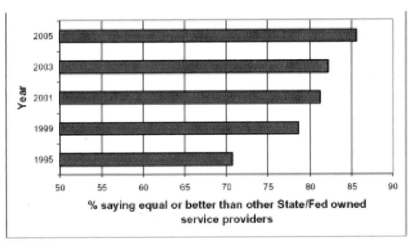

Cairns Peace Week

Local Area Multicultural Project (LAMP)

Local Governments around the world are facing the challenges and opportunities provided by increasingly culturally diverse communities. Current figures show that around 18% of the State's population was born outside of Australia. However, Queensland is becoming increasingly diverse through migration streams which include family reunion, skilled and humanitarian. In more recent years this diversity is spreading across regions that historically were not host centres mainly due to increasing skilled worker intakes.

In 1999 the Queensland State Government, in partnership with LGAQ, initiated the Local Area Multicultural Partnership (LAMP) program to assist Councils to make the most of the benefits of this increasing cultural diversity, to address barriers to full participation of migrants and refugees and to pre-empt possible divisions between communities. Now, with 16 Councils as partners, LAMP is a nationally recognised program focusing on economic, social and cultural outcomes for Queensland's communities, all of which are culturally diverse. From its base in Local Government, LAMP works across the whole community to develop greater cohesion and appreciation of the benefits of diversity.

Key aspects of the program include:

State and Local Government partnerships
Each partnering Council develops its own community relations plan that is based upon its distinct demographics, strengths and identified needs within that community. A full-time LAMP officer is employed within each Council. Over time, task-oriented partnerships have emerged between the three spheres of government and the community to address issues around employment, housing, health, policing, education, disaster management, corrections, domestic violence and racism. These partnerships have important local outcomes but also contribute to the development of a state-wide knowledge-base largely through the strategic role of LGAQ.

Transferability across 16 urban and regional centers
Whether Councils are large or small, this model has been able to produce workable results. It has also flexibly responded to the widely contrasting community demographics in each local government area.

Demonstrated local ownership yet state-wide implementation
Models developed in improved customer service delivery, policy development and planning arrangements are promoted through LGAQ's linkages to all Councils in Queensland and to other States and New Zealand. For example, the Queensland Department of Corrections, noting an increase in one particular ethnic group within its largest prison, requested the local Council to co-develop a program to better support their rehabilitation during incarceration. The request was based on the acknowledged work already done by the Council in other areas. This model is being used as a base for work in prisons across the State.

Community driven programs and contextually sensitive responses
Through LAMP, Councils have engaged with culturally diverse communities in new and dynamic ways which have provided opportunities for these communities to initiate and drive projects that meet both their aspirations and their needs. For example, Brisbane City Council developed a booklet Islam in Brisbane in collaboration with the city's Muslim community. The booklet aims to help Muslims feel welcome in the city and assists the wider community to better understand the Muslim community.

The LAMP program is a key strategy of the Queensland Government under its multicultural policy implemented in partnership with Local Government.

The Program won the Local Governments in Cultural Diversity national award for excellence at the UNESCO 2005 Transformations Conference, Canberra, Australia.

Speakout Youth Conference 2006

Youth Development and Local Government

People under the age of 25 constitute approximately one quarter of Queensland's population. They are a diverse group that makes a significant contribution to the economic, social and cultural capital of the community.

Queensland Local Government recognises providing services and programs for young people is part of Council's core business because:

- Young people are future voters and current citizens;
- Young people use public transport and community facilities;
- Young people use roads to ride bikes, to learn to drive and to travel to school;
- Young people have a role in caring for the environment; and
- Young people will inherit the consequences of the decisions that are made today.

In recognition of this important role the Queensland Government Department of Communities has worked in partnership with LGAQ to deliver the Youth Development Project. This project Speakout Youth Conference 2006 aims to build the capacity of Queensland Local Government to acknowledge and engage young people as community members who have the full rights and responsibilities of citizenship.

The aims of the project are to support and develop the skill and capacity of Councils to:

- Provide young people with positive experiences and opportunities within their community;
- Foster connections and networks;
- Advocate for effective and ethical youth policy and youth strategies;
- Develop Local Government engagement process and practice alongside young people; and
- Work developmentally to ensure connections to key organisational plans and policy.

Local Government is the closest form of government to the community. From a young person's perspective it is the most recognisable and accessible. Local Government's commitment to civic engagement with community members is sometimes challenged when attempting to involve young people as they are often defined as a 'hard to reach' group. To build trust with this highly mobile, sometimes skeptical and demographic group, the Local Government needs to rethink and reinvent its traditional methods.

At the 2006 National Awards for Local Government, three Queensland councils were recognised for their excellence, innovation and engagement of young people. Two projects are summarized as follows.

Sarina Shire Council

The Sarina Shire Council's 'Picture This Program' was awarded winner of the National Award for Innovation at the 2006 National Awards for Local Government for a council with a ratepayer base under 15,000.

The 'Picture This Program' engaged young people from small remote areas of the shire socially disadvantaged due to a lack of transport and recreational facilities. The project involved young people undertaking pictorial 'audits' of their community. These photographic representations were presented to Council so that they could 'view' the world through the eyes of a young person. Young people had identified barriers to their social inclusion and worked with Council to seek solutions.

The shire council is so pleased with the results that this process has become part of core business in engaging young people in the shire.

Brisbane City Council

On a bigger scale, Brisbane City Council's Inkubator is an initiative that targets young people under 26 years of age who are interested in self employment initiatives or starting their own enterprise. Inkubator is located in Brisbane City's award winning community hub for young people - 'Visible Ink'. The Inkubator has been an outstanding success. Over 10 enterprises have been started through this program, many developing a sustainable venture or project.

The initiative links young people to adult mentors, other youth entrepreneurs, emerging businesses, funding opportunities and subsidised rental. This combination helps an individual or an enterprise to develop a business plan and work strategically toward that plan within a supportive, flexible and creative environment.

Not only do these initiatives help to improve community wellbeing but also they actively engage young people in a process that builds important life skills. The engagement process with young people promotes a strengths-based approach built on dialogue and cooperation.

Roads Alliance: partnering for infrastructure

The Roads Alliance provides an excellent example of a partnership between the State and Local Government in the planning and provision of infrastructure.

The Roads Alliance is a commitment by Queensland Department of Main Roads and Local Government to achieve better value from all available road dollars through improved planning, increased capability, better resource sharing, joint purchasing, and more efficient project delivery. It is a shared initiative between Main Roads and Local Government to achieve smarter management and delivery of Queensland's road network.

In Queensland, both the State Government and local governments have responsibility for the construction and maintenance of the road network. Historically, these networks have been treated separately based on 'ownership'.

The Roads Alliance challenges this traditional thinking by focusing on road function and not ownership. Therefore, the development of the agreement required significant leadership by both the State Department of Main Roads and the LGAQ.

The fundamental premise at the core of the Alliance is that the community is not concerned about who 'owns' the road, but expects that roads of a similar function will be built and maintained to a similar standard across a region. Therefore, groups of local governments and the State Government should work together to deliver the best outcome for the entire region.

It empowers regional communities to set and deliver regional road outcomes. In the Roads Alliance partnership investment strategies and best practice road management processes guide decision-making on an agreed road network regardless of ownership.

Since its inception in 2002, the Roads Alliance has achieved its primary aim of establishing a collaborative approach to road network management and planning and the coordination of road projects. Both the State and local governments now jointly develop regional works programs to manage a network of approximately 32,000 kilometers of public roads, known as the local roads of regional significance (LRRS).

Eighteen regional road groups (RRGs) with representatives from local governments and Main Roads have developed regional works programs for the LRRS and will monitor their success with the view to improving the process over time. These works programs are reviewed annually to show 5 year road network priorities and demonstrate better funding allocations at a regional level.

This Alliance has re-defined how two spheres of government can do business with each other.

The Roads Alliance has celebrated some key achievements. In particular the completion of the 5 year regional works programs. This represented a very significant change for many local governments who previously only adopted one year works programs. Now there are 5-year programs that:

- Incorporate an agreed network of regionally significant roads;
- Address road safety across government boundaries;
- Give priority to projects which contribute to the economic and social development of Queensland's regions;
- Embrace 20 year investment strategies which take into account future demands on the road infrastructure; and
- Provide a clear direction for road investment in Queensland's regions.

The benefits to the community have been multiple:

- Better regional road network sooner;
- Improved access to social services within the region including schools and hospitals;
- A safer regional road network; and
- Improved regional economic development opportunities through reduced travel time and costs including tourism and freight movements.

For the two principal road owners benefits have also been derived locally from road management and investment decisions being made regionally which include:

- Best use of available resources;
- Economies of scale in various areas including plant and equipment;
- Improved Local Government road management, investment and construction capability;
- Access to better road management technology;
- Ability to produce a justifiable case for road funding;

- Continuing state government employment guarantees;
- Improved consistency in planning and investment; and
- Greater use of Local Government expertise.

In 2005, the Roads Alliance was recognized for its innovative and successful approach to inter-jurisdictional collaboration by receiving the International Road Federation's (IRF) Global Road Achievement Award for Program Management.

Social Capital Action Research Project

In 2001 the LGAQ brought to Australia renowned Harvard academic and social commentator, Professor Robert Putnam to deliver the keynote address at the LGAQ's Annual Conference. His visit generated vigorous discussion among Local Government and the wider community at a symposium in Brisbane on 11 September attended by over 800 paying participants. Putnam is well known for his commentaries on civic engagement and social connectedness or what he refers to as 'social capital'. His remarks during this Australian visit sowed the seeds for a collaborative social capital project between the Community Service & Research Centre (CSRC) at the University of Queensland and the LGAQ.

In his book, Bowling Alone (2000), Putnam documents a decline in social capital by referring to quantitative data that measures civic engagement and social connectedness across a range of activities. This decrease in the social capital stockpile, he says, has resulted in a measurable decrease in everyday quality of life.

Putnam says that social capital greases the wheel that allows communities to advance smoothly. When this is not in place there is a consequence - the result is a tangible cost to individual and collective health, wealth and wellbeing. The public sector is central to the functioning and welfare of any society and Local Government is no exception. The Australian Local Government Association (ALGA) Declaration on the Role of Local Government states -

"Local Governments are elected:
- To represent their local communities;
- To be a responsible and accountable sphere of democratic governance;
- To be a focus for community identity and civic spirit;
- To provided appropriate services to meet community needs in an efficient and effective manner; and
- To facilitate and coordinate local efforts and resources in pursuit of community goals".

While there are many commentators on the topic of social capital, and this work continues to grow, there are few documented examples of practice at an international or national level that relate to Local Government.

To help fill the gap in this research the LGAQ Executive (Board) approved a Social Capital Action Research Project in early 2003. The University of Queensland (UQ) Community Service & Research Centre (CSRC) was appointed to partner with LGAQ due to its sound record in applied or action research. It was important to the Association that this work had practical, tangible outcomes for Councils and their communities.

The purpose of the project was to:

1. Identify and document the roles, and potential roles, of Queensland local governments in building social capital;

2. Provide a clear direction for Queensland local governments to take up or continue undertaking the work of building social capital; and

3. Through undertaking the tasks above, continuing to strategically inform Queensland Local Government Corporate Planning Processes.

In addition the LGAQ wanted to build leadership and encourage confidence in government at a local level by supporting Councils to identify how best to engage their local citizens and incorporate community goals into sustainable decisions via planning processes.

The researchers called for expressions of interest and signed partnership agreements with five local governments representing diverse geographic locations, demographics and social composition. To obtain the required information the researchers conducted focus groups, interviews and developed a survey tool. Site visits were repeated several times to build upon the relationship being developed with each community.

A social map was developed on these local government areas including an examination of community values and aspirations. Because of the need to apply the research training and support workshops were conducted to provide feedback on the research findings. This helped staff and councillors better understand the principles and process of Social Capital. By providing Councils with these 'real world' skills ideas were developed on how to transfer the learnings into everyday Council operations.

The major outcome of the work, a Report titled 'What Makes Communities Tick?' [146] identified a need for more rigour to be applied to working with Local Government in the following areas: [147]

1. Fostering Leadership
2. Communication and Engagement
3. Sharing Learning
4. Measurement and Evaluation
5. Collaborative Partnerships.

LGAQ Community Engagement Framework

After the release of the Social Capital Action Research Project (SCARP) Report, LGAQ staff commenced another research project into what constituted good practice with regard to Civic Engagement. The SCARP Report sharpened LGAQ's focus on the significance of community engagement as a pillar of good governance. The report's findings supported the Community Satisfaction Survey results and consequently the need for Local Government to change and deliver on its commitment to participatory democracy.

It was realised that a cultural shift was required in the way Local Government perceived and approached community engagement. Local Government has a long history of the "public meeting" with little positive results and its approach to community engagement needed to change. The work that was about to commence had a strong philosophical base. At its core was the belief that the community is a resource, largely untapped, of ideas, solutions and potential – not a problem to be managed.

This decision resulted in another successful partnership. Along with a number of activist Councils the LGAQ collaborated with two key partners - the Queensland Government Department of Communities and the International Association for Public Participation (IAP2). These groups assisted in the development of a policy position and a comprehensive practice framework that would position Queensland Local Government for the future challenges of dealing with increasingly complex problems and diverse stakeholder groups.

A clear position was required that articulated what Local Government stood for. What followed was 12 months of discussion, a Discussion Paper, a Position Paper, a state wide consultation process and ultimately, a policy position was voted upon.

At the 2004 LGAQ Annual Conference in Mackay, Queensland, decision makers from the 157 Councils voted overwhelmingly to accept the following policy position.

---

[146]   'What Makes Communities Tick: A Local Government Social Capital Action Research Project'. LGAQ 2003.Woolcock, Renton and Cayave.

[147]   For more information go to http://www.uq.edu.au/boilerhouse/docs/Woolcock-et-al-What-Makes-Communities-Tick_LGAQ-FinalReport.pdf.

2.3 COMMUNITY ENGAGEMENT

2.3.1
Local Government recognises that community engagement is vital to the democratic process and contributes to building balanced healthy communities.

2.3.2
Local Government understands community engagement contains the core elements of information, consultation and active participation.

2.3.3
Local Government will apply the core elements of community engagement, where appropriate, to facilitate meaningful community involvement in the decision-making process.[148]

The democratic principles enshrined within this policy position provided the foundation for developing a set of tools that would build capability and confidence.[149] The IAP2 core values underpinned the process while the IAP2 code of ethics supported LGAQ's work as a practitioner.

It was learnt that community engagement draws upon many disciplines including social justice, risk management, education, conflict resolution, public relations. Also, there are numerous levels to engagement in applying the IAP2 Spectrum (see Annex B), and that for every level a promise or commitment is made. The IAP2 Spectrum was extremely valuable in that it provided a common language and 'demystified' the terms consultation, involvement and collaboration. For the first time, there was authority in the use of these terms and an understanding of the responsibility involved with each and the promise that was attached to it. Also, it was understood how important it was to develop a method for evaluating the process.

The value of planning for community engagement was learnt which involved a shift from developing project plans that incorporated community engagement as a line item to developing complementary community engagement plans. There was a perception that this meant asking an already over stretched workplace to do more and that the process implied elected members giving up their role and handing it back to the people. Neither was true. While there is a case for developing a complex engagement plan to support a complex project, there is equally a case for not undertaking 'consultation' where it is not warranted and indeed, for "piggy backing" on existing processes to achieve sound outcomes.

---

[148]   Adopted September 2004. LGAQ Annual Conference. Mackay, Queensland.
[149]   The LGAQ 'Framework' was recognised with an Asia Pacific Policy Award from IAP2 in 2005.

Elected members were given very clear messages that this was not about reducing their influence but about equipping them with maximum information and support to build the potential for positive outcomes and sustainable decisions.

Sustainable decisions are:

- technically feasible;
- economically viable;
- environmentally compatible; and
- publicly acceptable.

Another important aspect of the Framework was training. This commenced with a one day introduction to Community Engagement course specifically designed for Queensland Local Government. LGAQ actively recruited Councils to send a cross section of their organizations (Chief Executive Officers, elected members and staff) to the sessions. Over 400 people have participated in 19 locations across the state. The courses became so popular that they were opened up to State Government colleagues, particularly in remote areas, and key community partners.

Modeling this approach was essential to the success of the courses. Consequently, a methodology based on collaboration was adopted. The courses were led by an LGAQ officer and a private consultant and State Government regional officers were also invited to co-facilitate where appropriate. In addition, 'community engagement' were recruited.

These champions were identified by their peers as 'people who appreciated the value of Community Engagement'. LGAQ approached their respective councils and requested their involvement in the delivery of the courses on the following grounds.

- The participating Councils will be promoted as partners and as good practice agents in this area both on the training brochure and on the LGAQ website;
- The training will provide an opportunity for participating Councils to share their knowledge and expertise with neighbouring Councils and strengthen regional relationships; and
- The training course will provide a low cost and challenging professional development opportunity for the participating staff keeping their skills up to date.

All four Councils that were approached agreed. From the one day training sessions there was a critical mass on which to offer the five day IAP2 certificate training program. To date, some 50 people have attended the certificate program and have thus contributed significantly to the bank of knowledge across Queensland Local Government.

Community engagement is now understood as being decision oriented and goal driven. Also, a well developed engagement plan can facilitate a deeper understanding of the issues and encourages a richer, more meaningful conversation that is more open to the emergence of possible solutions.

The LGAQ has been very encouraged by the success to date. Not only has the community response to the Community Attitude Surveys improved but also several Councils have now won independently assessed national and state awards for their good practice.

Summary

This paper demonstrates the pro-active role played by Local Government in Queensland in the process of civic engagement and the leadership role played by the Local Government Association of Queensland over the past 10 years.

The paper also demonstrates at a practical level the significant role of community engagement in the development of place and people at the local level. It also demonstrates that delivering on the principles of community engagement requires a long term commitment if trust in government is to be developed and be sustained.

The Local Government Association of Queensland is in its 111th year of representing and providing leadership for its members - the city, town and shire councils of Queensland. Its success and longevity as a voluntary membership body is a measure of the trusting relationship with its members and its delivery on its mission of 'strengthening the ability and performance of Queensland Local Government to better serve the community'.

The paper also demonstrates the ease with which trust in government can be destroyed through the ill conceived use of political power for short term political gain. Notwithstanding this breach of trust the Local Government Association of Queensland will continue to engage the State Government to ensure that the interests of Local Government and the communities they serve are not the victim of a reform agenda devoid of any real commitment to civic engagement. This engagement will not be based on trust but on the need to protect and promote the interests of local communities.

Governments all over the world are facing more complex issues and increasingly 'wicked problems'. These issues are inescapable at the local level - drought, desalination, natural resource management, rural decline, water management, population control and sustainable growth. No one group or level of government has a mandate on the solution to these challenges. All stakeholders must work together in order to encourage the very best thinking and to promote the best decisions and therefore the best outcomes.

Annexes

Annex A

IAP2 Public Participation Spectrum

Developed by the International Association for Public Participation

INCREASING LEVEL OF PUBLIC IMPACT

INFORM	CONSULT	INVOLVE	COLLABORATE	EMPOWER
Public Participation Goal:	**Public Participation Goal:**	**Public Participation Goal:**	**Public Participation Goal:**	**Public Participation Goal:**
To provide the public with balanced and objective information to assist them in understanding the problem, alternatives, opportunities and/or solutions.	To obtain public feedback on analysis, alternatives and/or decisions.	To work directly with the public throughout the process to ensure that public concerns and aspirations are consistently understood and considered.	To partner with the public in each aspect of the decision including the development of alternatives and the identification of the preferred solution.	To place final decision-making in the hands of the public.
Promise to the Public:	**Promise to the Public:**	**Promise to the Public:**	**Promise to the Public:**	**Promise to the Public:**
We will keep you informed.	We will keep you informed, listen to and acknowledge concerns and aspirations, and provide feedback on how public input influenced the decision.	We will work with you to ensure that your concerns and aspirations are directly reflected in the alternatives developed and provide feedback on how public input influenced the decision.	We will look to you for direct advice and innovation in formulating solutions and incorporate your advice and recommendations into the decisions to the maximum extent possible.	We will implement what you decide.
Example Techniques to Consider:	**Example Techniques to Consider:**	**Example Techniques to Consider:**	**Example Techniques to Consider:**	**Example Techniques to Consider:**
• Fact sheets • Web sites • Open houses	• Public comment • Focus groups • Surveys • Public meetings	• Workshops • Deliberate polling	• Citizen Advisory Committees • Consensus-building • Participatory decision-making	• Citizen juries • Ballots • Delegated decisions

©2004 International Association for Public Participation

Annex B

AGENDA

7th Global Forum on Reinventing Government:
Building Trust in Government
26 – 29 June 2007
Vienna, Austria

THURSDAY, 28 June 2007
09:00 a.m. – 9:45 a.m.   OPENING SESSION

Organizational Matters and Brief
Introduction

Chairperson
Jacinto De Vera, Chief, Policy Analysis
and Coordination Unit, Socio-economic
Governance and Management Branch,
Division for Public Administration and
Development Management,
Department of Economic and Social
Affairs, United Nations

KEYNOTE STATEMENTS

Josef Moser, Secretary-General,
International Organization of Supreme
Audit Institutions (INTOSAI)
Delivered by **Gertrud Schlicker**,
Adviser, Austrian Court of Audit,
Vienna

INTRODUCTION TO THE THEME

Adil Khan, Chief, Socio-Economic
Governance and Management Branch
Division for Public Administration and
Development Management, Department
of Economic and Social Affairs,
United Nations

PARTICIPATORY GOVERNANCE FOR
EFFICIENCY AND EQUITY: AN OVERVIEW
OF ISSUES AND EVIDENCE
Siddiqur Osmani, Professor,
Development Economics University of
Ulster, U.K.

BUILDING TRUST THROUGH CIVIC
ENGAGEMENT FOR EFFECTIVE POVERTY
REDUCTION
Naresh Singh, Executive Director,
Commission on Legal Empowerment of
the Poor

FORMALIZING CIVIC ENGAGEMENT:
NGOS AND THE CONCEPTS OF TRUST,
STRUCTURE AND ORDER IN THE PUBLIC
POLICY PROCESS
Herrington Bryce, Life of Virginia
Professor, Mason School, College of
William and Mary, Virginia,
United States

09:45 a.m. – 10:30 a.m.   Discussion

10:30 a.m. – 11:00 a.m.   Break

11:00 a.m. – 12:00 noon   WELCOME STATEMENT
                                 Guido Bertucci
                                 Director, Division for Public
                                 Administration and Development
                                 Management, Department of Economic
                                 and Social Affairs United Nations

                                 SESSION I: INTERNATIONAL
                                 BEST PRACTICES

                                 Chairperson
                                 Adil Khan, Department of Economic
                                 and Social Affairs, United Nations

THE ECONOMIC AND SOCIAL COUNCILS:
ENGAGING MULTI-STAKEHOLDERS IN
POLICY DEVELOPMENT
Jean-Claude Pasty, President, Section of
External Relations, French Economic
and Social Council

CIVIC ENGAGEMENT IN PUBLIC
POLICIES: EXPERIENCE OF THE AUSTRIAN
SOCIAL PARTNERSHIP
Andreas Henkel, Secretary-General,
Advisory Council for Economic and
Social Affairs, Federal Economic
Chamber, Austria

CIVIC ENGAGEMENT IN NATIONAL
CONSULTATIVE COUNCILS:
THE EXPERIENCE OF KOREA
Hyuk-Sang Sohn, Professor, Director
for External Affairs
Global Academy for Neo-Renaissance
Ryan S. Song, Professor, School of Law
Kyung Hee University, Republic of
Korea

CIVIC ENGAGEMENT IN POLICY
DEVELOPMENT AT THE LOCAL
GOVERNMENT LEVEL: THE EXPERIENCE
OF NAGA CITY, PHILIPPINES
Jesse Robredo, Mayor, City
Government of Naga, Philippines

INCLUSIVE CIVIC ENGAGEMENT:
CITIZENS' VOICES IN POLICY MAKING
Tanja Timmermans, Consultant
Public Governance and Territorial
Development Directorate Organisation
for Economic Co-operation and
Development (OECD)

| 12:00 noon – 12:30 p.m. | Discussion |
| 12:30 p.m. – 2:00 p.m. | Lunch Break |

2:00 p.m. – 3:00 p.m.

CONTINUATION OF SESSION 1:
INTERNATIONAL BEST PRACTICES

Chairperson
Jacinto De Vera, Department
of Economic and Social Affairs,
United Nations

REBUILDING TRUST IN POST
CONFLICT SITUATION THROUGH CIVIC
ENGAGEMENT: THE EXPERIENCE OF
RWANDA
Protais Musoni, Minister, Ministry
of Local Government, Good
Governance Community Development
and Social Affairs, Rwanda

CAN CIVIL SOCIETY ENGAGEMENT
IN BUDGETING PROCESSES BUILD TRUST
IN GOVERNMENT?
Warren Krafchik, Director,
International Budget Project
Washington D.C., United States

OVERSIGHT OFFICES AND CIVIL SOCIETY
INSIGHTS: THE CASE OF INDIA
Amitabh Mukhopadhyay,
Joint Secretary
Parliamentary Financial Committees,
Lok Sabha Secretariat
New Delhi, India

The Role of Civil Society
Organizations in Public Governance:
The Experience of Korea
Eui-Young Kim, Dean, Office for
International Exchange,
Kyung Hee University, Republic of
Korea
BUILDING TRUST THROUGH PUBLIC-

PRIVATE PARTNERSHIPS: THE ECONOMY
OF COMMUNION PROJECT
Alberto Ferrucci, President, New
Humanity, Italy

3:00 p.m. – 3:30 p.m.   Discussion

3:30 p.m. – 4:00 p.m.   Break

4:00 p.m. – 5:00 p.m.   SESSION II: QUEENSLAND
(AUSTRALIA)
EXPERIENCE IN CIVIC ENGAGEMENT

Chairperson
Greg Hoffman PSM, Director,
Policy and Representation, Local
Government Association of Queensland,
Australia

CIVIC ENGAGEMENT IN QUEENSLAND:
PARTICIPATION IN ROAD SYSTEM
MANAGEMENT- A CASE STUDY OF MAIN
ROADS EXPERIENCE, QUEENSLAND
Neil Doyle, General Manager,
Organisational Positioning and
Stakeholder Relations, Department of
Main Roads, Queensland Government,
Australia
ROLE OF GOVERNMENT COORDINATION
IN CIVIC ENGAGEMENT: EXPERIENCE OF
QUEENSLAND, AUSTRALIA
Peter Oliver, Senior Research
Fellow, Engaged Government Project
Griffith University, Australia

LOCAL GOVERNMENT: A PRO-ACTIVE
PARTNER IN CIVIC ENGAGEMENT
Paul Bell AM, President Australia Local
Government Association of Queensland
and President, Australian Local
Government
Association, Australia
SIGNIFICANCE OF CULTURAL CONTEXT

for Civic Engagement
Michael Cuthill, Director and Senior
Lecturer Boilerhouse Community
Engagement Centre University of
Queensland, Australia

5:00 p.m. – 5:30 p.m.   Discussion

5:30 p.m.   Close of Day I

Friday, 29 JUNE 2007
9:00 a.m. – 10:00 a.m.   SESSION III: KEY ISSUES AND
                                     GENERAL Considerations in Civic
                                     Engagement

                                     Chairperson
                                     Jacinto De Vera, Department of
                                     Economic and Social Affairs,
                                     United Nations

                                     Civic Engagement and Public
                                     Sector Reform
                                     Paul Smoke, Professor and Director of
                                     International Programs Wagner
                                     Institute, New York University

                                     Shifting Mindsets to Promote
                                     Effective Civic Engagement
                                     Sonia Ospina, Associate Professor of
                                     Public
                                     Management and Policy and Co-
                                     Director of the Research Center for
                                     Leadership in Action, Wagner Institute,
                                     New York University

                                     Developing Capacity: The
                                     Reasonable Conversation of
                                     Representative Democratic Politics
                                     Patrick Bishop, Head of Department
                                     Administration, Department of Politics
                                     and Public Policy, Griffith University,
                                     Australia
10:00 a.m. – 10:30 a.m.   Discussion

10:30 a.m. – 11:00 a.m.	Break
11: 00 a.m. – 12:30 p.m.	SUMMARY, CONCLUSIONS AND FINALIZATION OF REPORT

Chairperson
Adil Khan, Department of Economic and Social Affairs, United Nations

Rapporteur
Robert Miles, Executive Director, Institute for Sustainable Regional Development (ISRD), Central Queensland University, Australia

12:30 p.m. – 2:30 p.m.	Break
AFTERNOON	WRAP-UP PLENARY SESSION

Presentation of key policy messages and reports on workshop discussions to all participants in the Global Forum

Jesse Robredo, Mayor, City Government of Naga Philippines

Annex C

Opening Statement

Mr. Guido Bertucci, Director, Division for Public Administration and
Development Management, United Nations Department of Economic and
Social Affairs

28 June 2007

Excellencies,
Distinguished Colleagues,
Ladies and Gentlemen,

I am sorry that I could not be here earlier. I had to address few unforeseen emergencies. I am glad that my colleagues have already got the workshop started. I am particularly delighted that Mr. Moser, Auditor General of Court of Audit of Austria and current President of INTOSAI was here this morning and delivered his valuable speech. At this stage, let me also recognize Minister Musoni of Rwanda who is here with us this morning. I also take this opportunity to acknowledge contributions of our five partners who are partnering with UNDESA in this workshop. These are, the Eastern Regional Organization of Public Administration   (EROPA), the Queensland, Australia Community Engagement Alliance, International Budget Project, Washington D. C., Kyung Hee University, Republic of Korea and the Wagner Institute of New York University, New York.

The theme of the 7th Global Forum has been chosen on the basis of a growing perception of falling trust in governments by their citizens. In recent times, surveys after survey are demonstrating this disturbing trend. The phenomenon of distrust seems to be pervasive and cuts across more or less all countries, developed and developing. There are several reasons that are attributed to the phenomenon of distrust.

Though reasons of distrust vary from region to region, the most commonly held perception is that of a growing gap that exists between what the citizens expect their governments to do and what governments end up doing.

Among other things, as Building Trust in Government is basically a phenomenon of citizen/government relationship, it is indeed very important that the issues of trust get looked at from citizen perspectives themselves. It is important to map out the causes of distrust and follow this up by exploring options and means that will build capacities to bring citizens closer to the government and government closer to the citizens. It is expected that proper understanding of barriers of trust and evolution of greater synergic relationships between government and the citizens will greatly help in instilling in public governance a sense of shared vision in development, a mutually reenforcing mechanism of transparency and accountability and in delivering services that meet priorities set by citizen themselves.

UN Secretary General Ban Ki Moon recently said "Trust between citizens, between member states, and in government itself is one of the most vital needs for peace and the prosperity of humankind. Our ability to work together to confront common threats and to promote mutually beneficial objectives—such as the Millennium Development Goals—requires that we nurture this invaluable commodity". (UN Secretary General – Ban Ki Moon)

The United Nations and its partners chose this topic because of its ever growing importance to governance and furthermore, it is recognized that of all the challenges facing governance and public administration systems worldwide today, none is more important and yet more daunting than the issue of building trust through civic engagement.

Democratic governance, a key tool in ensuring citizen trust is facing a number of challenges these days. The emerging political economy in societies is contributing to the elite capture of political power and consequently, distancing the citizens, especially the poor and the disadvantaged from the decision-making processes of the state.

Due to malfunctions, citizens in many countries are losing faith in democracy. Time may have come to take a fresh look at democracies and think of ways to make both its processes as well as its outcomes more inclusive and equitable. We must look for new and innovative mechanisms and new approaches for citizens' engagement throughout the processes of policy formulation, budget preparation, implementation of government programmes and delivery of services as well as the monitoring and evaluation of these programmes.

In order to rebuild citizen trust in government, several process as well as structure-related weaknesses in public governance need to be addressed. There needs to be a reinventing of the ways in which governments conduct their businesses. There must be a shift in processes that reinvigorates and enlists citizens into the structures and institutions of socio-economic governance of countries. And there must be new modalities and mechanisms that make governments more caring, listening and partnering.

Many of you who have gathered here are already aware of these needs and some are leaders in the concept of civic engagement. I am pleased to note that there are a number of "best practices" that will be presented at the Workshop. I hope these lessons of best practices and the knowledge of what works and what does not would assist us in devising options that can be tailored to each country's own requirements.

While we all agree that greater synergy between government and the citizens a sin qua non for building trust and for promoting pro-citizen development, the key challenges of civic engagement are: how do we go about it; what are the methodological complexities; what are the costs; and does approximating citizens in public governance necessarily build trust in government.

Hopefully, your workshop, "Building Trust through Civic Engagement" shall address some of these questions and advance further the understanding of and strategies for successful civic engagement in public governance.

I look forward to your conclusions and recommendations that will be presented at the closing plenary session on Friday afternoon. I thank you all!

Opening Statement

Josef Moser, Secretary-General
International Organization of Supreme Audit Institutions
28 June 2007

Ladies and Gentlemen:

I wish to thank the United Nations for inviting me to represent the International Organization of Supreme Audit Institutions – INTOSAI - and the Austrian Court of Audit in today's international workshop, which appropriately addresses issues of building trust through civic engagement.

As Secretary General of INTOSAI - and of course also as President of the Austrian Court of Audit, a Supreme Audit Institution with a long history of almost 250 years, permit me first of all to underline two very important parliamentary functions in building and maintaining trust through civic engagement.

The first refer to the so-called appropriations prerogatives of parliaments. In modern democratic social systems, parliaments on behalf of the people of their respective states as a rule have the constitutional right to decide on the collection, allocation and use of public revenues by act of Parliament.

Citizens, for their part, have a vital interest that public resources raised from the taxes they pay are put to the best possible use in terms of compliance with rules and regulations, economy, efficiency and effectiveness. To guarantee this, Parliaments usually also have another prerogative, the power of scrutiny and accountability, to back up their budgetary prerogatives. But in most cases, Parliaments do not fully exercise this scrutiny and entrust it to Supreme Audit Institutions.

Supreme Audit Institutions are independent of government and administration and are answerable directly to national parliaments. Worldwide 186 of them come together under the umbrella of INTOSAI. In the service of Parliaments, they exercise their independent audit and advisory functions in order to enhance public financial management and the economic and efficient use of public resources.

In this way, as well as by reporting their audit findings and recommendations to parliaments and by publicizing audit results via the media, Supreme Audit Institutions make a significant contribution to good governance, create a climate for public accountability and increase the confidence of citizens in public financial management.

Supreme Audit Institutions have always strived to strengthen the confidence of their parliaments, governments, citizens and civil society in the independence, objectivity, quality and cost effectiveness of their audit reporting as a contribution to their country's stability and economic growth, good governance and fight against corruption.

Scarcer public resources, the move from an authoritarian to a service-oriented state and growing empowerment of citizens in claiming public accountability and transparency of public financial management, create new challenges for public governance. These challenges are reflected in four targets to be achieved by state administrations, namely:

-   Performance targets (such as results, products, processes, case numbers, customer satisfaction, etc.);
-   Resource targets (for instance: organisation, financial means, optimising cost and time input, etc.);
-   Project goals (like constructing a public building, or introducing e-government services);
-   Behaviour goals (including friendliness or helpfulness of staff).

At subject-matter level, goals must be verifiable and quantifiable, free of contradiction and non-prescriptive as to how they are to be achieved. At staff level, goals should be motivating, challenging, and resolve conflicts. Target agreements are a management tool that makes it possible to interrelate targets and outcomes.

To achieve these goals, public administration uses new concepts, instruments and methods, such as New Public Management. This involves various innovations increasingly used in the public sector in recent years:

1. Reforms in the management of the public administration;
2. Development of IT technologies (IT tools); and
3. Development of a new output and resource-driven financial management.

The introduction of New Public Management (impact-oriented government) has shifted the focus to goals and targets, which are to ensure a more efficient and effective public-service delivery. In this process, it is instrumental to define objectives.

The challenge to Supreme Audit Institutions is to use modern methods to check and evaluate whether these goals of public financial management have been achieved in compliance with existing rules and regulations as well as in an efficient and effective manner.

Government audit is currently facing a global process of change. Therefore it is of special importance for the International Organization of Supreme Audit Institutions to tackle the question of how to best measure government performance and progress and communicate this to their national parliaments and public at large.

Prompted by soaring budget deficits and sustained austerity programmes, government administrations are facing mounting pressure from the public at large and from national parliaments.

By introducing modern, transparent, target- and service-oriented, and more efficient methods of management, virtually all reforms are designed to create a better image of government ("the company") with the citizens ("the shareholders").

"New Public Management" consists of a bundle of policy reforms and strategies that are driven by a micro-economic interpretation of how government is delivering service. The NPM reform model does not offer an exhaustive dogmatic catalogue of measures, but is often equated with privatisation and deregulation, the introduction of some entrepreneurial elements in the bureaucracy, and the adoption of private-sector management methods in government administration.

Cost and results accounting is an integral feature of the management process and used in order to verify whether the agreed targets have been reached at the end of an accounting period. Major elements of New Public Managements such as reporting, contact management, or controlling, are based on cost and results accounting.

Public audit can no longer confine itself to making recommendations to audited agencies to improve their administrative methods and meet the new challenges, such as recommending introduction of cost and results accounting systems as well as indicator systems on a wider scale.

Public audit institutions must define the value and benefits of their services, set out clearly the impact of their outputs for government and society, making them transparent, verifiable and credible. Bearing in mind that, as a rule, public audit institutions are financed by taxpayers, this should enable government audit institutions to meet their public accountability requirements vis-à-vis the citizens.

In the light of these ongoing challenges for government audit, INTOSAI, in co-operation with the United Nations, held an international Symposium on the value and benefits of Government Audit in a Globalised Environment, which took place in Vienna in March 2007, and which highlighted and discussed efficiency and effectiveness issues in government audit. The Symposium focused on the development of performance indicators to provide information on the delivery of the work of Supreme Audit Institutions. The Symposium also considered the issue of intellectual capital reporting of Supreme Audit Institutions, since know-how and do-how are essential elements to sustain the value and credibility of the audit and advisory activities of Supreme Audit Institutions.

Also, the Austrian Court of Audit, which hosts the INTOSAI General Secretariat since 1962, developed a system of indicators as a basis for its internal organisational planning and monitoring, and to assess its achievements and impacts.

As I mentioned in my keynote statement to the plenary session, it is the fundamental role of INTOSAI to help all SAIs around the world to achieve best results in government audit. Once again, the recent UN/INTOSAI

Symposium, which I have already referred to, has made this impressively clear.

The symposium proposed to INTOSAI that the work on the measurement of the value and benefits of government audit should be driven forward in collaboration with key stakeholders such as the UN, World Bank and the INTOSAI Development Initiative (IDI).

The longstanding excellent co-operation with the United Nations is not the only approach INTOSAI has tried and tested: Following its strategic plan, INTOSAI has established working groups and committees – such as the Professional Standards Committee, the Capacity Building Committee and the Committee on IT Audit, to mention but a few - to elaborate comprehensive and coherent guidelines and standards for the audit work.

As set out above, we at INTOSAI will continue to identify further measurements of the value which Supreme Audit Institutions deliver, and which could be used in future to demonstrate to Parliament and to citizens more widely the value and benefits from government audit. Doing so, Supreme Audit Institutions will contribute to improving trust in government and in the quality of governance.

A conceivable approach would be to establish a joint platform of NGOs, Civil Society Organisations and the International Organisation of Supreme Audit Institutions (INTOSAI). The platform should identify co-operation projects and then translate them into concrete action.

In fact, that course of action could be included into the recommendations of the Global Forum.

On behalf of INTOSAI, I wish all the distinguished participants a productive discussion in the further course of this meeting.

Thank you for your attention.

Contributors

Patrick Bishop
Senior Lecturer Department of Politics & International Relations
University of Lancaster, United Kingdom and Adjunct Fellow, Centre for
Governance and Public Policy, Griffith Business School, Australia

Dr. Bishop completed his PhD at University of Adelaide and has held teaching and research posts at University of Adelaide and Charles Sturt University. He has held visiting appointments at Virginia Polytechnic Institute and State University (US); the University of Melbourne and Lancaster University (UK). He is now also a research fellow with the Centre for Governance and Public Policy at Griffith University, and was Director of the Masters of Public Sector Management program from 1997 to 2005. He has been a Chief Investigator on four large Australian Research Council (ARC) funded projects on community consultation and democratic practice; ethical governance in the public sector; regional governance and, most recently, on E-democracy. He has also delivered numerous training courses for public managers through the Institute of Public Administration Australia (IPAA). Prior to his academic career he worked in local government in New South Wales for eleven years. Dr. Bishop has published works on public sector ethics, community cabinet process, public participation in the policy process and e-Democracy. He was the co-editor of the Australian Journal of Public Administration from 2002-2006 and has been a regular consultant to the Queensland State Government, working with a number of Queensland government departments.

Herrington Bryce
Life of Virginia Professor, Mason School, College of William
and Mary, Virginia, United States

Mr. Bryce is Life of Virginia Professor of Business at the College of William and Mary. Previously he served as a member of the Treasury Board of the State of Virginia, which issues Tax-exempt bonds and oversees cash management and custodial policies for state depositories. He also served as president of the National Policy Institute, president of the Carlogh Corporation, vice president of the National Academy or State and Local Governments, director of Research for the Joint Center for Political Economic Studies, and senior economist at the Urban Institute.

He was a fellow at the Institute of Politics at Harvard University, and economic policy fellow at the Brookings Institution, and a NATO fellow in Belgium. He has taught at the Massachusetts Institute of Technology, the

University of Maryland, and Clark University in Worcester, Massachusetts. He is author or editor of several books and articles, including op-ed pieces for the Washington Post, the Wall Street Journal, the New York Times, and the National Employment Weekly. Mr. Bryce teaches corporate financial strategy, corporate cost and profit-planning, and nonprofit finance and management.

Neil Doyle
General Manager, Organisational Positioning and Stakeholder Relations, Department of Main Roads, Queensland Government, Australia

Mr. Doyle has been appointed as General Manager for the Department of Main Roads, Queensland Government, Australia. He has held senior leadership positions in private and public sectors entities, including Telstra, Australia Post, Queensland Transport and Main Roads. Throughout his career, Mr. Doyle has been a champion for an improved and more responsive public sector, often leading major change initiatives. He has provided leadership at state, national and international levels for the transport and roads sectors through his many roles and affiliations.

As a senior public servant, Mr. Doyle's vision, dedication and hard work have helped shape the department's direction through the introduction of "Road Reform" in the early 1990s, the development of "Roads Connecting Queenslanders" in the late 1990s, and more recently through the "Roads Alliance". Each of these initiatives has held a common theme of innovation, relationships, citizen engagements and productivity.

Andreas Henkel
Secretary-General, Advisory Council for Economic and Social Affairs, Federal Economic Chamber, Austria

Since 2004, Mr. Henkel has been designated as Secretary-General of the Austrian Advisory Council for Economic and Social Affairs, Federal Economic Chamber of Austria. The Federal Economic Chamber is one of the four representative organizations in the Austrian Social Partnership. Prior to this appointment, he has held various significant positions in the Federal Economic Chamber. He previously worked with the Economic Policy Department where he was responsible for policies concerning SME, construction, corporate social responsibility, European Union enlargement, business ethics, European Forum Alpbach and social dialogue. In 2002, he was also a member of the Euro Cash Users Group, European Central Bank and the European Union Commission. Moreover, he served as a member of the Groupeuro from 1996 to 2001. Mr. Henkel earned his studies of jurispundence at the Vienna University in Austria.

Greg Hoffman
PSM, Director, Policy and Representation
Local Government Association of Queensland, Australia

Mr. Hoffman has had a long and distinguished career with Local Government. With over 40 years dedicated to Local Government, he has worked for three Councils including the position of CEO of Darwin City Council. He was the Executive Director of LGAQ for 10 years, the Local Government Commissioner for Queensland for 5 years, and for the last 10 years he has been the Director of Policy and Representation at the LGAQ.

He holds two Degrees - a Bachelor of Business with majors in Accounting and Management and a Bachelor of Arts, majoring in Community Studies and Media Relations. He is a Certified Practicing Accountant and a Fellow of the Local Government Managers Association. In 1994, he was awarded a Public Service Medal in the Australia Day Honors List for outstanding service to Local Government and in 2002 received a Centenary of Federation Medal.

M. Adil Khan
Chief, Socio-economic Governance and Management Branch
Division for Public Administration and Development Management
United Nations Department for Economic and Social Affairs

Mr. M. Adil Khan joined UNDESA in 2002 as the Chief, Socio-economic Governance and Management Branch. He is responsible for leading a team contributing to the normative, analytical and capacity building work of the United Nations, relating to participatory governance, MDG oriented public sector reform and restructuring, and championing the 'engaged governance' - citizen/government dialoguing concept for pro-poor policies.

His areas of expertise include policy analysis and policy development, high level negotiations and managing processes and preparation of policy documents/advice to the inter-governmental bodies of the United Nations, civil society networking, action-research on pro-poor governance initiatives, programme evaluation and evaluation capacity building, performance based management restructuring, post graduate level teaching and research supervision. He has authored numerous publications in the field of monitoring and evaluation, poverty and governance and is the founding editor-in-chief of the UK based international journal, Sustainable Development (1993-97).

Warren Krafchik
Executive Director, International Budget Project, Center on Budget and Policy Priorities, Washington D.C., United States

Mr. Krafchik is the Director of the International Budget Project at the Center on Budget and Policy Priorities. IBP works to enhance the effective participation of civil society organizations in public budgeting in developing and transition countries. Mr. Krafchik has worked with the IBP over the past five years, assisting budget organizations in Africa, Latin America and Asia by providing training and technical support and designing research programs. Krafchik joined the IBP in February 2001 after nine years at the Institute for Democracy in South Africa, where he founded the Budget Information Service in 1995 and directed it until moving to the IBP. Mr. Krafchik has a Masters degree in macro-economics, awarded with distinction, from the University of Cape Town and is the author of numerous publications on the role of the parliament and civil society in the budget process, the development of methodologies to track the impact of budgets on low-income and poor people, and international economic development.

Amitabh Mukhopadhyay
Joint Secretary, Parliamentary Financial Committees, Lok Sabha Secretariat, New Delhi, India

Mr. Mukhopadhyay majored in economics and sociology at the Delhi School of Economics and at present assists the parliamentary committees in India which deal with policies, legislation and accountability. He combines a wide range of experience in working with government and civil society institutions. As a member of the civil services in India borne on the audit cadre, he has served the Comptroller and Auditor General of India through various postings. He has led UN Audit teams for audit of UNHCR in Russia and Uganda in 1996 and also worked on secondment to FAO in 2003 for its emergency programme in Afghanistan. On deputation to the executive wing in India, he earlier worked in the Ministry of HRD on formulating programmes for mobilization of NGOs to implement projects for non-formal education of children as well as women's empowerment. Throughout his career, as a labour of love, he has associated himself with the anti-poverty campaigns for social audit and the right to information in India. He has published his views from time to time in academic journals like Yojana, Seminar and Economic and Political Weekly.

Protais Musoni
Minister, Ministry of Local Administration,
Good Governance, Community Development and Social Affairs
Rwanda

Mr. Musoni was appointed the Minister of Local Government, Community Development and Social Affairs in September 2004. He is responsible for the supervision of Government programs and policies related to territorial administration, good governance and the social well-being of Rwandan citizens. He previously served as Minister of State in the Ministry of Local Government, Information and Social Affairs and Secretary General in the Ministry of Local Government and Social Affairs. Minister Musoni participated in and chaired various commissions and Boards of Governors of different organisations and attended numerous seminars and workshops in both local and international fora on good governance, decentralisation and community development. He has also presented many papers in national and foreign high-level institutions on good governance and community development.

Peter Oliver
Senior Research Fellow, Engaged Government Project
Griffith University, Australia

Mr. Oliver is a Principal Natural Resource Officer with Queensland Department of Natural Resources and Water. His current role involves research on industry, community and government collaboration in natural resource management (NRM). He is also an Adjunct Senior Research Fellow in the Centre for Governance and Public Policy, Department of Politics and Public Policy, Griffith University and also serves as the Deputy Program Leader for Education and Training with the eWater CRC and is leading research focusing on stakeholder analysis, involvement and capacity building in relation to water planning and management issues. Mr. Oliver has over twenty years experience in citizen participation, citizen science, environmental education and natural resource management extension. He is a leader in water education, and was the first environmental educator in Australia to work with school students and community members to monitor the health of local waterways, initiating a national program of activities that is now known as Waterwatch. In 2000, the Department of Natural Resources and Water presented him with their Achievement Award for Queensland.

Siddiqur Osmani
Professor of Development Economics, University of Ulster, U.K.

From 1986 to 1993, Prof. Osmani was affiliated with the World Institute for Development Economics Research as a Senior Research Fellow in Finland. He also worked at the Bangladesh Institute of Development Studies in Bangladesh from 1971 to 1976 and initially started as Staff Economist, then as a Research Fellow and finally as a Senior Research Fellow. Prof. Osmani held noteworthy advisory positions at the UN High Commissioner for Human Rights, South Asian Network of Economics Research Institutes (SANEI), Poverty Reduction Network for UNDP and the Food and Agricultural Organization (FAO).

Among his recent publications include i) The Employment Nexus between Growth and Poverty: An Asian Perspective, Swedish International Development Cooperation Agency, 2005 ii) The Macroeconomics of Poverty Reduction: The Case Study of Bangladesh, UNDP, 2003. iii) Poverty and Human Rights: Building on the Capability Approach, Journal of Human Development, 2005. and v) Expanding Voice and Accountability Through the Budgetary Process, Journal of Human Development, 2002.

Vivek Ramkumar
Programme Officer
International Budget Project (IBP), Washington D.C., United States

Vivek Ramkumar joined International Budget Project in January 2005 as a Programme Officer.   Mr. Ramkumar has previously worked with the MKSS — an organisation that pioneered the Right to Know movement in India. The MKSS is best known for its innovative public hearing forums in which village communities track local budget expenditures. He has also worked with a Mumbai based NGO — SPARC — that is part of the Shack/ Slum Dwellers International. Mr. Ramkumar is a qualified Chartered Accountant and holds a Masters from the London School of Economics.

Desley Renton
Social Policy Advisor, Local Government Association of Queensland, Australia

Desley Renton is the Social Policy Advisor for the Local Government Association of Queensland Inc (LGAQ).   Her qualifications are in politics, literature and engagement (dialogue and deliberation).   In 2004, Ms. Renton developed a Community Engagement Framework for Queensland Local Government. This initiative was awarded the International Association for Public Participation (IAP2) award for 'Best Public Participation Policy Framework'.   Ms. Renton was elected President of the IAP2 Australasian Affiliate in August 2005.   She is a Fellow of the Saint James Ethics Centre having been one of 15 Australians to be awarded a Fairfax Ethical Leadership scholarship in 1997.

Jesse Manalastas Robredo
Mayor, City Government of Naga, Philippines

Mr. Robredo is a highly recognised expert in local governance. He is an *Edward Mason Fellow* and a graduate of Masters in Public Administration at the prestigious John F. Kennedy School of Government, Harvard University. In 1999, he also completed his Masters in Business Administration at the University of the Philippines. In 1988, Mr. Robredo was elected mayor making him the youngest City Mayor of the Philippines at age 29. He would later serve the city for an unprecedented five 3-year terms as local chief executive. As Mayor of Nagà, Mr Robredo energised the bureaucracy, dramatically improved the constituency's stakeholdership and participation in governance and restored Naga to its pre-eminent position as the premier city of the Bicol Region. During his incumbency, Naga was considered a model local government in the country and a laboratory of local government innovation. He was also a recipient of the 2000 Ramon Magsaysay Award for Government Service.